Fine WoodWorking *on* Hand Tools

Fine WoodWorking
on Hand Tools

38 articles selected by
the editors of
Fine Woodworking
magazine

The Taunton Press

Cover photo by Rosanne Somerson

First printing: September 1986
International Standard Book Number: 0-918804-53-1
Library of Congress Catalog Card Number: 86-50406
Printed in the United States of America

A FINE WOODWORKING Book

FINE WOODWORKING® is a trademark of The Taunton Press, Inc.,
registered in the U.S. Patent and Trademark Office.

The Taunton Press, Inc.
63 South Main Street
Box 355
Newtown, Connecticut 06470

Contents

Introduction

Of all the handcrafts, toolmaking must surely rank among the oldest. Long before man learned to fashion wood into the implements and weapons so crucial to his survival, he had first to devise crude hand tools to assist in the work. Even as recently as the turn of the century, when the Stanley Rule and Level Co. made a plane for every purpose, the skilled craftsman would often fabricate his own plane or gouge to accomplish some special task for which no manufactured tool existed.

Today, in a world dominated by motorized gadgets, you still need good hand tools to do the very best work. In this collection of articles from the first ten years of *Fine Woodworking* magazine, 29 practicing craftsmen pass on practical information about choosing, using and making hand tools for woodworking. You'll find sound advice on a wide selection of basic hand tools, including saws, edge tools, and marking and measuring devices. Planes and chisels are covered in a companion volume.

Paul Bertorelli, editor

Basic Blacksmithing

What a woodworker needs to forge tools

by Ray Larsen

Author files weld on shell auger.

The furniture maker ruins a mahogany table base while trying to cut a deep mortise in it. He is using the wrong chisel because the right one has been out of stock for eight months. The instrument maker applies pressure to the shell auger buried deep in the boxwood clamped in front of him. The bit snaps in his hand. The turner walks from his lathe, shaking his head. The poorly designed gouge has just ripped through the tulipwood bowl he's been working on all day. The sculptor lays down his mallet and puts his work aside in frustration. He can't get the effect he wants, although he's tried every tool in the catalog.

Such incidents, all too common in woodworking, have led to a resurgence of interest in hand forging high-quality tools, at least those special tools unavailable from even the best supply houses. This has developed a number of skilled blacksmiths able to produce special tools of the highest quality, and woodworkers need only avail themselves of their services. In addition, a growing number of serious woodworkers are taking up blacksmithing themselves. They are discovering that with a little perseverance they can forge their own tools.

It takes a substantial investment to set up a forge and a substantial block of time to locate equipment and learn the necessary skills. Each woodworker should ask himself how serious his need is for special, high-quality tools before deciding to make them. The devoted craftsman will quickly resent the time taken from his first love to produce tools he really doesn't need.

Once a woodworker learns blacksmithing, he never again need worry about tools breaking, or not holding an edge, or ruining the work. Less time struggling with tools means more time producing high-quality work. And the most exotic tools are readily available. Need a special shape for turning the inside of a box? It's there for the making. Many woodworkers find that a tool especially designed for a job enables them to produce pieces others can't, or to produce them faster or more economically. The right tool for the job means superior work.

After the initial investment, the blacksmith-woodworker saves time and money; others must wait until special tools become available, or run around searching them out, or pay the relatively high cost of having them made by a specialist. The woodworker who can make tools can also repair and modify them. A chipped screwdriver is reshaped at a fraction of the cost of replacing it; an old parting tool is reworked to turn a special configuration. In addition, the blacksmith-

woodworker can also forge special pulls, latches, hinges and other hard-to-find hardware. This ability is especially important to specialists in antique reproductions.

Equipment

I began blacksmithing with a homemade forge, two borrowed pairs of tongs, a $35 anvil and a beat-up grindstone. Most serious woodworkers already have several pieces of equipment essential to toolmaking, including a good grinding wheel or other sharpening system, high-quality bench honing equipment and a heavy-duty drill press. But additional equipment is required, including a forge, anvil, tongs, hammers, punches and chisels, fullers and hardies, swages, vise and quench tub. Start with a few pieces of equipment and master them before buying more.

The heart of the blacksmith shop is the forge, in which a blast of air applied to a coal, coke or charcoal fire heats steel to the high temperatures needed for forging. The sizes and styles range from big, permanent types costing well over $1,200 (all 1977 prices) to small, portable ones found in junkyards and secondhand shops for $50 to $200 depending on size, quality and your ability to bargain. The thrifty craftsman can make a forge with a discarded barbecue grill for the bed and the guts of an old vacuum cleaner or hair dryer for the blower.

Forging generates soot, smoke and dust that must be vented away from the clean areas of the shop, so I recommend a hooded, ventable forge over an open type. Some manufacturers have substituted stamped metal for cast iron in recent years, but cast iron remains best for the job because of its superior fire-resistant properties. Cranking the blower by hand may be romantic, but it isn't as efficient or as easily managed as an electric one. Respected forge manufacturers include Buffalo Forge Co. and Champion Blower & Forge, Inc. (the latter no longer makes blowers, so check secondhand shops).

Do not use the forge without first lining it with a suitable refractory, a non-metallic, ceramic material with heat-resisting properties that protects the forge bed from burning out. It comes in many forms but a powdered type, Kast-Set, made by A. P. Green Refractories Co., Mexico, Mo., is excellent; it is mixed with water like cement and cast in place. Such refractory will protect the forge and greatly extend its life at minimum cost (about $50 for the 100-lb. minimum order, about a four-year supply).

If the forge is the heart of the blacksmith shop, the anvil is its soul. No other single piece of equipment (save perhaps a favorite hammer) inspires blacksmiths to such heights of enthusiasm and such depths of despair. Like forges, anvils come in a wide variety of types, styles and sizes, from new but

Ray Larsen's company, Genuine Forgery, Inc., sells forged tools by mail (1126 Broadway, Hanover, MA 02339) and through dealers (e.g., Woodcraft Supply and Fine Tool Shops).

From *Fine Woodworking* magazine (Winter 1977) 9:58-61

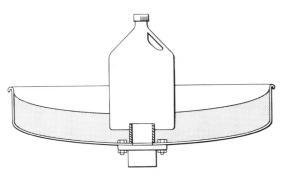

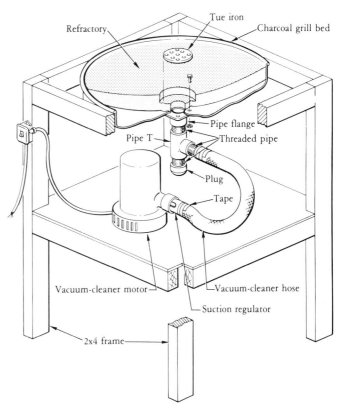

A serviceable forge can be constructed from readily available materials. The bed is built from a new or used stamped-metal outdoor grill. A hooded type (not shown here) makes essential venting easier. Or a hood can be made from sheet metal and a stovepipe. The factory-made tubular legs are discarded in favor of a heavy-duty 2x4 frame with braced 2x4 legs. The bed should be at workbench height. The center hole in the bed is enlarged to accept a 2-in. pipe flange; a T-fitting introduces air blast and a plug is loosely fitted beneath for ash clean-out. A vacuum-cleaner or hair-dryer motor with heating element removed is affixed to the frame; the blower outlet is linked to the T-fitting with vacuum-cleaner or hair-dryer hose. Adjustable clamps and duct tape ensure an airtight fit. A vacuum-cleaner suction regulator or similar device regulates the blast. Refractory is troweled around a suitable form, such as a plastic bleach bottle with 2-in. pipe inserted through its bottom, placed over the center hole (as above). A tue iron cut from heavy-gauge sheet metal and drilled or punched is laid over the 2-in. blast opening in the bed.

expensive all-steel types available from such supply houses as Centaur Forge Ltd., Burlington, Wis. (about $200 in 1977 for a 125-pound size) to traditional, steel-faced types available from secondhand dealers for $75 and up. The anvil should be mounted on a heavy tree stump.

When selecting an anvil, look for a smooth, flat face and unflawed horn. Use a steel straightedge to spot valleys. The quality of the work depends to a great extent on the condition of the anvil. Don't buy a used one with badly chipped edges on the face, a sure sign of misuse over the years. And don't buy an anvil whose steel face is separating from its cast or wrought-iron base. Improper welding of face to body is a clue to inferior manufacture. Two respected brands are Peter Wright and Hay-Budden; both companies are out of business but their anvils may be purchased through dealers or at junkyards.

Anvils come in many sizes, but the 125 to 150 lb. range is good for toolmaking. Anything smaller is too light to stand up to tool steels, while heavier anvils are too expensive and hard to transport. Before buying, strike the face moderately with a hammer. A good ring and strong bounce are signs of a strong, well-made anvil. Avoid limp clunkers.

Tongs, the long-handled tools used to hold steel while it is heated and forged, come in a bewildering range of sizes and styles. Early trade manuals, such as *Hand Forging* by Thomas F. Googerty (Popular Mechanics Co., Chicago, Ill.), suggest making one's own as a good way to learn the blacksmith's craft. There is a great deal of sense in that. But because tongs are readily available at junk shops and flea markets for as little as 50 cents, it is easier for the woodworker to buy them—at least at the outset. Pick a few simple sizes and shapes and purchase more pairs as needed.

There also are hundreds of new and used blacksmith, me-

chanic, farrier and other hammers on the market these days and each blacksmith has favorites (my own are an odd, one-pound cross-peen type that I use for delicate finish work and an old electric sharpening hammer that is excellent for hammering in blade edges). Start simply with several ball-peen and mechanic's hammers ranging from one to three pounds and fill in with special types as required. Buy only the highest quality (Sears' Craftsman mechanic's hammers are excellent).

Punches and chisels are special long or handled types which come in hot and cold versions for punching and cutting heated or unheated steel. They are available used from supply houses such as Centaur or manufacturers such as Diamond Tool and Horseshoe Co., Duluth, Minn. Prices vary. As with tongs and hammers, buy a few simple ones and fill in as requirements dictate.

Fullers and hardies fit in the hardie or square hole at the heel of most anvils. Fullers are used to draw steel, hardies to cut it. The metal is heated to forging temperature, then placed over the tool and struck with a hammer. Start with a few simple types from reputable supply houses or manufacturers and supplement as needed. Expect to pay about $10 each (1977 prices).

Swages come in two types. Bottom swages fit into the hardie hole and come in various round, square and other shapes. They permit the toolmaker to hammer hot steel to a desired configuration. Sets consist of matched bottom and top swages. The bottom fits in the hardie hole, and the top is handled like a hammer. Hot steel is held between the two and the top swage is struck with a hammer. This procedure generally requires a helper.

Supply houses stock only a limited number of swages. Secondhand shops, junkyards and tool dealers specializing in blacksmith equipment are better sources. Expect to pay $5 and up apiece. An alternative to buying a large number of swages is the swage block, a large block of cast steel with a variety of shapes on its four sides. The block is fitted to a special stand or placed on a heavy stump in the same manner as an anvil. Swage blocks, unfortunately, are expensive new and extremely rare used.

A good machinist's vise is satisfactory for the beginning toolmaker but he should consider buying a blacksmith's type as soon as possible. This vise has a steel leg that sets into the floor of the shop. The leg dissipates the shock of hammering steel in the vise. New blacksmith's vises are expensive compared to readily available used ones. Pay about $50 for one with five-inch jaws in very good condition.

Finally, a reservoir of water is essential for quenching tools. A large, galvanized washtub will do. Half a whiskey barrel is better.

Fuel

Some blacksmiths in England prefer coke for forging. Blacksmiths at Old Sturbridge Village in Sturbridge, Mass., use charcoal for authenticity. But the rest of us use "blacksmith coal," a soft, low-sulfur type especially suited for forge work. Blacksmith coal is available from Centaur and other supply houses but these are expensive sources. Try phoning a coal supplier in your area. Most dealers know who sells blacksmith coal and will quickly suggest a source. Buy 200 pounds to start (less than $10 worth in 1977). Pick it up at the yard—it's cheaper that way.

Steel

Domestic and overseas producers make a wide range of steels suitable for woodworking tools. New steel is preferable to used because the toolmaker knows what to expect when working it and can select the right type for the job. No matter how good the smith is at identifying used steel, there is always an element of risk in forging it. Because of producer restrictions on minimum order sizes, woodworkers will have to rely on local service centers or warehouses for the small amounts they require. If in doubt, select a company that advertises itself as a member of the Steel Service Center Institute (SSCI), an organization of highly reputable steel suppliers. Two basic families of steel are used in toolmaking: carbon and specialty.

Carbon steel is the single largest type of steel produced in this country and comes in many grades. There are two good reasons for using carbon steel: It costs considerably less than specialty steel, and it comes in many toolmaking shapes not readily available in specialty steels. Prices of carbon steels vary, depending on market conditions.

The amount of carbon determines the steel's hardenability and ability to do work. Only the high-carbon steels are of concern to the woodworker, those types whose carbon content exceeds 0.50%. High-carbon steel ranges from American Iron and Steel Institute (AISI) classification 1055 (containing

Author at work. Note rack of tongs by the forge and hardies mounted in slips around base of anvil, a 350-lb. Hay Budden.

Below, fuller in hardie hole of anvil speeds drawing down steel. Bottom, swage block gives steel round or gouge-like shape.

Spark patterns identify steels

High-carbon steel: Considerable bursting, sparking around wheel. Gold/white color.

Cast iron (not forgeable): Short, thin, brick-red streamers. Very slight sparking.

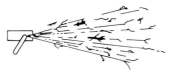

Medium-carbon steel: Some exploding or bursting sparks. Some sparking around periphery of wheel.

High-speed tool steel: Similar to high-carbon steel but with fine explosions. Reddish streamers. No sparking around wheel.

Low-carbon steel: Streamers thrown from wheel are straight, light straw in color. Some small amount of sparking.

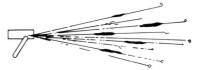

Wrought iron (inappropriate for blades): Very similar to low-carbon steel. Long yellow streamers. Practically no sparking.

0.55% carbon) to AISI classification 1095 (containing 0.95% carbon).

Decent, general-purpose tools can be forged from AISI 1055 steel, but its use is not strongly recommended. A smith forging high-carbon steels should work with the highest grades, 1085 and above. If these are unavailable, move up to a specialty steel rather than down to a lesser grade. High-carbon steel is recommended for screwdrivers, chisels, turning chisels and gouges, plane irons and carving tools.

Most of the specialty steels used in toolmaking are tool steels. They are expensive, some more than $3 a pound. Configuration is limited and finding small quantities can be a problem. They do make excellent tools, however. Commonly used types:

AISI W2 is a high-quality, water-hardening tool steel. As with high-carbon steel, it relies on carbon content (up to 1.40%, depending on producer) for hardness. Use it for tools that must hold an exceptional edge.

AISI O1 is a low-alloy, oil-hardening tool steel. It will not harden to quite the same degree as W2, but is easier to forge, harden and temper. Use it as an alternative to W2 where shape presents heat-treating problems.

AISI D2 is a high-carbon, high-chromium, air-hardening steel. Some cutlers consider it the best material for long, thin blades. It is especially good for bench knives and similar tools.

AISI S5, an oil-quenched, silicon-manganese tool steel specially designed for shock resistance, is difficult to forge but unsurpassed for tools subject to high impact. It makes excellent cold chisels.

AISI M2 is a molybdenum-type tool steel. Smiths report that it makes excellent planer and shaper knives.

AISI 440C Stainless is a high-carbon steel favored by most blade makers where exposure to the elements is a major consideration. It relies on high chromium content for its corrosion resistance. It will not hold as fine an edge as W2.

Used or recycled steel is attractive because it is cheap and some woodworkers may want to try it. Look for a scrap yard specializing in identified grades of high-carbon and specialty steels. These yards charge a premium, but knowing the exact qualities of the steel is worth it. Toolmakers can also rework certain steel implements manufactured from known types of high-carbon steel. Some typical items and the AISI steel they are made from:

Plow discs, plowshares and harrow discs, 1080; hay-rake teeth, 1095; leaf springs, 1085 to 1095; mower blades, 1055 to 1085; clutch discs, 1060 to 1070; and most heavy coil springs, 1095.

Toolmakers can apply the grinding wheel or spark test to steels of unknown composition. Steel is put in contact with a rotating grinding wheel and the resulting spark pattern is studied for clues to the nature of the steel.

Technique

There's no substitute for experience; woodworkers who want to make their own tools should train with an experienced smith. Most smiths will arrange for instruction and forge time. Several colleges and universities also offer courses in blacksmithing and farriery (horseshoeing). Reading is helpful; the bibliography below offers excellent starting points (1977 prices; for out of print books, check libraries). □

The Making of Tools and *The Modern Blacksmith,* both by Alexander G. Weygers (Van Nostrand Reinhold Co., 450 W. 33rd St., New York; $4.95 each, paperback). Weygers, a sculptor, began making his own tools when he became dissatisfied with available types. His suggestions for setting up shop economically, improvising equipment and using secondary materials are particularly good.

Blacksmithing for the Home Craftsman by Joe Pehoski (Stuhr Museum, Grand Island, Nebr.; $1.75, paperback). Pehoski is a working smith who believes in plain speaking and his book is packed with good advice. His troubleshooting section is especially useful.

Blacksmiths' and Farriers' Tools at Shelburne Museum by H. R. Bradley Smith (Shelburne Museum, Inc., Shelburne, Vt.; $5.00 paperback). To understand blacksmiths' tools is to gain insight into the subtlest techniques for using them. This is the best available book on tools.

The Blacksmith's Craft (Council for Small Industries in Rural Areas [CoSIRA], 11 Cowley Street, London, SWIP 3NA; $3.50 hardcover). Absolutely the finest book available on the techniques of blacksmithing for the beginner.

Drake's Modern Blacksmithing and Horseshoeing by J. G. Holstrom (Drake Publishers, Inc., New York; $4.95 hardcover). Holstrom is disarmingly folksy but his book contains a great deal of down-to-earth advice.

The Art of Blacksmithing by Alex W. Bealer (Funk & Wagnalls Publishing Co., Inc., New York; $12.45 hardcover). This book has come in for criticism in some circles for occasional inaccuracies and oversimplifications but still contains a wealth of good information.

Decorative and Sculptural Ironwork by Dona Z. Meilach (Crown Publishers, Inc., New York; $7.95 paperback). An excellent survey of the latest work and techniques of the country's best smiths.

Blacksmith's Manual Illustrated by J. W. Lillico (The Technical Press Ltd., London; $7.75 hardcover). An excellent advanced course in smithing with special emphasis on large, complex forgings.

Heat Treating

Making (or fixing) your tools

by Gordon S. Harrison

Cutting edges of unalloyed, high-carbon steel are essential to the woodworker's craft. Chisels, plane irons, axes, adzes, gouges, saws, knives, shaves, scrapers, rasps, and bits are just different configurations of a sharpened, carbon steel blade. The cutting edges of steel woodworking tools must be heat treated to give them the proper combination of hardness and toughness. It may become necessary for you to heat treat a cutting edge in your own shop. You may have spoiled the temper of a chisel by grinding; the factory temper of a gouge may not suit you because the cutting edge is either too soft or too hard; you may want to dress the edge of a large tool such as an ax or adze that is too hard to grind, in which case you must soften the steel by annealing to work it, and then re-harden it; or you may want to make a tool from an old file or leaf spring. Even if you have no occasion to heat treat a tool yourself, you should know how to tell if a cutting edge has been spoiled by overheating. In sum, a knowledge of heat treating is important to a self-reliant woodworker.

There are three steps to heat treating an unalloyed carbon steel cutting tool: annealing, hardening and tempering. Annealing is done by heating the steel to full cherry red and then cooling it very slowly by burying it in an insulating bed of lime or ashes. This softens the steel and prepares its grain structure for hardening. Hardening is done by heating the piece of annealed steel to a full cherry red and then quenching it suddenly in an oil, brine, or water bath. This makes the steel extremely hard and also extremely brittle. Tempering is done by heating the hardened steel to about

500° F. This reduces somewhat the hardness of the steel so it can be hand honed, as well as the brittleness so the tool will not break in use.

The photographs show the hardening and tempering of a drawknife I recently forged from a salvaged automobile leaf spring. First I annealed the entire forging blank overnight in the ashes of a dying fire in my woodburning shop stove.

Annealing eliminates the effects of previous heat treatment on the internal crystalline structure of the steel. Annealed steel has a fine grain structure and is soft, tough, ductile, and easily worked cold with files, hacksaws and abrasives.

A good portion of your tool, from the tip of the cutting edge back toward the handle, should be annealed. Even though it will only be necessary to harden and temper the tip of the tool, you want as much as possible of the remainder of the steel to be soft and tough so that it will not break in service. If you are working with a gouge, anneal at least 4 inches up from the cutting edge. If the gouge is a commercial product, the stem and tang are probably well softened already, but you should anneal the 4 inches anyway because you do not know how much of the tool was hardened at the factory. If you are starting to fashion a file or piece of spring steel into a tool, anneal the entire piece of stock.

To anneal a piece of high-carbon steel, you must thoroughly heat it to between 50°F and 75°F above its critical temperature and then cool it very slowly. When the critical temperature of a piece of carbon steel is reached, its crystalline structure is fundamentally transformed. The critical temperature, also known as the transformation point, depends upon the precise carbon content of the steel. However, the critical temperatures (or the transformation range) of the carbon steels you are likely to be working with are in a narrow range, from about 1350°F to 1400°F. Thus, 1450°F is hot enough to anneal carbon steel, and also to harden it.

There are several precautions to observe as you heat the steel to 1450° F. Heat it slowly so that the temperature rises gradually and evenly over the entire section to be annealed. Heat it thoroughly so the heat penetrates uniformly through its entire thickness. Do not greatly overheat the steel, for even if you do not destroy the steel by burning it (around 2200° F) you may seriously coarsen the grain, which will impair subsequent hardening and tempering. Most carbon steels will go to

Once forged and ground, the draw knife is heated with an oxyacetylene torch to a bright cherry red, or about 1,450 degrees. As soon as the steel is heated to cherry red, it is hardened by quenching rapidly in a bath of used crankcase oil (5-30 SAE).

From *Fine Woodworking* magazine (Fall 1976) 4:50-52

Temp. °F	Color
1125	dark red
1300	blood red
1350	low cherry red
1400	medium cherry red
1450	cherry red
1500	bright cherry red
1550	full red
1650	bright red
1750	orange
2100	yellow
2250	white

TEMPERING TEMPERATURES

Temp. °F	Oxide Color on Polished Surface	Woodcutting tool
450	straw	wood engraving tools
475	light orange ⎤	gouges, plane irons, drawknives, chisels, center punches, cold chisels, heavy tools
500	bronze ⎦	that are struck with a hammer
525	purple ⎤	wood borers, reamers, moldding and planing cutters for hardwood, axes, adzes,
550	full blue ⎦	wood bits, augers, thin or delicate carving knives, chisels, gouges, turning tools
575	medium blue	molding and planing cutters for softwood, saws
600	pale blue	
625	grey	

1700°F or more before grain coarsening damage begins. Do not direct the flame directly onto the bevel of the cutting edge. Rather, allow heat to penetrate this delicate area of the blade from the thicker adjacent material.

Use a torch for heat. It is possible to bring a small, thin piece of steel to its transformation temperature with a standard propane torch. However, you will have trouble sweeping a propane torch across an object of any size, because there is not enough heat in the flame to evenly raise the temperature of the steel. In this case the heat dissipates too fast, partly because the unheated adjacent steel acts as a heat sink. Thus, a tool about the size of my drawknife, needs an acetylene flame from a Turbo Torch, Prest-O-Lite torch, or oxy-acetylene torch. Use a neutral flame. Make the torch stationary and hold the work in both hands.

How do you determine that the temperature of the steel has reached 1450° F or thereabouts? The traditional method, used by blacksmiths for centuries, is observing the color of the heated steel in semi-darkness. Carbon steel reaches its transformation point when it glows a full cherry red. By the time it has become bright red it is well beyond the transformation point, and when it is orange it is near 1800°F.

Another way to determine temperature is with commercial temperature indicating crayons, such as Tempilsticks. Below its temperature rating, the crayon leaves a dry opaque mark; when its temperature is reached, the mark turns to a liquid smear. I have found Tempilsticks to be invaluable in tempering hardened steel. In the higher heat ranges, 1400°F to 1500°F which we are discussing here, the crayons are more difficult to use, and it is easier to rely on the color of the glowing steel. It is imperative to view the heated steel in a partially darkened room, because brightness will dull the color and you are sure to overheat the work.

When the steel has been heated to a full cherry red, it must be cooled very slowly. Bury it immediately in a bed of dry lime. If lime is not available, dry fine ashes may be used as a

The hardened knife shows oxidation rings, where the curve begins. Temperature-indicating crayon for 500° F is applied to the entire bevel and the blade is ready to temper with a propane torch (right).

The finished drawknife with walnut handles.

substitute. A small piece of steel may take several hours to reach room temperature. A stouter piece may take ten or twelve.

When the steel has cooled it is fully annealed. It is suitable for grinding, filing, and other cold working, and after that you are ready to harden the cutting edge. To harden plain carbon steel, you must heat it slightly above its critical temperature just as you did to anneal it, but instead of cooling it slowly, you must cool it rapidly. Plunge it into a quenching bath of water, brine, or oil. The quench stabilizes the molecular structure of the steel in a condition known to metallurgists as martensite. This particular structure imparts maximum hardness.

Only the portion of the steel that has reached the transformation point will harden when quenched. It is only necessary to harden the cutting bevel and an inch or so back from it. Observe the same precautions as when heating the steel for annealing: heat slowly and evenly; heat thoroughly; do not overheat; let the heat seep into the bevel from adjacent metal.

I prefer, and recommend, used crankcase oil for a quench. It is not as severe as water or brine and the relatively slower quench minimizes the risk of fracturing or distorting the steel. Plunge the heated steel into the bath absolutely vertically, blade first. Distortion will occur if the sides of the blade are quenched differently. There is a danger of igniting the entire bath of quenching oil only if the workpiece is large and contains a great deal of heat and the container of oil is small. This combination should be avoided in any case because it will not properly quench the workpiece.

When withdrawn from the quench, the cutting edge is extremely hard and brittle. It is still not ready to use because it is too difficult to sharpen and is liable to break or crack. The blade must be tempered.

Tempering softens the metal slightly from its state of maximum hardness, restoring a measure of toughness and ductility. To temper a piece of hardened carbon steel you simply heat it to a predetermined temperature below approximately 1000°F. The higher you heat it (below 1000°F), the softer and tougher it becomes. You can temper your tool to the degree of hardness that suits your tastes or needs. The harder the temper, the longer the blade will hold an edge but the more difficult it will be to hone; the softer the temper, the keener an edge the blade will take and the

easier it is to hone, but the quicker it loses its sharpness.

Most kitchen ovens will heat to 550°F, which makes th a convenient place to temper your hardened workpiec. Let piece soak thoroughly in the oven heat for 15 or 20 minu after it has reached the proper temperature. The rate at wh it cools after tempering does not alter its properties, so may quench it or let it air cool.

It is also possible to temper with a torch. The dange getting the cutting edge too hot before the heat has th oughly and evenly penetrated the entire hardened portio the workpiece. Therefore I use propane flame to temper cause the steel heats more slowly than it does in an acetyl flame. Also, I use a Tempilstik to tell me when the selec temper has been attained. Apply the crayon to the en bevel. When the dry crayon material turns liquid across width of the bevel, quench the heated portion of the too prevent more heat from running into the bevel and ruin the temper.

It also is possible to judge the temperature of the s visually as it is being heated. The clues are not the glow b spectrum of colors caused by oxides that form on the polis surface. Each color of the spectrum indicates a specific te perature.

As you apply heat well back from the cutting edge, oxidation colors will begin to run in both directions a from that point. Just as the color that matches the selec temper reaches the cutting edge, quench the tool.

I do not recommend this method of tempering. It is difficult to control, especially on long blades. Your kitc oven or a temperature indicating crayon will give a more curate result. However, you should learn the colors of oxidation rainbow, for it they suddenly appear on the edg a chisel that you are grinding, or on the teeth of a table blade that overheats in a piece of hardwood, the steel has its temper. A pale blue or grey would indicate signific softening of the blade.

Heat treating always leaves a ring of oxidation colors on surface of the steel. These can be removed with emery cloth a buffing wheel and emery compound. If they are obstina you can pickle the steel in a bath of sulphuric acid. I battery acid just as it comes from the service station (ca electrolyte, it is sulphuric acid that is about 64 perc distilled water by weight). Rinse in cold water and buff.

Before you set out to heat treat your favorite tool, prac with an old file or spring. Mild steel, of course, will harden; you must use an unalloyed, high-carbon steel suc is used in files and springs. Be sure you can recognize transformation point of the steel from its heat glow. Heat a quench a test piece at various shades of red, and attempt file the steel after each test. If a file does not cut the ste hardening occurred, which means the transformation po was reached; if it cuts, hardening did not occur and the tra formation point was not reached.

[*Author's note:* Tempilstiks are made by the Tempil Di sion, Big Three Industries, Inc., 2901 Hamilton Blvd., Sou Plainfield, N.J. 07080. These crayons are calibrated to m at systematically spaced temperatures from 100°F to 2500° They cost about $3.00 each (1976). Tempilstiks are availa in the transformation range of carbon steel at 1350, 14 1425, 1450, 1480, and 1500°F, and in the tempering range 450, 463, 475, 488, 500, 525, 550, and 575°F.]

A Blacksmith's Bleak View of Modern Tools
And how to go at hammer and tongs yourself

by Anders Richardson

By making this canoe knife out of a chunk of old sawblade, you can learn the techniques basic to hand-forging a range of woodworking tools.

America, you were sold a bill of goods back in '05 when they said drop-forging was the improved, modern way to make hand-woodworking tools. It was modern all right, but far from an improvement. Drop-forging merely favored mass production, encouraging the design of tools that could be machine-made out of alloy steel instead of true, high-carbon tool steel. Toolmaking, once an industrial art, was reduced to brutal economics; companies that produced barely tolerable tools at the lowest cost survived the competition. We became a nation of buyers instead of makers.

Accustomed as craftsmen were to the superior edge-holding qualities of hand-forged tools, they could tell the difference and said so. Since the turn of the century, research metallurgists have busied themselves with the task of making drop-forging better. Because of the sudden, violent shock of the drop hammer's swat, forging is incomplete, and the steel is left unrefined and full of stress. Many of these tools would crack if subjected to a proper hardening process. Instead, they're made thicker than they should be, out of inferior (but tough) alloy steel. Hardening is minimal. Tempering of the tool—softening it slightly to strengthen the metal and to ease sharpening—is rarely done, despite factory claims to the contrary.

The best way to make an edge tool is with 1% carbon tool steel. You forge it by hand, anneal it (soften it for working) and then grind or file it to shape. Heating the metal and immediately quenching it in water or oil hardens the tool; reheating the cutting edge to a lower temperature tempers it. Hardening and tempering are separate operations in fine toolsmithing. Only the blade should be hardened, not the entire tool, as is done in hit-or-miss factory ovens. None of this applies to cold chisels, wrenches, hammers and the like. These shapes can be made of alloy steel to good effect, if edge-holding is not an issue.

I'll admit that if everything were done conscientiously, fac-

tory tools could be much better. But the assembly line is numbing and factory production so fragmented that workers cannot take care. In olden days, smiths truly competed, striving for thinner, stronger tools or ones with keener, harder-tempered blades, or making more shapes and sizes than did the forge down the street. Tools used to outlive the men who made them and those who originally bought them.

But it's not as though there's nothing to be done about it. You can still buy serviceable old tools, or redress damaged ones. Lots of junk-store and flea-market finds need only handles and sharpening to be good as new. You can patronize your local blacksmith, or take up the hammer yourself. Even the novice stands a good chance of forging better tools than he can buy. Tool steel has never been cheaper, more available, or of better quality than today's water-hardening 1% carbon drill rod. Buy it new at the local machine shop or steel jobber—it's the cheapest stuff around. Coal should be so good and so plentiful.

If you want to forge things for real, you can make a simple forge and burn coal, coke or hardwood-lump charcoal. Experiment. Old-timers in the Pacific Northwest supposedly used Douglas fir bark scales for fuel. There are now electric forges and gas furnaces, too. What's handiest for the half-serious toolsmith is the Bernzomatic Jet II torch (#JTH-79), available by special order from the local hardware store (about $25 in 1984). It will do a lot more than just heat tool steel to forging temperature. I use mine to harden the tools before tempering and to anneal pieces. It also brazes. Put two opposite each other; you'll have all the heat of a coal fire.

But let's get on with it. You'll have to do some research. You'll want to read about the basics, analyze that information, experiment, and then see for yourself what you want to believe. Look at Alexander Weygers' books (see p. 11).

You've got to start someplace, so try a canoe knife—a handy style of crooked knife capable of fast stock reduction,

A canoe knife in five steps

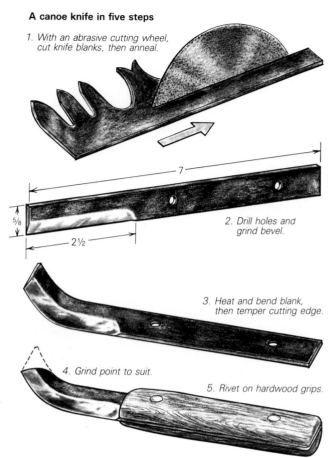

1. With an abrasive cutting wheel, cut knife blanks, then anneal.

2. Drill holes and grind bevel.

3. Heat and bend blank, then temper cutting edge.

4. Grind point to suit.

5. Rivet on hardwood grips.

originally used to make canoe thwarts and paddles. Get an old crosscut-saw blade, rusty, even pitted some. Cut it lengthwise into strips with an oxyacetylene torch (or have the local garage do it for you), or with an abrasive cutting wheel on your tablesaw. Anneal the metal in a woodstove by tossing the strips into a good fire, heating them to a bright orange-red, and then cutting the draft, letting the fire die overnight. That's the best, slowest method. Fish the pieces out of the ashes before you fire the stove the next morning.

Now cut the strips to the shape of a knife-blade blank, as in the drawing above. Use a hacksaw, cold chisel, hot chisel, grinder, or abrasive cutter in a tablesaw. On one side of a strip, grind or file a flat bevel (20° to 25°) for 2½ in. from one end, but don't make it too sharp, else the thin edge will heat too quickly later. File the other side of the strip dead flat, if it isn't that way already. Remove nicks, pits and scratches near the cutting edge. Drill two or three holes at points along the other half of the blank's length, where you'll later rivet on the handle.

Grip the blade with a pair of vise-grip pliers and heat the first ¾ in. to 1 in. of the business end with a propane torch. Bend the end up toward the beveled side by pressing down on a benchtop, or by tapping lightly with a hammer. Work it soft and easy. Let it cool, and then grind a point that suits your fancy, or wait until you've tempered to grind the point.

Now, with two torches or an oxyacetylene rig, evenly heat the entire cutting edge, turning the blade over and moving it back and forth in the fire until the metal glows orange-hot along the 2½-in. length of the cutting edge. Touch a magnet

to the blade—it shouldn't stick. If it does, heat the knife blade hotter and test again with the magnet. At the proper moment, the color will suddenly brighten right before your eyes, and the magnet won't stick. Now, quick, plunge the blade into a pail of water, horizontally, either edge-first or back-first, and agitate it up and down. The blade, if it didn't crack or warp, is now successfully hardened. If there's a sharp corner on the edge of the knife, scratch a window. The edge should be harder than glass. Yes? Congratulations.

Now polish the steel all over where it has been hardened. Use sandpaper, a disc sander or belt sander, or, better yet, a buffing wheel.

Go you now to the kitchen for tempering. Turn on the electric range or hot plate. Or put a piece of ¼-in. steel plate over a gas flame. Or use the top of the woodstove the next time you see it red-hot. When the heating element of the range burner is glowing righteously, take the blade, vise-grips still attached, and hold it with the back flat on the element. Move it around so that it heats slowly and uniformly. Watch the blade closely, in natural light if possible. The shiny metal will begin to turn vaguely yellow down near the source of heat first. That color will move up the blade toward the beveled edge as the back turns brown. These colors indicate oxidation of the shiny metal surface at temperatures much below where the metal begins to glow visibly.

Look out! You don't want to go too fast here. Remove the blade from the heat and inspect it—if the colors proceed on their own, let them go no further than purple overall. Maybe tinged with blue, but not all the way to gray. Purple at the back with dark brown at the cutting edge suits me best. If you have to stop the progression before it goes to the purple color, quench as before in water.

That's it, you've done it. Rivet on a couple of hardwood scale grips, draw a burr when you sharpen, and it's done—a canoe knife, more or less. Depending on which side of the blade you put the bevel, it's either right- or left-handed. No matter, this first one is just for learning. Likely as not, some step didn't go as well as it might have. Next time you'll get the whole thing right and smart. By the time you've made five or six such items, they'll be heirloom-quality tools.

Steel stock up to ⁵⁄₁₆-in. can be heated with the Jet torch—that's plenty of metal for tools ¾-in. to 1-in. broad, for chisels and gouges. For bigger stuff, you'll need a hotter torch, or a forge. You'll need an anvil, too—a scarce item today. Could take months or years of looking and haggling.

There's much more to the blacksmith's trade than this, of course, but you can still get started in the garage, shop or basement. Learn the refinements (secrets) yourself as you struggle along—it's largely a matter of developing personal superstitions and acting accordingly, looking always for improvements. There are hammering techniques to discover: "packing the steel," "double-fullering," and "drawing out over the horn." There's learning how to analyze scrap metal, and learning how to treat various alloy steels. If you can, find old craftspeople and artists to learn from—they can teach all this, and more.

Enough said. There should be thousands, if not millions, of blacksmiths in this nation. Hobbyists, at least. It's fun for me, what else can I say? □

Anders Richardson operates Savage Forge in Clear Lake, Washington.

Drawing: Dan Thornton

Alexander G. Weygers: a woodworker's blacksmith

by J. Petrovich

I first became acquainted with Alexander G. Weygers through his books. In clear, direct prose, they describe the metalworking principles and processes you need to fabricate hundreds of items, from a small engravers' burin to the fittings for a one-ton trip hammer. As a woodworker, however, what captured my interest were Weygers' fine chisels, gouges and knives, all logically designed and elegantly made. It didn't take long for my imagination, stimulated by Weygers' books, to supply some of the tools I would otherwise have bought from the foot-high stack of "wishbook" catalogs I keep on hand.

Weygers' three books, *The Modern Blacksmith, The Making of Tools* and *The Recycling of Tools* (all published by Van Nostrand Reinhold Co.), are modest in size and cost. Together, they tell a remarkably complete story of toolmaking, full of the anecdotes and tricks learned over a lifetime in the shop, yet rich in the fundamentals as well. All three books are illustrated with Weygers' own lucid pencil drawings, many of which are informative enough to stand alone, without text.

As my reliance on his books grew into successes at toolmaking, I wondered if it would be possible to study with Weygers. His home in Carmel Valley, Calif., is not that distant from my own in Salinas, but I had read in a newspaper feature that he had undergone open-heart surgery. Figuring it couldn't hurt to ask, I phoned Weygers in February 1982. Mrs. Weygers answered. Yes, she said, Alex was going to teach one more class. It would be his last, and it would start in mid-April. I was delighted, but a little concerned, imagining a frail old man passing along his trade secrets with his final breath.

My concerns proved groundless. The class met or exceeded all my expectations, and it wasn't without its surprises. Though 83 years old, Weygers wields hammer and tong with the precision and enthusiasm of a man half his age. Far from the elderly invalid I had imagined, he works nearly every day, forging tools or creating the wood sculptures and engravings that have earned him an international reputation. Born in Java and

At 83, Alexander Weygers is still an active toolsmith. He has chronicled the theory and technique of his craft in three books, all illustrated with his pencil drawings, like this one of a carving gouge (reprinted from The Making of Tools*).*

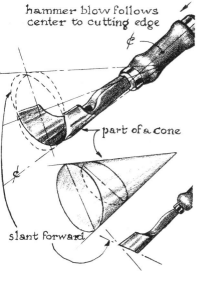

hammer blow follows
center to cutting edge

part of a cone

slant forward

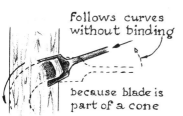

follows curves
without binding

because blade is
part of a cone

educated in Holland as a marine engineer, Weygers exudes resourcefulness.

There were no lesson plans, no blackboard or even notes. We were carried through projects by demonstrations and the kind of hands-on training that teaches you what a book cannot. Weygers spoke as he worked, a Dutch accent adding crispness to his speech. "First we must upset the steel. We will upset it here for the blade and here for the shoulder of the tang. First we strike hard, then correct, correct, correct. We are constantly correcting, little corrections. A tap here, a tap there. Little corrections. With the little corrections, we avoid the big corrections."

If the man, an active octogenarian blacksmith, came as a surprise, the week that I and ten other students spent with Weygers was a continuing revelation. I had secretly suspected that many of the tools illustrated in his books were products of a talented pencil and a fertile imagination. I was wrong. Everywhere I looked around Weygers' spacious forge and shop, I saw the marvelous products of this man's skill—real and functional objects, not prettified pencil drawings. Watching him work, I gained an appreciation for his apt comparison of hot metal to wet clay, even if my own efforts made it seem as though the glowing steel had a mind of its own.

I still refer to Weygers' books constantly. The number of tools I've made and modified from them would pay for dozens of copies of each, and I've gained an understanding of sharpening and cutting edges I never could have accumulated if I had bought all my tools. Beyond the economics and versatility of the forgings are the designs themselves. From the large and graceful gull-winged gouge to the small engravers'-style chisel, each tool seems aesthetically independent of its function and yet enhanced by it. Each is the result of what Weygers would say is "doing what we are doing because it is the most important thing in the world . . . or else we wouldn't be doing it." □

J. Petrovich is a professional furnituremaker in Salinas, Calif. Photo by Jim Ziegler.

Testing Wood Chisels
Lab finds no secrets in the steel

by Bill Stankus

A wood chisel is a very simple tool, but there are so many brands to choose from, and such a wide range of prices, that deciding which one to buy is anything but simple. It helps if you can examine a chisel, try the edge with your thumb, and heft the tool to feel how well the handle fits your hand. It's important that a chisel *feel* right. But what about the most important part— the steel? Are the more expensive chisels made of better steel? Just by looking, there's no way to tell how a chisel will sharpen or hold an edge. Advertising copy isn't any help, either. Some tool-sellers' claims notwithstanding, there hasn't been a magic blade forged since Excalibur.

As a tool consultant and woodworker I've used many chisels over the years, and I've noticed that they don't all perform in the same way. Determined to find out why, I enlisted the help of Paul Horgan, a metals quality-control manager and amateur woodworker. We decided to run a series of metallurgical tests on chisel blades to see if steel quality differs between brands and, if so, what effect this has on sharpening and edge-holding properties. *Fine Woodworking* agreed to pay for the tests, which were conducted by Anderson Laboratories, Inc. in Greendale, Wisconsin, and confirmed by another Wisconsin lab. We don't claim our tests to be the last scientific word on tool-steel metallurgy, but the results do shed some light on a confusing subject.

We couldn't test every chisel on the market, so we chose 11 popular brands: Craftsman and Stanley (United States); Footprint, Marples and Sorby (England); Hirsch and Spannsage (West Germany); Iyoroi, Oiichi and Sentora (Japan); and Mifer (Spain). So we wouldn't base our findings on a chance bad chisel, we tested two of each brand bought from mail-order and retail outlets around the country. To correlate the lab analysis with performance, I sharpened the chisels on waterstones (800-, 1200-, 4,000- and 8,000-grits) and worked with them at the bench.

Despite the wide range in price (from $7.60 for the Footprint to $31.95 for the Oiichi in 1985), the tests showed that 8 of the 11 chisels tested are made of very similar water-hardening tool steels. The lab tests did show some variations in carbon content and alloys, but no significant differences except for the Sorby, which was a different type of tool steel, and the Sears Craftsman, which was a plain carbon steel with a low carbon content. The other U.S.-made chisel, the Stanley, was made of a plain high-carbon steel. Differences that directly affect how the tool sharpens and holds an edge—hardness and grain size—were more pronounced and quite noticeable during sharpening and use, suggesting that the type of steel probably has less to do with how well a chisel works than does how carefully the factory forges, grinds, and, most importantly, hardens and tempers the tool.

To make sense of the lab tests, it's helpful to understand a little about tool metallurgy. To cut well, a wood chisel needs steel hard enough to hold an edge for a reasonable time but soft enough to be sharpened on benchstones. It also has to be tough enough to resist chipping when hammered through dense wood such as maple. Mild steel, the stuff found in angle iron and I-beams, won't do the job because there's no practical way to make it hard enough.

Adding carbon to steel—anywhere from 0.45% to 1.40%— makes steel hardenable. Plunged red-hot into water, brine or oil carbon steel's crystalline structure changes to a brittle, harder form. A cutting edge made from this brittle steel would fracture so the hardness is reduced slightly by reheating the steel to a lower temperature. This is called tempering and makes the steel much tougher. Tool steels, which were actually developed not for hand tools but for industrial applications such as stamping dies and metal cutters, are a type of high-carbon steel that has been alloyed with metals such as chromium, manganese and vanadium to improve hardenability and wear resistance. The main difference between plain high-carbon steels and the tool steel commonly used for chisels is in the quality control. Tool steel is manufactured to a more rigorous set of quality standards than is ordinary high-carbon steel. Its chemical makeup is constantly tested, and each batch is routinely inspected for microstructure, cleanness, hardenability, and surface and internal flaws. This consistency means that the consumer is less likely to get a bum tool, but it also makes things easier for the manufacturer since theoretically, each batch of steel will react about the same way when it's forged and hardened, thus producing tools of identical quality.

We had the labs perform three basic kinds of tests on the chisels: chemical analysis, hardness testing and inspection of the steel's microstructure. First, they mounted the $300 worth of new chisels on an abrasive cut-off wheel and sawed them up into small chunks in order to get at the steel inside. A spectrographic analysis of the pieces revealed their chemical makeup to be very similar. It's worth noting that steel standards vary from country to country, but all of the foreign-made chisels closely matched the U.S. definition of a family of tool steels called W-type water hardening, except for the Sorby, which is a shock-resistant S-type tool steel. Both U.S. chisels were non-tool-steel grades of carbon steel. Carbon content of the 11 tools varied widely, from a barely hardenable 0.50% in the Sears to 1.24% in the Footprint.

Hardness, the quality most discernible at the bench and that which most governs a tool's edge-taking and edge-holding properties, was measured with a tool called a Tukon tester. Here

From *Fine Woodworking* magazine (March 1985): 51:44-48

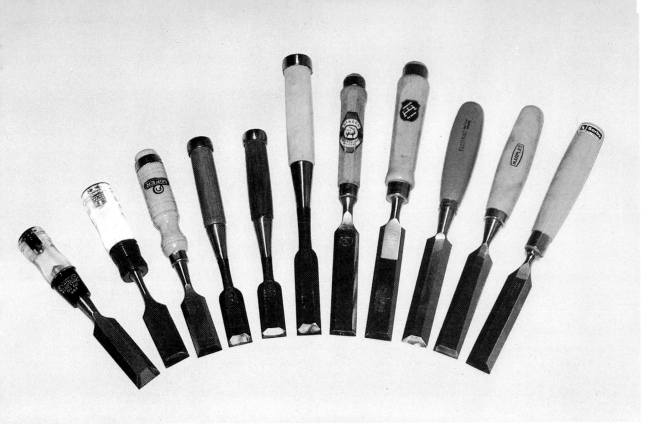

...test chisels had a wide range of handle styles and blade lengths—both important factors to consider when selecting a chisel. From ...Stanley, Craftsman, Mifer, Sentora, Oiichi, Iyoroi, Hirsch, Spannsage, Footprint, Marples and Sorby.

...measure hardness, two slices from each chisel were cast in plastic and polished, then they were mounted on the Tukon tester ...ove right), which calculates hardness by measuring the penetration of a diamond stylus.

...y the test works: One longitudinal and one transverse slice of ...h chisel's blade are cast into a small disc of thermosetting ...tic. The sample is polished and mounted under the tester's ...roscope. A tool with a tiny, diamond-tipped stylus called a ...op indenter is next placed on the steel. Weighed down by a ...-gram weight, the indenter penetrates minutely into the steel; ...deeper it goes, the softer the steel. The depth of the nick is ...asured and converted to a hardness number on the Rockwell C ...le. The microscope allows the technician to place the indent-...away from soft spots or contaminants that might give a false ...ding. For our tests, three separate readings were taken near

the cutting edge on each sample and the results averaged.

As the chart on p. 14 shows, the chisels varied in hardness by as much as 7 points on the Rockwell C scale (RC), which ranges from 20 to 70. At 52 RC, the Sears Craftsman was the softest of the test chisels—too soft to hold an edge. The three Japanese chisels were the hardest at more than 60 RC.

Hardness tells only part of a tool's metallurgical story. Peering through a microscope, a metallurgist can learn a lot about a steel's properties just by looking at it, reading its texture just as a wood technologist might study pores to identify a wood sam-

Chisel Characteristics

	Brand name	Price (1-in. chisel)	Steel	Average hardness at cutting edge*	Carbon content	Grain size	Blade thickness at top of bevel	Handle	Edge-retention rating
United States	Stanley	$10.25	High-carbon (AISI 1095), trace of carbides	59.5 RC	0.94%	#11	9/64 in.	Plastic, round	Very good
	Sears Craftsman	$ 7.99	Plain-carbon (AISI 1050), no carbides	56.0 RC	0.50%	# 9	5/32 in.	Plastic, round	Poor
England	Footprint	$ 7.60	W-type tool steel	59.0 RC	1.24%	**	9/64 in.	Beech, oval	Very good
	Marples	$13.15	W-type tool steel	60.0 RC	1.18%	# 6	1/8 in.	Boxwood, round	Fair (edge breaks down when dull)
	Sorby	$11.75	S-type tool steel, no carbides	57.5 RC	0.57%	#10	11/64 in.	Boxwood, round	Very good
West Germany	Hirsch	$14.95	W-type tool steel, no carbides	58.5 RC	0.80%	#11	3/32 in.	Ash, octagonal	Very good
	Spannsage	$ 9.25	W-type tool steel, no carbides	59.5 RC 62.0 RC	0.81%	#11	9/64 in.	Ash, round-flats	Very good
Japan	Iyoroi	$27.95	W-type tool steel, mild steel back	61.5 RC	1.04%	# 8	7/32 in.	Boxwood, round	Excellent
	Oiichi	$31.95	W-type tool steel, mild steel back	63.5 RC	1.09%	# 9	11/64 in.	Red oak, round	Excellent
	Sentora	$ 9.95	W-type tool steel, mild steel back	60.5 RC	0.81%	#10	3/16 in.	Red oak, round	Excellent
Spain	Mifer	$ 8.10	W-type tool steel	59.5 RC	1.10%	# 8	9/64 in.	Boxwood, round	Fair (edge breaks down when dull)

*Knoop indenter, 500-gram load. Average of three readings.
**Not determined.

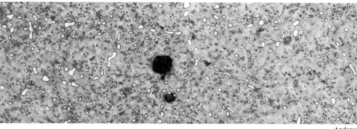

The chart above lists significant chisel characteristics. The prices given are the retail prices paid for the test chisels; current prices may vary. The edge-retention rating is based on the results of the bench test. The micrograph at right (magnified 100X) of a section of the Marples chisel shows the steel's microstructure. The small white particles are primary carbides, a hard-wearing combination of carbon and iron that improves edge retention. The large dark island is an oxide inclusion.

Andersc

ple. The lab tests sought two important microstructures in our chisels: carbides and grain. Carbides are a compound of carbon and iron present in the steel as it comes from the mill. Ideally, when the chisel is heated and quenched, some of these very hard carbide particles will disperse throughout the crystalline structure of the steel. The higher the initial carbon content of the steel, the more likely it is that the heat-treated chisel will contain carbides. Carbides are desirable because they greatly increase the wear resistance of the steel. In theory, a blade with fine and evenly distributed carbides will hold an edge longer than will a blade of the same hardness with no carbides.

Grain refers to the crystalline particles that make up the steel. The size of the grain is a measure of the "fineness" of the steel. A fine grain is important for edge retention and, in combination with evenly distributed carbides, will give the longest edge life. Grain is measured on a numerical scale: #1 is extremely coarse, #10 or above is extremely fine. Any steel with a grain size of 8 or higher can be considered a fine-grain steel.

Again, the results of the laboratory tests more or less agreed with my findings at the bench. But the really interesting thing that the microstructure analysis showed is that hardness alone doesn't necessarily mean the best edge retention. After sharpening each chisel, I pared away at a variety of hardwoods and pine

until the edge dulled, then I resharpened. I noticed a consi able difference in edge retention between brands. The six c els that contained carbides (Footprint, Marples, Mifer, Oi Iyoroi and Sentora) seemed to take an excellent edge from waterstones. With their hard edge and evenly distributed bides, the Japanese chisels held keen edges longer than an the Western chisels. The Hirsch, Spannsage, Sorby and Stanl all fine-grained but slightly softer than the Japanese chisels— and held very good edges. The Mifer and Marples are aln as hard as the Japanese chisels, yet when dull their e seemed to fragment and become ragged. It took longer to them sharp again because more steel had to be removed du the sharpening process. This is due, I suspect, to their tively coarse grain. The Sears Craftsman chisel fragmented b as it dulled.

A common complaint about Japanese chisels is that the brittle, and tend to chip. I experienced this once when I c mortise with a new Japanese chisel without first sharpenin Perhaps because I removed a fair amount of steel at the in sharpening, however, chipping wasn't a problem with any of Japanese chisels in the test.

The lab examined each steel sample for impurities suc slag. These are called inclusions (photo, above). From a m

visit to a chisel factory

Bros. has been making woodworking
in Millbury, Mass., since 1853, when
les and Richard Buck picked out a
with good water power. Water and
turned the wheels at Buck Bros. un-
e 1940s, but today wood chisels are
uced on modern machines. The fac-
also makes carving and turning tools,
vdrivers, scrapers, crowbars, spade
hatchets, and pitching horseshoes.

st summer I visited the firm to see
wood chisels are made. According to
company manager, J.C. Cort, Buck
manufactures all their chisels from
high-carbon steel (AISI 1095) with
ganese added to improve hardenability.
specify carbon and manganese con-
(each about 1%), and rely on their
supplier for quality control. Buck
does not test the steel.

isels are rough-formed by forging,
ny romantic notions I might have had
t wheezing bellows and ringing an-
were soon put to rest by what I saw.
-forging—at least for production tools
e in the United States—is a thing of
ast. Today, chisels are drop-forged in
part dies.

e blacksmith's modern counterpart is
hammerman. He works in semidark-
as his predecessor did, but instead of
mmer and anvil, he presides over a
ng drop hammer that packs a 1600-lb.
ch. Judging the temperature of the
by the color, the hammerman seizes
of the long steel rods from the gas fur-
at his side. With the timing and
d of a juggler, he brushes off scale on
e wheel, then places the glowing end
e rod in the bottom half of a two-part
Quick as thought, the hammer slams
n, rises and slams down again, bring-
he die halves together. The first blow
h-forms the blank, the second fin-
it. A good hammerman handles two
at once and can forge as many as
chisels in an eight-hour shift.

rning to a press, the hammerman sep-
s the chisel from the rod and flash,
xcess steel that squeezed out of the
The still-glowing chisel travels down
veyor and drops into a wheelbarrow.
hen cool, the chisel is ready for heating. First, the front, back and edges
round by machine to remove surface
erfections. The chisels are heated in a
ce called a high-frequency induction
r coil. Twelve chisels are placed on
in a fixture. In a few seconds they're
ed to a temperature of 1800°F. After
econds at this temperature, the chis-
automatically drop into a tank of

quenching oil. A circular conveyor lifts
out the hardened chisels and drops them
into a soda wash to remove the oil. At this
point, the steel has a hardness of about
64 to 65 RC. The clean, hardened chisels
are then loaded into gas-fired air draw furnaces for tempering at 440°F. When the
chisels come out, they have a hardness of
59 to 60 RC throughout.

Before 1950, one highly skilled man
ground the entire chisel by hand. Today,
it's done by machine in five separate
steps: edges, front and back, side bevels,
barrel, and cutting bevel. There's a separate automatic watercooled grinding machine for each operation. The loading and
unloading of the machines was the only
handwork I saw.

The machine that grinds the front and
back holds forty-five 1-in. chisels in a circular fixture called a spider. The spider
spins horizontally under an abrasive wheel.
When one chisel face is finished, the chisels are manually turned over and ground
on the other face.

After grinding, each finished blade is inspected by eye, and any rejects are cast
aside. The ones that pass inspection are
hand-wiped with oil to prevent rust. Then
the blades are ready for handles.

Most of the chisels get plastic handles.
These plastic-handled tools are intended
for mass-market sales, so the blades get
dipped in lacquer to prevent rust. Many of
these chisels are packaged on cardboard
cards, others go as sets in plastic pouches.
A small percentage of the blades get
wooden handles, but none were being fitted the day I visited.

I was surprised to learn that only about
15% of the total chisel production carries
the Buck Bros. trademark. Some of the remaining 85% might carry the Great Neck
brand (Buck Bros.' parent company). Others will carry the brand of the hardware or
discount-store chain that ordered them
(not Sears, however—Craftsman-brand chisels are made by Western Forge in Colorado
Springs, Colo.). There's no difference in
steel, manufacturing process or quality
control—just a different name on the plastic handle and, most likely, a different
price, too. Funny, before my visit I equat-
ed the name Buck Bros. with high quality,
but who ever heard of Great Neck? I
would have turned up my nose at the
discount-store chisel, thinking that it
was inferior.

I've never owned a Buck Bros. chisel, so
I don't know how the blade stacks up to
the German and Japanese chisels I use for
fine work, or the 15-year-old Sears chisels

At Buck Bros., chisels are drop-forged in two-part dies. The monstrous drop hammer above slams the die halves together with a force of 1600 lb., squeezing the hot plastic steel between them. Two quick blows forge a chisel.

I carry in my carpenters' toolbox. From
what I saw, Buck Bros. makes a chisel
carefully and efficiently. The manager is
well versed in metallurgy and knows what
a woodworker expects from a tool. His di-
lemma is to try to satisfy the skilled user
and at the same time avoid injuring the
chap who grabs a chisel to pry open a
paint can. This dichotomy dictates the tool
he makes. When asked how his chisels
would be different if serious woodworkers were his only customers, Cort replied,
"We'd increase the hardness. The edge
would be brittler, but much keener." □

*David Sloan is an assistant editor at
Fine Woodworking.*

lurgical viewpoint, inclusions are a red flag because they often indicate sloppy quality control in the steel-making. The Sears Craftsman was the only chisel we tested that had a metallurgically unacceptable level of inclusions. The tests turned up some slag in the Iyoroi and Sentora chisels, but in the welds, not in the steel itself. Adhering to tradition, the Japanese make their chisels by forge-welding (often by hand, with a power hammer substituting for a sledge-wielding apprentice) a hardenable tool-steel blank to a mild-steel billet that forms the tool's front face. Chemical segregation was another steelmaking quality-control problem that turned up in the Mifer, Spannsage, Sentora and Iyoroi chisels. This means that elements in the steel that should be thoroughly mixed weren't.

Apart from the metal quality and hardness, we noticed some other things about the chisels that shed some light on how carefully they are manufactured. The Japanese chisels were carefully prepared at the factory. They came accurately ground to the 30° bevel recommended by the manufacturers. Setting the steel ring on the handle was the only "tune-up" that these chisels required. The Western chisels, however, were less carefully prepared. Some were ground to a bevel that was way off the 25° most woodworkers aim for, and this required quite a few minutes at the benchstone to correct. The Stanley had a double-bevel knife-edge grind, so the back had to be ground down to remove the extra bevel. I found the Hirsch to be buffed so heavily that the edges were rounded, making it difficult to see if the cutting edge was square to the body or shank.

I always hand-sharpen chisels, and to me it's important for a chisel to have a perfectly flat back, especially in the area immediately behind the cutting edge. Stoning the bevel leaves a wire edge that must be removed by lapping the back of the chisel. If the back isn't flat, part of the wire edge won't contact the stone and may not be completely removed. A flat back rests solidly on the benchstone and eliminates the possibility that you might unintentionally lift the handle and stone a slight second bevel on the back of the chisel. A flat back also provides a bearing surface when you're using a chisel for paring. Except for the Sorby and

the Japanese chisels, which came from the factory wit backs, all of the chisels failed the flatness test—some mise The backs of the Craftsman and Stanley chisels were so wav it was very difficult to remove enough steel by hand to get flat. In contrast, the Japanese chisels all have hollow-g backs, which makes deburring easy.

Having read the lab reports after actually using the to came away with some very definite ideas about chisel b The main thing to consider, I think, is your attitude t sharpening. With one exception, the Sears Craftsman, a these chisels properly tuned and sharpened will work ade ly. If you're satisfied with your sharpening skills but aren't fussy about getting the best possible edge, any of the W chisels, except the Craftsman, should do fine. The steel similar in five of the eight Western chisels that only a very s sharpener could consistently tell the difference between That said, you might just as well let tactile factors such a tool's weight and balance, blade length and handle shape g your decision. Or the price.

If you're adept at sharpening and strive for the keenest the Japanese chisels may be for you. As the tests showed are harder and made of fine-grained steel with evenly distri carbides. But as with all Japanese blades, they require c hand-sharpening and they won't tolerate being bashed a loose inside a toolbox.

So which would I buy? My favorite Western chisels we Footprint and the Hirsch. Both had very comfortable handle good edge retention, and at $7.60, the Footprint is an exc value. For the very sharpest edge and the best retention, vorite was the Oiichi, although at $31.95 it was the most e sive of our test chisels.

Bill Stankus is a tool consultant, lecturer and woodwork Bayside, Wis. John Boyzych of Kelsey Hayes Labs and Mayer of Anderson Labs assisted in the preparation of thi cle. For more on tool steels, see Tool Steel Simplified *by Pa Luerssen and Pendleton, Chilton Company; and* Tool S *from the American Iron and Steel Institute, Washington,*

A second opinion

by Paul Horga

My initial interest in this article was as a technician. My background is in metals quality control, so I was suspicious of the high-flown claims in some tool catalogs. My intent in researching this article was to determine if the large differences in chisel prices were due to some measurable, physical difference in the tools. In my view, there is no measurable difference. The materials are all similar and the methods of manufacture aren't different enough to justify any substantial difference in price.

The lab rejected all tools softer than 59 RC, but I feel that this judgment is excessively harsh in the case of the Hirsch and Sorby chisels. The softer steel may require frequent sharpening,

but in my view this is a minor consideration. Besides, differences of up to four points on the Rockwell C scale are not necessarily significant because of variables in hardness testing.

The laminated Japanese chisels we tested were made in a style once found in Virginia in the 18th century. Steel was scarce then, so only a small piece was used for the cutting edge of the chisel. Iron was used for the body because it was less expensive. The Japanese continue their traditional practice of laminating blades for what I see as two reasons. First, the Japanese respect and revere tradition. Second, they understand the interest we in the United States have for the Orient, and for very

good business reasons they are explo ing the differences between our too making traditions. In selling laminat tools they are selling something diff ent. These chisels are very well ma but their initial expense and the time quired to maintain them makes them appropriate for the beginner or the p duction professional, in my opinion.

My advice? Don't let the steel dete mine which chisel to buy. Pick any ch el that's reasonably priced and fe nice. Sharpen it as well as you kno how. Any differences in the steel are subtle that most woodworkers won't r tice the difference.

Paul Horgan lives in Torrance, Cal

Steeling away
Starting from scratch

by John Gallup

Lately I've been dissatisfied with the quality of the steel in tools I get at the local True Value, so I decided to make my own. The process is quite simple, and with practice anyone can get good results. To get started, you'll need 20 or 30 tons of high-grade iron ore, 15 tons of low-sulfur coal, oxygen, and a dab of molybdenum.

The iron ore I use comes from the Mesabi range in northern Minnesota. Taconite, a low-grade pellet with less iron content, will work, but you'll need more of it. A coalyard should be able to fix you up with the coal, but if you prefer to use charcoal, refer to Eric Sloane's *A Reverence for Wood* for instructions on how to make it. The oxygen is essential to the Bessemer process, which results in a better steel, and you can order as many tanks as you need from a welding supply house. You'll need the molybdenum only if you're going to make sawblades and the like; I get mine from the big Climax, Colo., facility.

Okay, now we're ready. Load a few tons of coal into a coke oven battery and heat it for about three weeks. The natural-gas tap to your house may not be big enough, but you can dig it up out to the street and run a larger pipe in from there. Check with the local utility company about getting a larger meter, and watch out for sparks. When the coal is cooked, it's called "coke," and makes the hot fire you'll need in the blast furnace. Using tongs and heavy potholders, transfer it there, and hurry so it doesn't cool off. Specially designed railroad cars are quicker.

Load the furnace with ore and start heating. When it's molten, the various impurities will cook off or be left as slag. Experiment will teach you just how much oxygen to inject and when. Pour the white-hot steel into molds for five-ton pigs, and hustle them over to your rolling mill. I built mine out of scrap, but be sure to use good-quality metal—the rollers are under quite a bit of stress when they squeeze that squarish 2000° pig out into the bar stock you'll need to make plane irons and chisels. If the steel cools off before you've finished working it, drop the pig into a firebrick-lined pit and cook it some more. You can't be too careful here. When those five-ton pigs are shooting back and forth between the rollers they sometimes get loose, and there go your insurance rates, right through the roof.

Now you've got about five tons of bar stock. Give it a few days to cool (if you do this in the winter it will really help the heating bill). A trip hammer is handy for cutting it to length. Don't forget to allow for tangs on your chisels. Take a piece over to the Rockwell hardness tester and check it. If it's below C60-64, you didn't add enough carbon back when the steel was molten. But don't worry. You can always melt it down and start again.

Once you get the fundamentals down, all kinds of possibilities open up. A few years' apprenticeship with a tool-and-die maker in a foundry will teach you all you need to know to cast your own plane bodies and saw tables. A drop forge is handy for making flat pieces, and will save you a lot of tedious anvil work. Once you start making your own steel, you will never again be frustrated with nicked chisels and broken router bits. □

Tools Are Where You Find Them

Luthier borrows lots of help from other trades and crafts

by Michael Dresdner

My shop, where I repair and restore musical instruments, is filled with paraphernalia that you won't find in the average woodworking catalog. Over the years I've confronted innumerable jobs that required some special tool that didn't seem to exist in my field, and often I've had to invent a tool to do the job. But it's easy to forget that what may be a rare and unlikely job for one craftsman is another's bread and butter. I am reminded of a luthier who painstakingly made a small aluminum riser for a guitar repair job. Upon showing off his invention, he was told that he had made a piano string jack, a 3-in. high tool readily available in piano repair shops. I've had enough similar experiences that I now check out other trades' tool catalogs before I set about to reinvent the wheel.

STRING JACK

Local specialty stores, such as jewelry suppliers and medical and dental suppliers, are often very helpful. They not only have access to scores of wholesale outlets and manufacturers who don't want to bother with small retail sales, but they also have a good idea of the range of tools and possibilities, and they give good, pithy advice. Look in the Yellow Pages, and scan the ads in specialty magazines. The Tool Works, 111 Eighth Ave., New York, N.Y. 10011, has a good catalog, but the place is even more valuable for the tools the catalog has no room to list. Owner Bart Slutsky has steered me in the right direction more than once. Among other things, he turned me on to a set of machinists' round-edged joint files, such as those drawn below. If you ever need to make round-bottomed grooves of specific widths, such as for guitar strings, these are just perfect.

Catalogs I rely on because of their broad range include Techni-Tool, 5 Apollo Rd., Box 368, Plymouth Meeting, Pa. 19462; William Dixon Company, Division of Grobet File Co. of America, Carlstadt, N.J. 07072; and Brownells, Inc., Rt. 2, Box 1, Montezuma, Iowa 50171 (gunsmithing). Also, affiliated local hardware stores usually have a monster catalog of things they can't stock but will order. My neighborhood store isn't very big, but their catalog has almost 2,000 pages, lists over 30 manufacturers, and has illustrations—a great help if you don't know what something is called, but have a good idea of what it should look like.

The cleverest suggestions, however, always seem to come

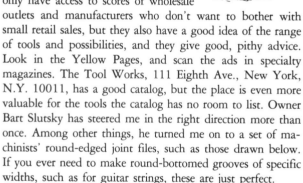

ROUND-EDGE JOINT FILES

from mechanics. I had been complaining to my friend Barry about the inadequacy of the available turntable mechanisms to provide me with a portable, heavy-duty, spray-booth turntable. A few days later, he handed me a 20-lb. chunk of metal that turned out to be a transmission bearing from a junked Pontiac. It consisted of two plates, already drilled with four evenly spaced holes, connected by a *very* heavy-duty bearing. It took only minutes to attach a board on the top plate and set the mechanism on a base, and I was spraying with a smooth, sure turntable that is, so far, impervious (due to the protected, greased bearing) to clogging by spray dust.

Here's another tip from the automotive field: Sometimes I have to steam open old glue joints, and one of my favorite aids is a small cappucino maker, a steam generator that produces very hot, dry steam under a good deal of pressure. It has a built-in safety valve and a cut-off valve. To get into tight spots, I extended the output stem by adding a length of surgical tubing, with a basketball air-fill pin as the tip, and secured both with hose clamps. As I was using it one day, I watched in horror as the tubing suddenly ballooned out. As I made a grab for the cut-off valve, the bubble burst, spewing steam and pieces of rubber all over me and the shop. The oven mitts on my hands prevented injury, but the incident shook me up. I set out to the nearest auto supply store, and came back with some reinforced heat-resistant fuel line hose. It's been holding like a trooper for more than two years now.

Although surgical tubing was a "bust" as a steam hose, it's still indispensable. It's no secret that random lengths make fine tie-offs for holding things, and that this tubing can act as a rubber-band clamp. But it has other uses as well. I keep a split length handy to protect the soundhole of a guitar from being marred by metal clamps, and I usually slip a strip onto a bar clamp to protect the wood from the bar. The hose comes in various diameters and, because it's latex, it will not mar or react with lacquer finishes. Strips of tubing can be slipped over metal hangers that are to hold finished wood, and the larger diameters attached to the fingers of a drying rack make a cushiony support. A loop thrown onto a rough tabletop will allow you to float a finished board on it while the other side is being worked on.

Don't walk out of the medical equipment store yet. Surgical gloves are more sensitive and less clumsy than grocery store rubber gloves, especially for aniline staining and French polishing, when you need to feel the pad. Various surgical clamps and hemostats make fine extra hands and mini-clamps for small or delicate parts. Even the humble petroleum jelly (Vaseline) is handy as tapeless masking for lacquer, as well as being a must for lubricating spray guns. Vaseline won't mess up a finish if a drop of it migrates, as will some oils. Surgical jelly has similar properties and is water-soluble as well.

From *Fine Woodworking* magazine (September 1983) 42:58-59

GUNSTOCK VISE

There is a versatile gun-stock vise, such as shown at right, on just about every luthier's workbench. It rotates 360° and its jaws pivot to grip non-parallel stock. Most luthiers pad the jaws with leather or suede, and a rubber band draped between the jaws will protect the stock from dropping onto the metal guides. While you are checking out gunstock vises, take a look at checkering tools too. They make a whole range of handy little chisels of odd shapes and sizes, great for getting into tiny spots to clean up intricate carvings. And for the backgrounds of those carvings, remember that leather stamps work just as well on wood. Leather punches are also very handy. They'll make clean circular holes in veneer or plastic, or else cleanly cut-out dots, whichever you happen to need. Don't overlook leather workers' files and rasps either. They work superbly on wood, are generally finer-cutting than woodworking ones, and often come in different, handy profiles. Machinists' files add to the arsenal. Many of them cut on the pull stroke rather than the push stroke, which is great for tight spots. Speaking of fine cutting and versatility, dental bits and burs can't be beat. The burs will fit a Dremel, and come in an astonishing array of sizes and shapes—far more than the motor tool companies offer. Catalogs of jewelers' tools usually list them.

For pearl inlay work, you need something that draws a constant, narrow line, unlike a regular pencil whose point gets thicker and thicker as it dulls. I used to curse my way through six or seven pencil points while drawing on pearl, and one day I finally stomped out and steamed my way over to the local art supply store. There I saw a heartwarming display of mechanical drafting pencils. They take leads of a dozen different diameters and all degrees of hardness. I chose a 0.3mm pencil and a medium-hard lead, and I now use it for all marking and drawing where scribing is impossible or the scratch line undesirable. On my way out of the store, I asked for a thinner masking tape than was on display, and got accidentally introduced to another worksaver. They sold me a paper tape used in drafting, and I soon found that while it masks every bit as well, it doesn't lift off old, checked finishes the way masking tape invariably does.

Spray adhesive, also from the art supply store, has simplified many temporary holding jobs. It makes working with pearl or other small inlays much easier. I spray-glue the back of the inlay and stick it on the surface where it will go. Then I spray the surrounding area with a contrasting color of tinting lacquer—a mixture of almost pure pigment and solvent that has virtually no binder. After I lift off the inlay, I can rout out the wood within the crisp, colored outline. Mineral spirits loosens the adhesive without affecting the lacquer. Lacquer thinner removes both adhesive and color.

Years ago, I went out to buy a ³⁄₃₂-in. router bit, for cutting bridge slots. The salesman looked at me as if I were crazy, and sold me an end mill instead. I took it home, set it up in my slower drill press (rigged up like an overarm router), and found that its spiral cutting edges made a clean, burn-free cut. It works especially well in hard woods such as ebony and rosewood, causes less chipping, and, because it's made to cut metal, has outlasted every router bit in my shop.

My friend Barry, the bearer of clutch bearings, has been my main guide to metalworking tools. One frequent job I'm asked to do, installing a larger set of guitar tuners, involves enlarging all or part of a hole already drilled. My old method had me plugging the hole, finding the center, and drilling a new hole. It was time-consuming and inaccurate. Then Barry introduced me to the counterbore, shown at right, a metal bit with a removable pilot in its center. Any size pilot (with a standard shaft) will fit in any size bit, so you can enlarge or partially bore any hole from any other one, and the pilot ensures that the hole center remains the same. In addition, the bit makes a clean, uniform hole, with no chipping.

Don't overlook the trash can. I make a regular practice of raiding the local glass cutter's rubbish for scraps of clear plastic sheet. It shows up in several thicknesses, and I tote them all back to my shop. As clamping cauls, they let you see how the seam underneath is lining up, saving many repeat jobs, and wood glue will not stick to them. But it is the larger pieces that are really indispensable—they become my instrumentmaking templates. The plastic lets you see through to line up the grain the way you want it, or to include the prettiest figure.

Having borrowed so much from other trades, perhaps I can give something back. We've all learned that lining a jig with face-up sandpaper stops things from sliding around, but a common item from my own trade, violin rosin, works just as well and does less damage to the piece. It crushes into a fine, sticky powder which will cling to the jig and provide just the right tack. Mineral spirits cleans away any residue. Also from my workbench is a small clamp, shown at left, used for repairing cracks in soundboards. The objective is to glue a tapered cleat beneath the crack. The clamp, made from a guitar tuner and angle iron, works by pulling up on the cleat, leveling the crack at the same time. When the glue is dry, the guitar string is simply clipped off and pulled out, leaving a tiny hole.

One final word of warning when accumulating what seems to be free for the taking. I have several sandbags in my shop that I use for bedding curved or rounded objects on the drill-press table. One day I asked my wife to fill one for me, as she was on her way to the beach—living on the Jersey shore, with its over 100 miles of beachfront, I assumed there would be ample sand to spare for my small bag. But the bag came back empty. After mutely watching my wife fill the bag and lug it to the car, a policeman had stepped up and ordered her to take it back and dump it on the beach. Apparently, in New Jersey, you can take home only as much sand as you can unwittingly carry in your shoes and bathing suit. □

CLAMP
CRACK
GLUE.

COUNTERBORE

Michael Dresdner, of Red Bank, N.J., came to instrument repair via an apprenticeship in antique restoration.

Knife Work

Make the knife and carve a spoon

by Rick Mastelli

Winter nights are long in Sweden. When farmers go into the forest to cut the year's firewood, they make a point of also collecting bent limbs and crotches, blanks from which to whittle spoons in the evening months. In rural Sweden many men still wear knives, not as weapons but as ready tools, and it is part of the ritual of conversation to punctuate a sentence with a shaving from a stick. In some parts of the world whittlers carve figures or ornaments, and there are always some who just make chips. In Sweden spoons are traditional, and still popular. The centuries have yielded a deep understanding of hand-tool techniques, as well as of the form of the wooden spoon—together they evidence a refined simplicity.

A week-long workshop I attended last summer focused on these hand-tool techniques. The place was Country Workshops in Marshall, N.C., and the teacher was Wille Sundqvist, a wiry, 57-year-old Swede whose relationship to craft is long and thorough. As a boy he learned to carve by watching his father and grandfather, both of them farmers and winter woodworkers. When he was six years old, he discovered the first principle of knife work while squabbling with his brother. His brother grabbed the knife's handle and he gripped the blade, and when they pulled, he learned indelibly how knives slice. At 20 Sundqvist hurt his back in a forest accident, and so had to find a career other than farming. He went to wood-

Sundqvist uses innumerable knife grips and strokes. These two are among his most powerful, because they slice away from the body and require no 'safety stop' to protect the carver from the blade. At right, the hand that holds the blank rigid is lodged above the knee cap. The knife is held at an angle in the hand such that the stroke leads with the handle, the tip of the blade trails. The slice is powered from the shoulder and back, the elbow and wrist locked. Above, the slice is also from the handle toward the tip, but here leverage against the chest helps power it.

Photos: Rick Mastelli and Drew Langsne

From *Fine Woodworking* magazine (January 1983) 38:84-88

Sundqvist demonstrates the grip and stance for grinding an ax. The backing board helps to maintain even pressure on the ax head as it is run diagonally over the grindstone.

artisan's work increases directly with his understanding of and respect for his tools. Thus Sundqvist began by having us make knives. We spent a full day fitting a 3½-in. long, laminated Swedish steel blade into a chunk of applewood, then shaping the wood to fit our own hands. We took another day fitting the knife into a wooden sheath with a leather collar we sewed wet around the knife's handle. After the leather dried and shrank, the knife could be eased out and snapped securely back into place, and afterward it hung from our belts to remind us how handy a knife can be.

We sharpened our tools so there was no rounding at the edge, and no secondary microbevel, for the surfaces that produce the edge have to be flat. Dubbing is right for edges that are meant to split wood; dubbing keeps the tool from sticking in the wood. And a microbevel is okay for a chisel, whose flat back registers the cutting edge. But for a knife, the bevel itself is that registration plane. When it is flat on the wood surface, the edge must be there too, ready to cut. These blades were manufactured by Erik Frost in Sweden and are called Sloyd knives by most woodworking supply outlets. You can see the lamination line halfway up the bevel. The softer steel sandwiching the harder makes the knife less brittle and easier to sharpen. We sharpened to a greater angle than is usually recommended: 25° for knives and gouges, 28° for axes. For knives, the bevels on either side of the blade are equal. For axes, if you are right-handed, you sharpen the left-hand bevel longer than the right, for more surface with which to guide the cut. Axes can be honed by moving the ax head over a stationary stone, but I found it easier to clamp the ax upright in a vise and move the stone over the bevels in small circles. Sundqvist showed us how to keep our eye on the bevel opposite the stone, looking for a thin line of honing oil to be scraped off the stone's surface and to run down the edge. Maintain the finest flow of oil, and your bevel will be flat. This technique also works for honing the carving gouges used to hollow the bowls of spoons. You hold the tool upright in one hand, bevel away from you, and rub the face of a stone

working school, where he apprenticed with the illustrious furniture designer Carl Malmsten. Later he taught woodworking at Malmsten's school, and in various elementary and preschool programs, then for ten years he taught others to be woodworking teachers. Since 1969 Sundqvist has been consultant to the Handcraft Society in the province of Västerbotten, researching traditional handcrafts and helping the disabled and the elderly become productive craft workers.

In Sundqvist's hands, ax and knife are powerful, precise tools. Throughout the week at Country Workshops we ten students were awed. Sundqvist could waste thick, measured slabs from an ornery dogwood branch, or with the same surety scribe vigorous detail into a spoon handle. Every inch of the knife blade or ax edge, every contour of their handles, had its purpose and right use. He showed us a profuse variety of traditional grips and strokes—useful not only because they direct the cut but also because they provide built-in safety stops, in that the cuts end when part of the hand or arm comes in contact with the work (or part of the carver's body), thus keeping the knife from slicing flesh. When you are sure of your stop, you can work with confidence and direct more energy into the cut. Not only his hands, but the whole of his body worked. Barefoot, shirtless, in shorts, he showed the interaction between thrust and safety stop, brace and swing, grip and lever. He did not say much; English does not come easy for him. We learned by watching him work.

It's shocking how much we modern craftsmen underestimate the basic tools. Knives sold for carving come with spindly handles and stubby blades, their bevels dubbed round by the buffing wheel. Axes are sold with their bevels made bulbous by a sanding belt, and with handles so skinny that your fingers bottom out on your palm. No wonder we figure these tools are good only for hacking at firewood. The quality of an

Fig. 1: Plans for a Sloyd knife handle

Side view

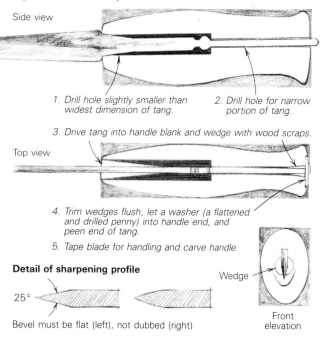

Top view

1. Drill hole slightly smaller than widest dimension of tang.
2. Drill hole for narrow portion of tang.

3. Drive tang into handle blank and wedge with wood scraps.

4. Trim wedges flush, let a washer (a flattened and drilled penny) into handle end, and peen end of tang.

5. Tape blade for handling and carve handle.

Detail of sharpening profile

25°

Bevel must be flat (left), not dubbed (right)

Wedge

Front elevation

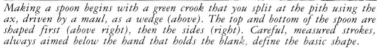

Making a spoon begins with a green crook that you split at the pith using the ax, driven by a maul, as a wedge (above). The top and bottom of the spoon are shaped first (above right), then the sides (right). Careful, measured strokes, always aimed below the hand that holds the blank, define the basic shape.

up and down, flat against the bevel. Rotate the tool slowly back and forth to present the whole of the bevel to the slip stone, all the while looking for the dribble of oil to leak over the edge. To remove the burr, slip the round edge of the stone up and down, flat against the inside of the gouge.

Any close-grained, dense wood will make a good spoon. The natural curves of branches make for a stronger utensil, because the grain can follow the shape. We had a pile of green crooks and crotches to work: rhododendron, dogwood, black birch, apple. At times it seemed that the spoons we were making were only vehicles for practice with knife and gouge. Eventually the tool and hand would work effortlessly for a while, and the infinite possibilities of the spoon would replace the challenge of simply using the tools. How make a lump of wood hold food, be comfortable to the hand and mouth, please the eye, enjoy use? The bowl of the spoon needs to be thin, to fit the lips, and so for strength it ought be oriented to minimize end grain. The stem of the spoon should position the bowl below the plane of the handle, and to satisfy the eye it should be narrow, so for strength it ought be thick and continue down like a spine, supporting the bowl. The top of the handle should be thin, to fit the hand, so for strength and visual balance it should be wide. A wide

surface calls for decoration, so at the top ("to keep the eye from flying off," as Sundqvist puts it) you need a finial. Making a spoon, you learn how deep is the challenge—design that is infinite with possibilities, all coordinated by tradition and function. Suddenly, the wooden spoons you buy at the supermarket are two-dimensional.

It's surprising how much like a spoon you can shape a branch with only an ax. First the ax splits the branch in half (you drive it with a maul, like a wedge), to ensure that the pith will not be part of the spoon. The trick for the rest of the ax work is to support the blank solidly on the chopping block and far enough forward so that an overswing will not end in your leg. Hold the blank so that the thrust of the stroke is below your fingers. You shape the side view of the spoon first, including most of the bottom of the bowl, then you define the outline of the bowl and handle. This order gives you more stock to hold on to longer. The strokes that shape the stem near the beginning of the bowl are the most critical, because an overswing here can easily crack the bowl. For a more mincing stroke, you hold the ax closer to its head.

Now you sit down with your knife and a couple of gouges. The green wood cuts like cheese. The diverse grips for safe, forceful knife and gouge work are recorded in the photos of

Fig. 2: Plans for a Swedish spoon

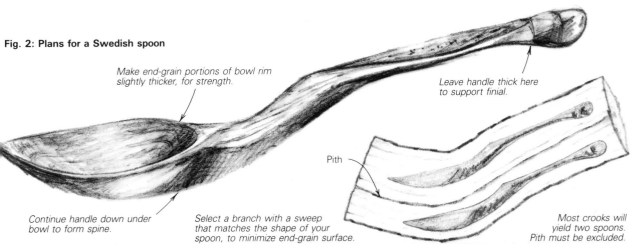

Make end-grain portions of bowl rim slightly thicker, for strength.

Leave handle thick here to support finial.

Pith

Continue handle down under bowl to form spine.

Select a branch with a sweep that matches the shape of your spoon, to minimize end-grain surface.

Most crooks will yield two spoons. Pith must be excluded.

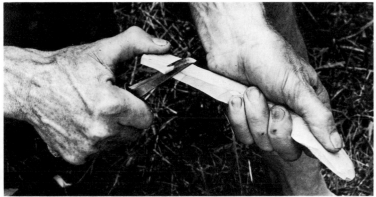

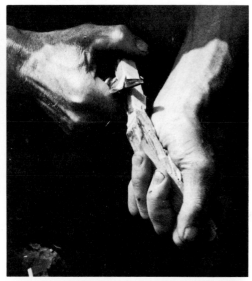

Most of us pare by slicing from the stout end of a knife toward the tip. Sundqvist gets greater power arcing the blade from tip to handle, often using his thumb for leverage. Each stroke has its safety. Above, the thumb is held out of the knife's direction on the spoon end. At right, Sundqvist modifies this stroke to slim the middle of the spoon's handle by repositioning the thumb 90° to the stroke and rotating the knife in the palm about 30° toward the blank. Short, arced strokes stop before the thumb is touched.

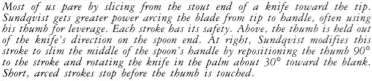

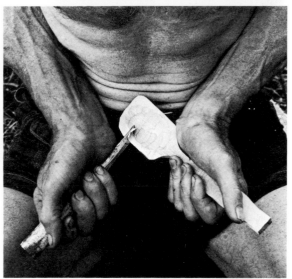

It doesn't take long to shape the blank with the knife before it's time to hollow the bowl. Gripping the gouge as shown at left keeps the stroke short and safe. Most of the strokes are cross-grain, and they stop when the hand contacts the spoon. The rim of the bowl calls for special grips. The knife grip above may look dangerous, but it has its safety and is surprisingly controlled. The trick here is to put your little finger on the flat of the blade, which positions the heel of the hand along the back. Then both arms are braced against the ribs, and the hands move together like a pair of scissors. With the wrist cocked, it is not possible for the knife to reach the body.

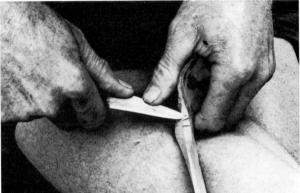

These two strokes are both powered by the hand not holding the knife. They show how Sundqvist uses the whole length of the blade: the stout portion for heavy cuts, the tip for fine work. At top is the still-green blank. Wet wood is easier to shape, but to smooth the surface, the spoon is first dried overnight. Dry wood, above, frays less.

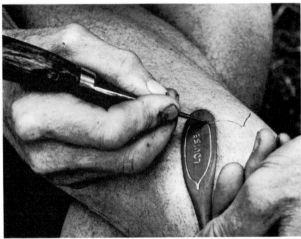

Gift spoons warrant decoration. Sundqvist first pencils in the shapes and letters, then uses the tip of the knife locked at about 60° to the surface, first in one direction, then the other, to remove a triangular chip of whatever length.

Sundqvist at work. Most of these positions feel strange at first, but by the time the calluses form, you have a physical memory. Your body reaches for the necessary posture to handle that excess of wood at the rim. For the underside of the handle, it reaches for another position. You don't think about it, you feel for it. But each time before you power the stroke, you think, *where is this edge going to stop?*, and you balance the tensions, or you adjust your hands so the edge doesn't end in your flesh. It's absorbing work. The conversations I enjoyed late into the night, unable to release my work for the day, were indeed punctuated with shavings.

When the shape of the spoon is there, you rub the blank with a boiled potato to fill the pores and forestall checking. The blank dries over the stove until morning. Green wood is easy to carve, but it is trouble to smooth. The next day you lightly go over your dry blank with the knife, and then you sand, until your spoon is fit for hand and lip.

Sundqvist was a remarkable teacher. He would devote himself entirely to one student at a time. He would listen to your question or watch you work for a moment. Then, unable to tell you what to do, he would show you. It was unnecessary to explain to him what shape you had in mind. He would see it in the blank. It may have taken you half a day to realize what you were doing, but he knew in half a minute—you would see what force could be exercised, how much wood could be made to disappear, if only you held the knife *this* way. It was unnerving at first to hand over that precious lump of wood, with all your feeble little nicks in it, and then watch great chunks of it fly. But it was your own vision Sundqvist handed you back. And then he would hold your hands in his and shape them to the task.

He cared about every piece of worked wood. The more effort that had gone into it, the more valuable it became. There were no mistakes we could make nor defects in the wood we could uncover that did not summon his healing energies. I watched him painstakingly patch a misbored hole in a knife handle, even an incipient check in a spoon bowl. The pieces hardly seemed worth the trouble—they still looked like ax offal. But he saw them as works, and his fixes made them all the more valuable. When finished, they were special pieces, marked by their making. Craftsmanship, Sundqvist demonstrated, is measured as much by the mistakes you correct as by the ones you avoid. □

Rick Mastelli, formerly associate editor of Fine Woodworking, *is video producer and director for* The Taunton Press.

A Sundqvist spoon, traditional craft.

Antique Tools

A buyer's guide to many you can use

by Robert Sutter

The latest tool catalog has arrived, so you settle down with the "wishing book" in eager anticipation. But oh, those prices: sixteen dollars for a saw, twenty-two for a brace, sixty for a plough plane (1976 prices throughout). It sure puts a damper on your ardor to fill your shop with all those wonderful-looking objects in the pages of that catalog open across your knees.

Well, how do you go about getting your heart's desire while preserving as much of your bank account as possible? One way is to budget a realistic sum of money for your basic tools and then make additions only as the need arises. Buy the best you can get in the way of edge tools and saws. If you must, you can acquire inexpensive yet less soul-satisfying hammers, pliers, screwdrivers, files, etc. at the local hardware store. Beware of special house brands and bargains, though; you only get what you pay for. Shop carefully and compare with your wishing book; you may find that a small price difference will procure a more trustworthy item than the bargain bucket at the local hardware emporium.

Another way to build your journeyman's kit is the antique tool route. There is certainly a big kick to be gotten out of finding a half dozen peachy chisels at the back of the antique shop for just two dollars apiece. That sort of bargain may be easy on the budget, but old isn't necessarily good, and if they turn out to be made of Swiss cheese, you can't exchange them. Realize that when searching for old tools you compete with the tool collector and that chances are he knows a lot more about the tricky business of buying antique tools than you do.

Recognize, too, that sellers of antiques keep informed about trends in their field. They know that competition between collectors for new acquisi-tions raises prices, and they are aware that old tools have recently been touted as preeminently collectible. Dealers also know the worth of old tools on the current market, so don't expect to find an antique dealer who doesn't know what he has in that box of rusty old tools lying half out of sight under the dropleaf table in the back of the store. He knows, and he put that box where it is on purpose.

Okay, let's assume that in spite of my admonitions you decide you're going to look around for some old tools. What can you expect to find and what will the results of your search cost? I'll try to answer those questions from experience garnered in fifteen years of collecting and over thirty of buying tools for my workshop.

Braces

The first braces were naturally form-ed tree limbs of the proper shape. Next came factory-shaped wooden braces with brass reinforcement plates. Such items are in the seventy to one-hundred-fifty-dollar class—more if unique. Metal braces with rudimentary screw chucks were in use side by side with wooden ones. Later on in the 19th century, and early in the 20th, braces with universal shell chucks and ratchet sweeps began to be manufactured. Stanley braces from 1900 on can often be found with ten to fifteen-dollar price tags, which, if sound, will function perfectly today. Check the chuck to be sure it closes all the way and is concentric. See that the wooden parts are not split and that the metal is bright under the dirt. If so, you've got a usable tool for a reasonable price.

A word about rusty tools here. A lit-tle rust easily scraped away to expose bright metal is okay and can be cleaned up. Discoloration due to use and han-dling likewise. But eschew the item encrusted with rust. It won't clean satis-factorily no matter the effort, and the metal will bear pit marks and deep-seated rust pockets for evermore. While

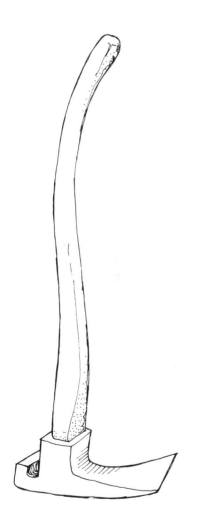

ADZE

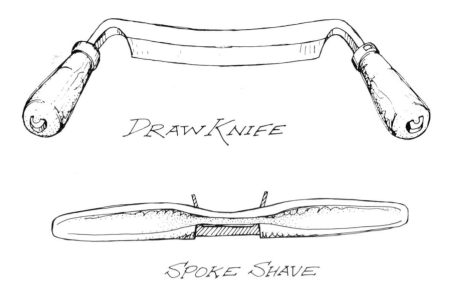

DRAW KNIFE

SPOKE SHAVE

dles, for the only way to sharpen them
is to remove the handle. To use an adze
requires a very sharp edge on the adze
and a very sharp skill on your part.
Have someone who knows show you
how to use it, and then practice on
scrap timber before working on anything important. Watch out for your
toes as the tool is swung towards them.

Drawknives, etc.

Another archaic but useful tool is the
drawknife. Anyone who has visited one
of the restoration villages has undoubt-
edly seen a drawknife in use or at rest
on a shaving bench. For quick shaping
of round and curved work, this tool is
hard to beat. Since the depth of cut is
dependent on how the tool is held
relative to the work, some practice is required to cut a long, uniform shaving.
There is also an element of risk in pulling a large, sharp knife towards your
stomach. Safer and more easily controlled is the spokeshave which operates
on the same general principle as the
drawknife but has the mechanics of a
plane to control the cut. Spokeshaves
come in brass, iron or wood bodies with
straight, convex, concave, or rounded
soles. Sometimes two differently
shaped soles, each with its own blade,
were mounted side by side in a single
handle. New spokeshaves are easily obtained from purveyors of fine tools
through their catalogs or as antiques.

merely unsightly in some cases, such
pits and pockets on edge tools affect the
edge-holding ability of the tool.

Saws

You may find some good, usable old
saws, but I doubt it. Old, all-steel saws
are often temptingly priced since they
are not very popular with collectors,
who prefer frame and turning saws. In
years gone by, a craftsman bought a saw
and used it until it was worn out from
repeated sharpening and setting. He replaced broken handles and rivets as
they were needed for the steel saw
handles. When the saw was past using,
it was discarded—for you to pick up.
Therefore resist the temptation to buy
an old saw even though it costs but
three or four dollars. Purchase the highest grade new one you can and take care
of it. It will serve you well just as the
four-dollar relic served its owner when
it was shiny and fresh from the store.

Adzes

The adze is one of the oldest tools in
the woodworker's kit. Paleolithic specimens are to be seen in museums, but
today the adze turns up more often in
crossword puzzles than in real life. For
the unfamiliar it is a sort of mashie-
niblick axe with an oddly curved
handle. An adze is a smoothing and
shaping tool used for finishing large
areas of wood such as floors and beams
as well as for all sorts of chores in ship-
yards. The adze is no longer a common
item on the shelf of hardware stores in

this country, even though still available in most of Europe. Should you
decide you can't live without one, you
will have to purchase it as an antique.
The Collins Axe Company made adzes
out of good steel with proper balance
until a few years ago. They were jap-
anned black and sold without handles,
as were all adzes, since the handle is a
matter of individual design. You can
often find a good, quite new Collins
adze head lying about for perhaps eight
to fifteen dollars. Those that have
handles and are older will be more expensive. By the way, adze heads are
never permanently fixed to their han-

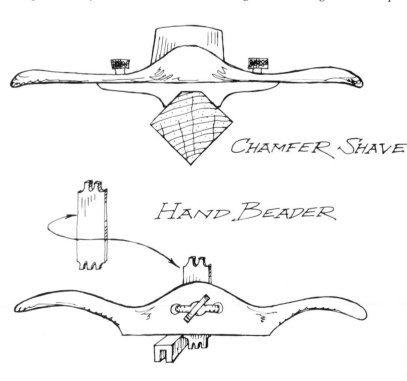

CHAMFER SHAVE

HAND BEADER

Prices run from six or seven dollars for a modern spokeshave to twenty dollars for 19th century iron ones. Wooden shaves were commonly made out of beech or box woods, but occasionally you will see ebony or cherry or other fine cabinet woods used. Beware of wooden spokeshaves as the throat wears easily and makes them difficult to set. Because of this deficiency, many wooden specimens have brass or even ivory set into the throat to provide a hard, less easily worn surface. Towards the end of the 19th century, Stanley and others produced a chamfering spokeshave which is most useful and worth some hunting about for.

Another branch of this large and useful family of tools is the scratch stock or universal hand beader. It is really a scraper of sorts with handles like a spokeshave. The hand beader has a thin steel blade with a shaped edge held almost vertically to the plane of the work piece. When pulled, the blade scrapes a bead or other shape out of the wood. A scratch stock will cut moulded edges on curves, and works well regardless of grain direction or complexity. Since it scrapes, there is practically no tendency to tear the wood. Unfortunately, this tool can now be found only as an antique.

Chisels

There are more varieties of chisels than there are herring dishes in Finland. In one catalog I counted twenty flat carving chisels and one hundred and thirty gouge shapes, fishtails, allonge fishtails, spoon, and backbent chisels. In addition there were bevel-

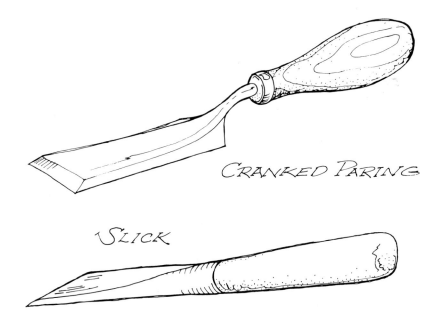

CRANKED PARING

SLICK

edge paring chisels in several grades, long and strong hooped chisels, in-cannel gouges and mortise chisels. Prices ranged from under four dollars to over ten. Antique chisels are available in all the variety of the newer ones plus others long out of production such as slicks, framing, and corner chisels. Except for slicks and corner chisels, not many collectors are interested, so prices vary from under a dollar to ten or twelve dollars, with exceptions running up in the twenty-five to fifty-dollar range.

Framing, corner, and hooped chisels are for pounding on as are mortise chisels. Paring chisels, in-cannel gouges, and slicks are for pushing. The latter will take a razor edge while the former (somewhat softer to withstand the stresses of being pounded) take a little coarser edge. Chisel making is an

art. Good steel, well forged and properly heat-treated to be hard at the edge and tough in the body and tang is what you will be seeking, often in vain, in modern tools.

Chisels are really the only case in tool acquiring where I would suggest antique over new because the older handmade tools are more likely to have the qualities required. Of course, shapes and sizes must be found one by one, and often just what you need is unavailable, but seek out the old steel and you'll likely have a winner. Many older chisels have inlaid edges, a piece of very hard, brittle steel for the edge welded onto a softer, tougher steel shank. Buy old chisels with as much intact blade and inlay as possible. Picturesque, well-worn, short-bladed tools are useless because they are probably ground back past the hardened portion at the business end of the blade. Tools by Buck Brothers, Barton, Isaac Greaves, Wm. Butcher, Underhill Edge Tool Co., and many Sheffield, England, companies are pretty sure to be of high quality. Don't let the words "cast steel" confuse you. The blades weren't cast, for cast steel in the 19th-century context refers only to a type of tool steel of high quality.

For those woodworkers who are always looking for the best tool to do the best job, there is an aesthetic quality to tools used by generations of craftsmen before our time which is as satisfying as the keen edge or comfortable fit of a new tool. Perhaps it is justification enough for the search. I often think so. □

CORNER

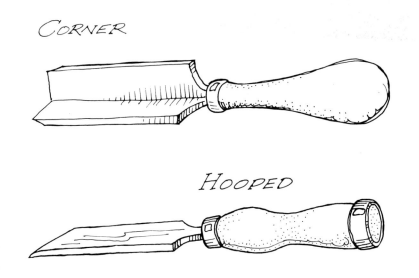

HOOPED

A Carver's Tricks
Three methods from a period-furniture maker

by Eric Schramm

One of the most valuable additions to my collection of carving tools is a set of four round-nose chisels. Originally they were ordinary butt chisels, but I re-ground them to rounded profiles and hollow-ground the bevels to a length of about ⅜ in., as the factory-ground bevel was too steep for carving. I use these four chisels in place of many gouges having different sweeps and widths. Used with the bevel down, the 1-in. and ¾-in. chisels are excellent tools for wasting wood fast in relief carvings as well as roughing-in a carving in-the-round. Used with the bevel up, all four chisels work well for shaping and smoothing convex surfaces. The ½-in. and ¼-in. chisels eliminate the need for a large number of gouges when setting-in a line. For example, setting-in a simple scroll can take up to eight different numbered gouges, as shown. But this scroll can be set-in using only one or two round-nose chisels.

To maintain a razor-sharp edge on my carving tools, chisels and plane irons, I made a rotary hone from a disc of ¼-in. plywood covered with 3/16-in. thick leather which is cemented in place. I bored a hole in the center of the disc and mounted it on a work arbor (available from Sears or a well-stocked hardware store); with the arbor chucked in my drill press and the leather stropping surface charged with white rouge (available from Sears), I can hone chisels and gouges quickly, without having to interrupt my work by getting out and setting up a lot of sharpening equipment. The drill press should run at its lowest RPM. You can also use tripoli or jeweler's rouge, but neither is as effective as white rouge.

For sanding sculptured furniture parts, I devised a pinwheel sander, which I make up from worn stroke-sander belts that I get free from a local cabinet shop. I cut the belt into 8-in. dia. circles and cut a ½-in. hole in the center of each. Then, using a paper pat-

tern and scissors, I cut eight evenly spaced slits from the outside toward the center. These stop about 1½ in. from the center hole. Next I fold one corner of each slit over the center and secure the pinwheel on a work arbor, whose collars hold the folded ends in pl[...] little piece of double-sided tape [...] folded corner will keep the pinwh[...] gether until it's secured on the [...] Take care that all the folds go [...] right direction in relation to rotati[...]

Photos: Robert

For doing the work of many carving gouges—roughing-out relieved areas and smoothin[...] vex surfaces—Schramm made this set of round-nose chisels by re-grinding standar[...] chisels. The long hollow-ground bevels are especially well suited for carving.

To make honing quick and tidy, Schramm constructed this rotary strop (above left) [...] plywood and leather. He mounts it in his drill press and charges the surface with white ro[...] simple arrangement for keeping a razor-edge on all his tools, without the mess ma[...] oilstones. Pinwheel sander (above right), when chucked in lathe or drill press, is good for [...] ing contoured furniture parts like cabriole legs.

Eric Schramm is a professional cabinet-maker who builds reproduction furniture in Los Gatos, Calif.

A Set of Carving Gouges
Grind the profiles you need

by Fred J. Johnson

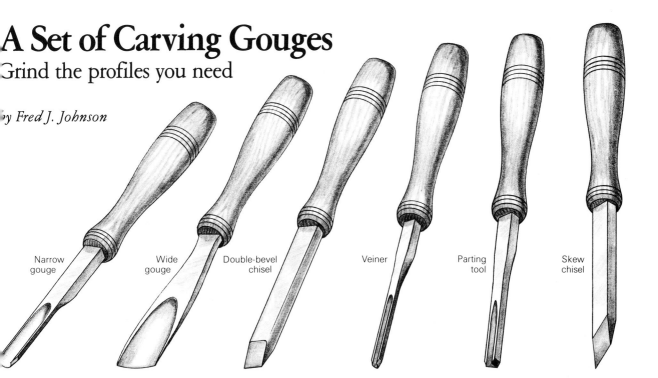

Narrow gouge   Wide gouge   Double-bevel chisel   Veiner   Parting tool   Skew chisel

About six years ago I reached that stage in my furniture making where I wanted to stop whittling and start carving. I had read and reread A. W. Marlow's *Fine Furniture for the Amateur Cabinetmaker,* and wanted to do what Marlow described. The only thing I lacked was a set of carving tools, which I couldn't afford, so I decided to make my own. Here is how I went about it.

Before starting to grind, I had to decide what tools to make. The 1974 Woodcraft catalog listed 116 different tools in their "professional" category; there are 148 now. This was confusing. So I reread Marlow again, looked at all of the pictures and sat down to design the set of tools I would need.

My gouges would have to outline scrolls and spirals with fair, sweet curves. This would require their edges to be arcs of circles. With a compass and a circle template, I laid out a series of increasingly smaller arcs spaced at regular intervals (drawing, bottom right). I had previously learned that any arc of greater diameter than 12 in. could be cut with a series of short, straight lines. I ended up with 21 diameters and decided to make 24 gouges, the extra three being narrow duplicates of the 2-in., 1-in., and ½-in. curves for removing backgrounds. These diameters refer to the cross section of the gouge at its edge, not to its width. The wide, flat gouges are often called "sweeps," the small, tight ones, "veiners." The rest of the set would consist of two *V*-shaped parting tools (one 60° and one 90°), five sizes of single-bevel chisel (¾ in., ½ in., ⅜ in., ¼ in. and ⅛ in.), two double-bevel chisels (½ in. and ⅜ in.), and a ⅜-in. skew chisel, 34 tools in all. I already had two shallow bent gouges that I had used in gunstocking. I bought enough steel for three extra blanks, so if the need for a particular shape arose, I could grind it. So far, I've found the set to be entirely adequate.

A friend who knows about metals recommended oil-hardening tool steel. It will crack and deform less with quenching and is easier to harden than some of the other choices. The only oil-hardening tool steel that we could locate in small quantities was the precision-ground stock that is sold in metalworking tool supply houses for making tools and dies. It comes in a wide variety of rectangular cross sections, in a dead soft state. I already had a ⅛-in. by 1-in. by 6-in. length of this material, so I made a gouge with a 6-in. diameter cutting edge to try out the process. It came out just fine.

I decided to go ahead. I bought a Sears grinder on sale with an extra 6-in. by ½-in. carborundum wheel and a wheel-dressing stick. The steel sold locally came in 18-in. and 36-in. bars, and since two cuts would make three blanks out of the 18-in. length, that's the size I bought—eleven bars of it. The current price (1980) would be about $10 per bar, maybe $3.50 per tool.

Shaping the steel — The procedure consists of these steps: saw the bars apart; shape the steel and grind the steel; finish-grind, file and stamp; harden and temper; clean up and maybe polish the steel; make and attach the handles; and sharpen. It's time-consuming only because there are so many tools in a set.

You need a template for each gouge. For the large sizes above 1⅜ in. in diameter, cut templates from cardboard. Save both the inside and the outside of the arc. The concave part is for checking the curvature of the wheel, and the convex part is for checking the tools. For the smaller arcs, use a draftsman's circle template like Pickett No. 1200, about

The cross sections in a set of gouges are a series of 21 circular arcs.

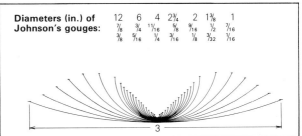

Diameters (in.) of Johnson's gouges:	12	6	4	2¾	2	1⅜	1
	⅞	¾	11⁄16	⅝	9⁄16	½	7⁄16
	⅜	5⁄16	¼	3⁄16	⅛	3⁄32	1⁄16

$1.50 (1980). Cut it apart on the center marks to make semi-circles. Dress a ¾-in. wide, 60-grit wheel to the required curvature for the largest diameter and after grinding, progressively re-dress the wheel to the next smallest size. Dressing a grinding wheel is like scraping on the lathe. Rest the dressing stick on the tool support and press it gently against the wheel. Keep the stick moving and check only after turning the grinder off. Resist the urge to touch the template to a spinning wheel. If the wheel seems to run forever after you turn it off, slow it down with the dressing stick. When you get to the ½-in. tools, switch to the ½-in. grinding wheel—not as much material to remove.

1: Steps in shaping a gouge

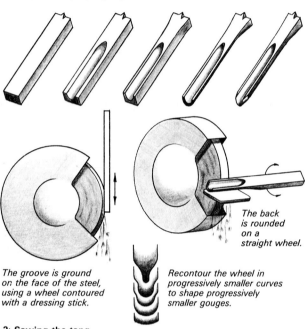

The groove is ground on the face of the steel, using a wheel contoured with a dressing stick.

The back is rounded on a straight wheel.

Recontour the wheel in progressively smaller curves to shape progressively smaller gouges.

2: Sawing the tang

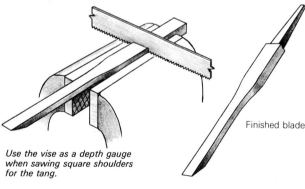

Finished blade

Use the vise as a depth gauge when sawing square shoulders for the tang.

3: Fitting the handle   **4: Carver's mallet**

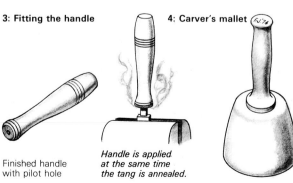

Finished handle with pilot hole

Handle is applied at the same time the tang is annealed.

Grind the hollow of each gouge by holding the steel vertical, tang end up (figure 1). Start at the bottom and grind a shallow groove. Then lower the steel to extend the groove toward the tang. Slide the steel up and down on the wheel, keep it moving, and don't use a lot of pressure. Keep the groove centered on the steel and parallel to its sides. Narrow deep grooves are far easier to grind than wide shallow ones.

Now you need to decide how long to make the groove. Most commercial tools are forged. It is just as easy to stamp a long groove as a short one; thus the groove usually runs almost to the tang. You can grind your tools this way, but I made the grooves of mine only about 1½ in. long for three reasons. First, it saved grinding and wheel-dressing time. Second, I will never sharpen that much steel away in my lifetime. Third, and most important, a tool is more comfortable to hold and easier to control with the left hand if its shaft is rectangular with nicely rounded corners.

After the blank is ground to the proper width and depth, check its curvature with the circle template held against the bottom end of the groove. Keep in mind the way gouges are sharpened. Most have a large bevel on the outside, a few have all of the bevel on the inside, and some are in between. The outside bevel is convex, not straight and not hollow ground. Then there is a smaller bevel on the inside, put there during sharpening. This is no accident—the double bevel makes the tool easier to control, and its edge more durable. The way each gouge is to be sharpened will determine the diameter of the groove that you grind. A fully sharpened tool with a profile of ⁵⁄₁₆-in. diameter may start with a groove of ⁹⁄₃₂ in.

After you grind each groove, shape the grinding wheel to the next smaller size. Contouring the wheel is easy, but messy—wear a mask to keep from breathing the dust, and vacuum it up promptly. When finished with the gouges, reshape the wheel to the angles chosen for your parting tools.

After you have put the groove in the face of each gouge, veiner and parting tool, clean them up with files. This is especially important for the parting tools if a sharp angle rather than a radius is wanted at the bottom of the groove.

Next, round off the back of each gouge to match the curve of the front. This is done by first hogging off the corners and then by rolling the blank in your hands while moving the steel back and forth across a straight wheel. Hold the gouge horizontal, 90° to the wheel, and keep it moving with a light touch. Check it often, then file everything smooth and grind each gouge to an almost finished edge. Make the straight chisels by grinding and filing their sides to the required width and thickness. Then grind the desired bevels and clean up with files. But don't make the cutting edges sharp enough to cut yourself with until the very last step.

Now the tools are ready for forming tangs. A 1½-in. tang that is ³⁄₁₆ in. by ¼ in. at the base and tapers to about ¹⁄₁₆ in. by ⅛ in. at the tip will do. Lay out on all four sides of the steel, clamp it in the protected jaws of a vise and hacksaw to the required depth on all four sides (figure 2). This will make a square shoulder for the handle to abut. Grind the tang to the approximate dimensions on a coarse wheel and finish with a coarse file. Keep in mind when handling and clamping tool blanks that they are soft and easily scratched.

Put as much finish on the tools as your sense of fitness demands. At least, round the edges and smooth the surfaces. Rust forms more readily on a rough surface than on a smooth or polished one. I marked each of my gouges with the diam-

From *Fine Woodworking* magazine (September 1980) 24:73-75

Johnson's tool case holds 40 carving tools. Right, piecrust table carved with them.

eter of the cutting edge, using a set of number stamps and stamping near the handle.

Hardening and tempering — Each bar of oil-hardening tool steel comes in an envelope with hardening and tempering instructions printed on it. Heat-treating specialists (look under Heat Treating—Metals in the Yellow Pages) will harden and temper this many tools for about $20, their minimum (all 1980 prices). Tell them what kind of steel you have and the hardness you want. But there is no magic to heat-treating, just temperature control, and you can do it yourself.

First heat the metal to 1,450°F to 1,500°F, then quench in hot oil (120°F to 140°F). Motor oil will do, but be ready to put a lid on the oil if it catches fire; proper quenching oil has a higher flash point. Don't let the tools get hotter than 1,500°F and don't leave them at that temperature. You can buy temperature-indicating pellets (about $3.50 for 20) or crayons (about $3.50 each) from the supplier who sold you the steel. Quench by plunging the tool straight down into the oil, then move it around, keeping it under the surface. Plunging vertically minimizes distortion. Your heat source might be a forge, an acetylene torch, a kiln or a heat-treating oven. Unless you have experience with a torch, don't heat the tools directly. Put them in a small firebrick oven or on a steel plate and heat everything, being careful not to get above 1,500°F.

Clean the oil off the tools and wire-brush them. Then temper according to the instructions that came with the steel. Most carving tools are tempered in the range of 56 to 60 on the Rockwell C-scale. I followed directions to obtain 57 Rockwell for my tools. The harder they are, the better the edge. If they are too hard, though, the edge breaks off. If they are too soft, they won't stay sharp. The instructions specify a tempering time of one hour at 400°F to get about 60 Rockwell, at 500°F for 58 Rockwell, and 550°F for 56 Rockwell. This can be done in your kitchen oven, but unless you know that its thermostat is correct, use temperature-indicating pellets or crayons. Now you can smooth, buff and polish to your heart's content.

Handles — I turned handles out of scrap oak (railroad dunnage) that was thoroughly dried. I made them 5 in. long when finished. You can make them any shape you like, and

out of any wood that is strong and appeals to you. They are your tools and your hands, so experiment to find what feels good. Make some prototypes and try them out.

To mount the handles, drill a pilot hole in the wood and clamp one of the blades in a metalworking vise with all of the tang pointing up (figure 3). Heat the tang with a propane torch until it is red hot. Press the handle firmly down on the tang. Stop short of the shoulder by 1/16 in., remove the handle and let it cool. You may have to heat the tang more than once to get the handle on. When the tool is cool, clamp it firmly in the vise and drive the handle down against the shoulders. Heating the tang serves two purposes. It anneals the tang so that it is not brittle and subject to snapping off, and it fire-hardens the handle hole. To get a handle off requires quite a tug. If you ever have a handle loosen, put some plaster of Paris into the hole. That will mount the blade firmly again. I varnished one handle and found that I preferred the feel of the raw wood. Since your tools will have a reasonably well-formed edge on them, ground before they were hardened, they will be easy to sharpen.

There are really two more things to do before you can consider your toolmaking project complete. One is to make a carver's mallet (figure 4) and the other is to make a case to hold the carving tools (photo, above left). I made a case for forty tools that consists of four trays of ten compartments each, plus a cover. They are all hinged together on the back and latched on the front with small brass hooks. The sides of the trays have rabbets for 1/8-in. hardboard bottoms and slots for hardboard dividers. A handle screwed to the top finishes the case.

I discovered why carvers use round mallets the first time I tried to use a square-faced one. You don't have to look at them when you strike. A square head glances off if the angle is not just right. I turned light and heavy mallets out of oak and they seem to hold up well. The head of the mallet should curve a little from the top to the handle for the same reason that it is round. I enjoy and treasure my tools very much. They suit my carving needs and they give me a feeling of pride and satisfaction because I made them. □

Fred Johnson works as a package designer and makes furniture for his home in Long Beach, Calif.

Spoon Bits
Putting 17th-century high technology to work

by David Sawyer

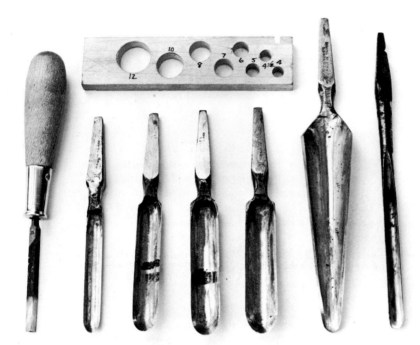

At left, a Windsor chairmaker's toolkit. The hardwood hole gauge provides references when sharpening. Lined up from left to right are the sharpening scraper, four spoon bits for mortises, a tapered reamer for leg-to-seat joints, and an old shell bit for back spindles. As shown above, bits are soft enough that you can sharpen them easily by scraping with an old file honed to a keen edge. They are tough enough to remain sharp for a few dozen holes.

For the last couple of years, Conover Tools has been selling a set of eight spoon bits and a tapered reamer in a neat canvas roll. They are copies, made in Taiwan, of a fine old set in Michael Dunbar's Windsor chairmaking toolkit. The bit sizes are six, seven, eight, nine, ten, eleven, twelve and sixteen sixteenths, with spoons about 2¾ in. long. The reamer tapers a hole at a 10° included angle, quite useful for chair leg-to-seat joints—although I'd prefer 8°, since 10° barely "sticks."

As bought, these spoons are straight-sided doweling bits, which were a mainstay for many craftsmen, such as coopers and brushmakers. Chairmakers either used the bits straight, as in Dunbar's set, or modified them into duckbill bits for boring the large-bottomed mortises found in so many old green-wood chairs. John Alexander, author of *Make a Chair from a Tree* (Taunton Press), explains the advantages of this joint on p. 34. Old-timers also used open-end spoon bits, called shell bits, which look almost like "ladyfinger" gouges. They are easier to sharpen than spoons, and cut nearly as well, even in dry hardwood chair backs. This is fortunate, since a used-up spoon bit will become a shell bit.

When you first unroll Conover's bits, they're beautiful. Upon closer inspection, they're kind of lumpy and bumpy, apparently finished in a hurry with a belt sander. Fear not—with a little tinkering and sharpening, they will work just fine. A lot of folks object to having to tune up new tools, but I find that this is a great way to learn all about the tools and make them truly your own.

How a spoon bit cuts—The spoon bit cuts on only one side of its semicircular lip. No other part needs sharpening. The cylindrical portion guides on its outside, clears chips on its inside, and must not have a diameter greater than the cutting edge, to avoid binding or reaming a tapered hole.

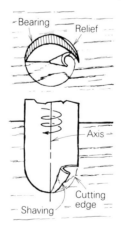

Any cutting edge must have some relief on its underside. What I call the "lead" of a cutting tool would be the progress per revolution in a drill or a reamer, or the thickness of the shaving a plane takes. For a plane, lead is regulated by how far the blade projects beneath the sole; for an auger bit, it is regulated by the leadscrew. A machinists' twist drill is like a spoon bit with a straight cutting edge, and if you can visualize how it cuts and how it is sharpened, this will help you understand the spoon. Try to imagine the spiraling development of the hole and the bit following it. In a spoon bit, lead depends entirely on how much relief you grind into it—if too much, the bit gets too hungry. The relief space shown above is exaggerated for clarity. It will be gradually used up as the bit is resharpened, and then the outside must be reshaped. The bearing surface gives stability in the hole.

As we all know, you can force a dull twist bit, or one that

From *Fine Woodworking* magazine (November 1983) 43:70-72

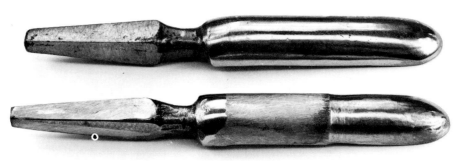

The spoon bit at top is as it comes from the manufacturer. The one below it has been modified into a duckbill for boring the chairmakers' mortise, shown at right. When shaping the bit, maintain full diameter just behind the cutting lip, but relieve the sides so that the bit can pivot in the hole to enlarge the bottom without enlarging the opening. The mark on the bit is a depth gauge.

has lost its relief, to drill a hole if you press hard and compress the material. No doubt you can also do the same with a spoon bit, but it's more pleasurable to sharpen correctly and let the bit follow itself through the hole.

Tinkering—To avoid slop when boring, the axis of the bit must be right in line with the brace handle. At least one of my bits came with a misaligned tang, easily corrected with some vigorous taps on the anvil. Flattening the surfaces of the tang and some grinding at its base will improve the fit in the chuck. I use a Spofford (split-chuck) brace, and try various bit orientations to cancel errors. Then I mark the tang so that it goes in the same way every time.

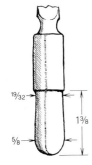

Conover's bits are hardened to Rockwell C45-50, which is soft enough to cut with a file but hard enough to drill numerous holes between sharpenings. A 10-in. mill smooth file is fine for truing up bits. You can eyeball the bit's diameter with a ruler, but vernier calipers are better. As an additional aid, make a hole gauge as shown in the photo on the facing page, or use draftsmen's circle templates, which come in $\frac{1}{32}$-in. and $\frac{1}{16}$-in. increments. By testing the bit in a series of round holes, you can judge its roundness and relief. A metal-cutting scraper sharpens the inside of the cutting edge by removing shavings like a one-tooth file. My scraper is an old broken-off triangular saw file, with teeth ground off two sides to yield a 60° straight cutting edge, which is then honed sharp.

First make the cylindrical portion of the spoon bit truly straight and round. Don't worry about maintaining diameter, because tenons can be made to fit. Then shape the outside of the point for relief and bearing, checking by eye with various diameters in the hole gauge. I would normally aim for clockwise rotation. My $\frac{9}{16}$-in. bit has an imperfect left lip, which would have shortened its working life, so I sharpened it to turn counterclockwise. Now do some scraping on the inside and light stoning on the outside to remove the burr, and try some boring. After you've got the bit working well, you can convert it to a duckbill if you like. I relieved my $\frac{5}{8}$-in. bit back about $1\frac{3}{8}$ in., as shown at right, to accommodate inch-long tenons.

The reamer—At first glance I thought the reamer was a disaster, since the tang is not cranked over to the centerline as on the spoon bits. But Michael Dunbar said no, just put it in the brace and ream holes, and sure enough it works fine. You just have to gently bend the tang until the reamer's axis aims dead on the brace handle. Don't even look at the chuck! The tang has a tiny waist and I noticed some twist in Dunbar's. So less brute force and more sharpening.

The reamer's cross section has a lot of hogback, which makes for too much lead and encourages a scraping rather than a paring action. It's also somewhat barrel-shaped. All this is easily fixed by filing or grinding. There's plenty of metal, but you can check with calipers if you get nervous. After shaping, you can sharpen with stones and do some scraping at the point. If the point is sharp, the reamer works like a shell bit, and you need no pre-boring in softwood seats. It does a neat job of breaking through on the other side, too. You can bore and ream seats like mad, in one operation.

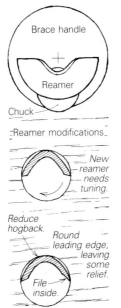

Making chairs—I worked up a kit for Windsor chairs and proceeded to put together two Federal period chairs using 17th-century high technology. After another dozen chairs I may see no need for Forstners, augers or brad points. I have a $\frac{5}{8}$-in. duckbill for stretchers, $\frac{7}{16}$-in. and $\frac{1}{2}$-in. spoon bits and the reamer for seats, and a $\frac{5}{16}$-in. shell and $\frac{3}{8}$-in. spoon for spindles.

With a little practice, the bits start easily. To bore at an acute angle, it's best to start straight and change direction after the full cutting edge is in the wood. The chips are marvelous, tightly cupped spirals, like pearly-everlasting flowers. On through holes, you will be pleasantly surprised by the neatness of the break-through. Stretcher mortises can be enlarged at the bottom by canting the duckbill bit. You can do this nearly as well with a straight (doweling) bit. In either case, you will have to sharpen part of the side of the bit as well as the round point, to help the side-reaming action.

Tenons can be turned green, oversize, and dried in hot sand—a wonderful method I learned from Dunbar. This way, you can have green mortises and bone-dry tenons in the same piece. Drying takes four to eight hours (depending on size) at 200°F. Over 200°F causes too much internal checking; at 400°F you get charcoal. Check dryness by rotating the tenon between your fingers: when it won't get any more oval, it's dry. With a little experience, you can turn just oversize enough so that joints will pop together (with a large hammer) with no further fitting. The larger diameter fits *tight* against the mortise end-grain; the smaller diameter is just snug on the sides. For ⅝-in. tenons, I allow ³⁄₆₄ in. oversize (7½%). You can start there, and adjust for your woods and bits.

For an angled joint, you can chamfer the shoulder of the tenon and one side of the mortise. Make the mortise extra deep so that the shoulder will seat. Shrinkage may open the joint a little, but it will still look good.

The same process of green-turning and sand-drying works with tapered leg-to-seat joints. I ream the hole in an air-dried pine seat, then fit the tenon with a cabinetmakers' rasp. With the leg properly oriented (major diameter against end grain), I rotate it back and forth a little. Then I file off the shiny spots, just like lapping the valves in a car. Repeat this until the leg feels really solid in the seat and is at the proper depth. Some angular correction is possible, and often needed. □

Dave Sawyer, who has taught green woodworking at Country Workshops in Marshall, N.C., was trained as a mechanical engineer and now makes Windsor chairs. You can get spoon bits from Conover Woodcraft Specialties, Inc., 18125 Madison Rd., Parkman, Ohio 44080.

The incredible duckbill spoon bit joint

by John D. Alexander

There is no one way to drill round holes in round sticks. I have used auger bits, Forstner bits, Power Bore bits, multi-spur bits and spade bits to make chair joints, and I have a few more ideas. Modern bits, however, have drawbacks. You don't want a leadscrew or a point projecting ahead of the cutting edge, where it will poke through the other side of the chair leg before the mortise is deep enough. You don't want a flat-bottomed hole—because its bottom profile limits the size of the tenon, as explained below. Nor do you even want the hole to be truly round, because an oval hole conforms better to the tenon. Chairmakers traditionally used the duckbill spoon bit, and its peculiar quirks combine to make the ideal mortise for green-wood chairs. The duckbill even turns the spoon bit's main shortcoming, boring slop, into a virtue.

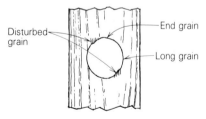

Disturbed grain — End grain — Long grain

Spoon bits cut deeper in end grain than in long grain, producing an oval hole with characteristic tearout where the cutting edge makes the transition from a paring cut to a scraping cut.

Square-bottomed mortise — Weak point — Round-bottomed duckbill mortise

Rounded corners in round stock make for a stronger chair. If the mortise were square-bottomed, both mortise and tenon would have to be smaller.

By canting the duckbill bit during boring, you can cut the lower and upper walls of the mortise deeper, into a dove-tail shape, without enlarging the opening or the sides.

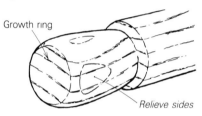

Growth ring — Relieve sides

Tenons are turned green, then dried. The tenon shrinks to an oval cross-section during drying, which automatically helps it conform to the oval mortise. In side view, the tenon should be shaped to conform to the mortise's dovetail profile, so that it will bear tightly against the end grain in the leg. The end of the tenon is larger than the mortise opening, but the green wood in the chair leg is compressible enough that the tenon can be pounded home. The sides of the tenon are relieved, so as not to split the chair leg as it dries and shrinks.

If a joint does not split when a tenon is pounded home, or very shortly thereafter, it is most unlikely to split later, unless the mortise is near the end of the stick. In a test piece, drive home a series of increasingly larger tenons until the leg splits, listening to the difference in sound as the peg seats. When it comes time to make the chair, drive home the size tenon just smaller than the one that split the mortise. One caution: Immediately after assembly, the dry tenon absorbs moisture from the green leg and swells, while the chair leg shrinks tighter against the sides until the leg is fully dry—if the sides of the tenon have not been relieved enough, the leg will split, starting in the areas of disturbed grain left by the spoon bit.

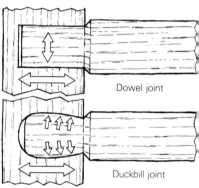

Dowel joint

Duckbill joint

With cyclical changes in humidity, the mortise depth lengthens and shortens as the leg shrinks and expands. The length of the tenon, however, does not change. In the ordinary dowel joint, this creeping mortise eventually breaks the glue joint. In the duckbill joint, because of its dovetail shape, as the mortise changes, the tenon tends to remain wedged tight because it swells and shrinks in height. The duckbill joint does not rely on a glue bond, although glue doesn't hurt.

The joint, once assembled, can't be easily taken apart. If something goes wrong during assembly, the only solution is to saw off the tenon at the mouth of the mortise, bore it out and start again.

In extremely dry weather, the tenon may rattle in the mortise, but its shape prevents it from coming out. Because of all its virtues, you might think this joint would last forever, but if the joints are too dried-out, the chair will be wobbly, and the leverage effect at and within the mortise will eventually break the joints down. In a similar manner, extremes of humidity, such as in outdoor use, will sooner or later destroy the chair—there is opposing wood movement built into chair joints, and wood, once its compressible limit has been exceeded, cannot recover to normal size. □

harpening Screwdrivers

by Michael Podmaniczky

1964 I was blessed with a Latin teacher who was as happy to avoid the drudgery of classical studies as his charges e. His nonacademic interests were wide and varied, and was easily sidetracked by his resourceful students. On one h rambling day, while discoursing on the development of internal combustion engine by BMW, he observed that in er to make some vital adjustment, a properly sharpened ewdriver was necessary. This brought a back-row dozer to den, albeit sleepy, attention:

'Sharpen a screwdriver, sir?''

'Indeed, scholar Westcott. . .sharpen a screwdriver.''

don't remember just what tangent we managed to steer the ewdriver tale toward, but the vignette came back to me other day when I was asked about the same thing.

The first requirement for a screwdriver is that its blade itively engage the slot of a (wood) screw well enough to remain in place while you turn and tighten the fastener. The ond is that this must be accomplished without mangling the rounding wood, or, if the screw is to be countersunk and gged (as is usually the case in boatbuilding), without deming the bung hole. Screwdrivers straight from the hardre store don't perform either task very well, but with a little aarpening'' they will.

Since the screw manufacturer kindly provides a slot across whole width of the screw head, you might as well take advantage of it. You therefore want a screwdriver tip that's exactly as wide as the screw head and that fits tightly in the slot, so as to bear along its entire width. Thus you really need a *set* of drivers, individually matched to each and every screw size you use.

A screwdriver tip that's too wide will overhang the ends of the slot. When driving a countersunk screw, it will ream out the bung hole, resulting in a poorly fitting and unsightly bung. If you're trying to tighten down a screw flush with the surface, that last turn will score the wood around the head, or raise nasty burrs on brass hardware and fittings.

Most manufacturers make screwdrivers with spade-shaped tips, which means that the blade will make the hole even bigger as it goes deeper into the wood. You can prevent this by grinding the tip to a constant width.

Grind away.

A screwdriver tip that's too thin will bear only at its corrs, defacing the screw slot and increasing the likelihood that e tip will jump out of the channel and gouge the woodork. This problem, bad enough with flat-head screws, is even orse with round-heads because the slot is so shallow at the tremes. Ask yourself why you push so hard when tightening fastening with a stock tool. The answer is that you're trying keep the tip from parting company with the slot. Because the threads of a screw do all the work, pulling it

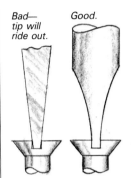

Bad— tip will ride out.

Good.

tightly into the wood, you should have only to apply torque; forward pressure should be unnecessary. But the faces of a stock screwdriver taper slightly, preventing the blade from squarely contacting the slot's sides, and the tip therefore tends to ride up and out when torque is applied. The harder you twist, the greater the tendency of the tip to pop out, and the greater the force required to keep it jammed in place. If the tip does jump out, all the force you're exerting will be directed at the surrounding wood—too bad! Yankee-style screwdrivers can apply only as much "push" as the spring is strong, and they invariably pop out if not dressed properly. The result is a less-than-decorative "Yankee doodle" across your pride and joy.

The solution is to dress the tip of the screwdriver so that its faces are parallel to the sides of the slot. Bits designed to be power-driven with an electric drill are invariably ground this way by the manufacturer—they would be lethal otherwise. You can grind a screwdriver to the correct shape as easily as you would hollow-grind the bevel on a chisel. The tip will wear in use, and now and then you'll have to go to the grinder to square up rounded edges. Such touch-ups will gradually shorten the blade, but you should be able to drive a few thousand screws before you have to hollow-grind the blade again.

For major-league screw installation, such as in boat planking, maximum torque is supplied by a brace and screwdriver bit. Once in a great while, this may even break a screw, but a properly sharpened screwdriver bit will engage the slot so well that even a screw that's been broken above the threads can be coaxed out of the bung hole by turning it counterclockwise with the brace and gently pulling it. Try that with a stock bit.

Trim corners.

The ultimate touch, the *pièce de résistance* of the craftsman's ego, is to ever so slightly grind away the corners of the sharpened tool to make the tip conform perfectly to the beveled edges of the screw slot.

There you have it. The screwdriver with the right stuff is actually one of a set, each driver ground to match a particular screw size. You can take virtually any old screwdriver and true it up to do its job, but I prefer to begin with what are variably called "cabinet" or "cabinetmakers' deluxe" screwdrivers. These have a constant-dimension round shank for literally generations of sharpening. With one of these, you're halfway to having a well-dressed screwdriver already. □

Michael Podmaniczky is a boatbuilder and Windsor chair maker. He lives in Thomaston, Maine.

Auger Bits
How to tune these deceptively simple tools

by Richard Starr

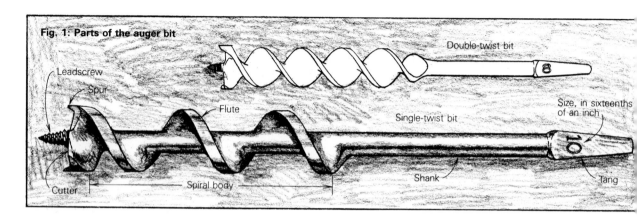

Fig. 1: Parts of the auger bit

Leadscrew — Spur — Flute — Cutter — Spiral body — Double-twist bit — Single-twist bit — Size, in sixteenths of an inch — Shank — Tang

I once knew an auto mechanic who didn't believe in gremlins. He felt that it was natural for a car to run well—if it didn't, there was a good reason. Like a car, an auger bit should work well. If you have a bit that has lost its bite and requires hard pushing to get it to drill, you needn't put up with its misbehavior. There's nothing mysterious going on; something specific is amiss, and it usually can be fixed. Even new bits can be tuned to cut more smoothly and easily.

The auger bit has probably the most complex shape of any piece of steel in the shop, with several parts that must work in concert. First into the wood goes the leadscrew, which pulls the bit forward with enough force so that once it gets a bite, no further pressure is required on the head of the brace. Next, the spurs score a circle in the wood, severing fibers across the grain so that the cutters, which follow the spurs, can lift a shaving without tearing the walls of the hole. The spiral flutes lift the shavings away from the cutters, while bearing against the walls of the hole to keep the bit running straight and true. To allow the bit to turn freely, the spiral body of an auger must be slightly smaller than the hole diameter. The diameter of the hole is determined by the distance between the tips of the spurs, so the manufacturer makes clearance for the flutes by flaring the spurs outward slightly.

There are many variations on this basic design. Some are intended for rough construction work and for power drive. The two varieties suitable for use in a hand brace are the solid-center single-twist bit and the double-twist Jennings type (figure 1). The double-twist is reputed to do a better job of lifting shavings from a hole, and it has more flute surface bearing on the walls of the hole to keep it boring true. On the other hand, the single-twist bit is less likely to bend, because of its sturdy core, and is cheaper to manufacture. In practice, the differences are insignificant.

While many rough-construction bits have a single cutter and one spur, workbench bits have two of each. Each of the paired parts does only half the work that a single cutter or spur would have to do. Because wood is removed more gently

this way, less effort is required and a smoother hole results. well-tuned bit is balanced: the spurs do equal work and th cutters take shavings of equal thickness.

The pitch of the leadscrew determines how fast the bit w cut. Bits available at hardware stores are usually single-twi types with coarse-pitch or fast screws, while most of th double-twist bits have fine-pitch leadscrews. The slow-lea bits take thinner shavings and leave a smoother surface. Fa bits are harder to turn because they take a bigger bite, and harder woods the effort required may be excessive. By using brace with a wider sweep (twice the radius of the crank), yo can reduce the amount of force required to turn any bit. Mo braces today have a 12-in. sweep, but I prefer a 14-in. swee for bits larger than ¾ in. in diameter. These braces are n longer made, though they can be found at flea markets.

Auger bits sold in the United States are made in ¹⁄₁₆-i increments, from ½ in. to about 1½ in. in diameter. The b diameter is usually stamped on the tang with a number th represents sixteenths of an inch: a number 14, for example, a ⅞-in. bit. Most auger bits are made to cut ¹⁄₆₄ in. oversiz unless they are designated as doweling bits (made by Th Irwin Co., PO Box 829, Wilmington, Ohio 45177), whic are sized right-on. Doweling bits are shorter than regular au ger bits, being about 4 in. to 5 in. long, with flutes abou 2½ in. long.

If an auger bit doesn't drill well, any of the three cuttin parts—leadscrew, spurs or cutters—may be the culprit. Firs check the screw. It should have a sharp point and clean, un damaged threads along its full length, or it will load wit ground-up fibers, preventing it from biting. Bent threads ca sometimes be straightened with the point of a knife. If th fails, true them with a small jewelers' file. Remove as littl metal as possible but as much as necessary—a low section o thread will cause less resistance than a pinched section. Eve broken points can sometimes be filed to shape.

Spurs are often too long and thick, even on new bits. long spur, by scoring the wood much deeper than the thick

From *Fine Woodworking* magazine (January 1984) 44:62-6

The single-twist auger on the left is new, while the bit on the right is a well-cared-for veteran with modified spurs. Starr drilled sample holes in cherry with these bits, then cut the wood in half (below). You can see the difference in scoring depth—the new bit scored too deeply. The thinner, shorter spurs of the modified bit made the smoother surface at right.

Fig. 2: Auger-bit file

This end is safe on the edge.

This end is safe on the face.

Fig. 3: End view of auger bit

To cut evenly, the cutter edges should be parallel.

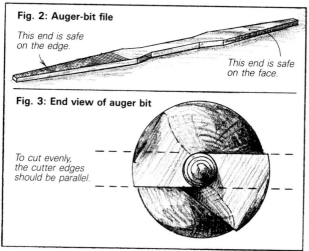

When sharpening a cutter with an auger file, it's easy to file accurately if you support the bit against a piece of scrap wood.

ness of the cutter's shaving, wastes effort. A thick spur wedges its way through the wood rather than cutting cleanly. On the other hand, if the spurs are too short, the cutter will reach the surface of the wood first and tear out unsevered fibers, leaving rough walls. A spur that's too thin will dull quickly and may bend. Since the spurs are flared to provide clearance for the flutes, shortening them reduces the hole diameter slightly, but since most auger bits are designed to cut $\frac{1}{64}$ in. oversize, this may not be a problem.

Use an auger-bit file (available from mail-order tool suppliers and hardware stores) to sharpen or modify the spurs. Its tapered ends let you work on wide or narrow surfaces. One end has no teeth on the face, while the other end is safe on the edge, as shown in figure 2. This allows you to file without damaging adjacent surfaces. You can finish up with an auger-bit stone, but I'm satisfied with the edge I get from the file.

To file spurs, I secure the shank end in a vise and support the upper end of the bit with my left hand. Since the spur is thicker at its base than at its tip, you should file the entire inside surface to avoid thickening the spur's profile as the spur gets shorter. If you wish to thin down the entire spur, file the base thinner first, then work all of the inside surface. Though only the tip actually cuts wood, any nicks along its leading edge will scrape the walls of the hole, so these should be filed out. Never file the outside edge of the spur, except to gently brush away burrs. To check that the spurs are of equal length, drill into a board with the bit square to the surface, watching to see if one spur touches the wood first. If it does, shorten that spur slightly and try again.

Dull cutters make a bit difficult to turn, and may even cause the leadscrew to slip and load up. Even new cutters may need a touch-up, but be sure to file on the flute or bevel side, not on the leadscrew side. Most problems with cutters come from filing the wrong side. To file, I hold the bit in my left hand, and press its business end firmly against a piece of scrap wood for support. A 30° bevel angle is about right. A damaged cutter may be filed back quite a bit, but be sure you file both cutters to maintain balance. You can judge this by looking at the end of the bit—the cutter edges should appear parallel, as shown in figure 3. To fine-tune, drill a hole, compare the shavings made by each cutter, and file a little more off the cutter that makes the thicker shaving. If the cutters are filed back a lot, check the spurs for depth of cut; they may need to be shortened.

Have you ever noticed how difficult it is to drill into end grain with a regular auger bit? The spurs are the problem. They have no function in end grain, and just get in the way. You can recycle a damaged auger bit for use in end grain by grinding off the spurs. The leadscrew does tend to follow the grain, so for really accurate deep holes in end grain, grind the leadscrew off too. Then use a file to angle the cutters toward the center where the leadscrew was, so that the end of the bit resembles the point of a machine drill. You'll have to start the hole with another bit that still has its lead.

It takes experience to get the hang of filing auger bits. Practice on some worn or damaged ones. If the back of your tool cabinet doesn't contain the usual pile of ineffective bits, you can probably pick some up cheap at a flea market. You'll be surprised how easy it is to resurrect them. □

Richard Starr is a teacher and the author of Woodworking with Kids *(The Taunton Press). Photos by the author.*

Doweling Jigs

Putting nine to the test

by David Sloan

When you're starting out in woodworking, the dowel seems like the perfect answer to every joinery problem. Drill a couple of holes, dribble in some glue and bang in those little wooden nails. If the dowels and holes don't quite line up, a little muscular persuasion will put things right. And if the surfaces aren't exactly in the same plane, the belt-sander offers a quick remedy.

Before long, however, the aspiring woodworker will learn that dowels won't do everything. They are mostly worthless where there is much cross-grain wood movement, or any amount of racking stress, as in chairs. Sure, dowels work well when glued into end grain, because the dowel's fibers line up, and move, right along with those of the main board. Dowels are also great for aligning edge-glued joints where long grain is being mated to long grain, and they keep things from sliding around while you're clamping. They're good for quick frame joints or for lightly stressed rail-to-leg joints, and they work fine in stable, man-made boards. But in most applications, to get the best results with dowels, you need some kind of jig to get the holes lined up and square.

The various doweling jigs on the market are designed to do just that: guide a drill to make accurate, perpendicular holes in the edge, end or face of a board. Most also provide a way to drill mating holes in two boards. A few jigs can make only one type of joint, others can make several, and some are extremely versatile. Deciding which one to buy can be tough.

I tested all the commercially made doweling jigs I could find, nine of them, by making as many different joints as I could with each. I used $\frac{7}{8}$-in. thick, 3-in. by 12-in. poplar boards, factory-made birch dowels (both fluted and spiral—I found no obvious advantage to either type), brad-point bits and yellow glue. I evaluated each jig for accuracy, versatility, ease of operation and quality of construction.

In addition to the jigs, I tested a dowel-former—a $\frac{1}{4}$-in. thick, hardened steel plate that produces a crude, but functional, dowel when you bang an oversize piece of wood through the appropriate hole ($\frac{1}{4}$-in., $\frac{5}{16}$-in., $\frac{3}{8}$-in. or $\frac{1}{2}$-in.). This $15 tool could be handy if you run out of dowels in the middle of a job, or want dowels made of your primary wood. I also tried dowel-centers—metal plugs with a point on one end. These are great for curved work that doweling jigs can't handle, and they also work well on flat stock. You drill a hole, insert the right-size plug and press the piece you want to join against the point, which leaves a nice clear center mark for the other hole. You may seldom need a dowel-center, but they're cheap enough ($4.50) to keep on hand.

• • •

After finishing my tests, I had several favorites. The Dowl-it #1000 was hard to beat for speed and convenience on edge or end joints, and the Dowel-Master and Dowel Magic were really fast on corner joints. These jigs center automatically—I like that. Most times I want a dowel on center, and for the few times I don't, I can use a shim to nudge the Dowl-it off-center. With the Dowl-it and either of these other two, there aren't many jobs I couldn't tackle. But if I could have only one jig, I'd buy the Record. It takes a long time to set up, and its loose bushings are easy to lose, but no other jig can make as many different joints.

David Sloan is an associate editor at Fine Woodworking. *All prices and availability information are as of date of original publication, March 1984.*

Each jig will make the joints shown in white.

Dowl-it #1000	Sugg. price $27.95	Dowel sizes $\frac{1}{4}$, $\frac{5}{16}$, $\frac{3}{8}$, $\frac{7}{16}$, $\frac{1}{2}$

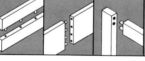

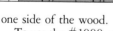

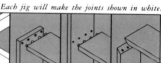

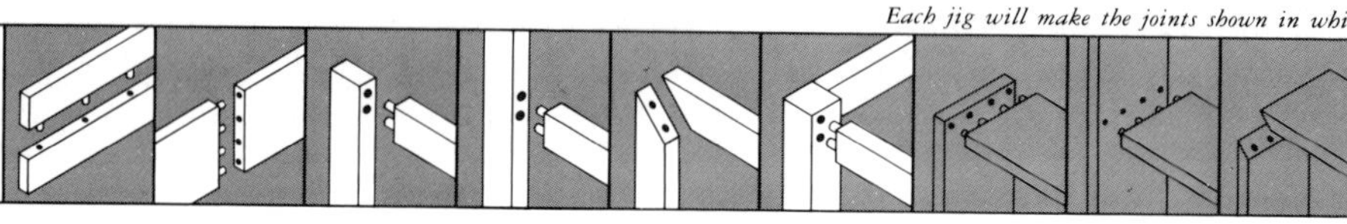

Dowl-it Model #1000—The Dowl-it jig I got didn't look like the one pictured in the mail-order catalog—the gizmo I remembered from junior high school shop. The manufacturer says it's "improved." I'm usually skeptical of "improvements" (translation: cut manufacturing costs and, most of the time, quality), but this time I was pleasantly surprised. The American-made Dowl-it is a durable tool of nicely machined steel and extruded aluminum. The hardened-steel drill guide has five holes ($\frac{1}{4}$-in. to $\frac{1}{2}$-in.), with sizes clearly stamped into the metal. There are no loose parts to lose and no extra clamps required. A large T-handled center screw clamps the extrusions around boards up to $2\frac{7}{16}$ in. thick, and centers the drill guide automatically and accurately. You can drill holes off-center by putting a spacer on one side of the wood.

To use the #1000, you first mark the board where you want dowels, then line up the jig's index marks with your pencil lines. You have to read these marks through a slot, which is difficult with overhead light, but this was the only design flaw I found.

Of the nine jigs tested, the Dowl-it #1000 was the handiest and most accurate for edge- or end-doweling, and it's the only one that can be conveniently used on round or odd-shaped stock.

I didn't test the Dowl-it #2000, which is basically the same as the #1000 except for six screw-in bushings that allow you to drill two identical holes parallel to each other, without moving the jig. It's easy enough to do this by moving the #1000, and besides, who needs those loose bushings?

From *Fine Woodworking* magazine (March 1984) 45:48-51

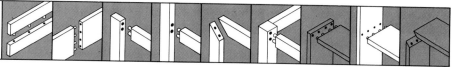

Dowl-it #4000	Sugg. price $72.95	Dowel sizes ¼, ⁵⁄₁₆, ⅜, ½, ⅝, ¾, 1

Dowl-it #4000—Weighing just under 4 lb., this behemoth was, at $72.95, the most expensive jig tested. Like the #1000, its quality is high. Two clamping heads and a steel drilling guide slide on two rods. A T-handled screw then tightens the heads. There are seven drill sizes (¼-in. to 1-in.), the three smallest in the form of pairs of threaded bushings that enable you to drill two identical holes without moving the jig. The four larger drill sizes are permanent holes.

Unless you improvise with spacer blocks, the #4000 will drill holes only in the face of a board, or in the edge or end of boards thicker than 1½ in. It can drill anywhere on the face of a board as wide as 12 in., and wider if you add longer rods. It was the only jig tested that could accommodate ¾-in. and 1-in. dia. drills.

Alignment marks incised on the jig are easy to read on wide stock, but on narrow stock, parts get in the way. No instructions came with my jig, and it doesn't center automatically, but the thing I like least about this one is that you need an Allen wrench (not supplied) to make all the adjustments. Knurled screws, which could be finger-turned, would be a great improvement.

This jig is hard to beat for drilling holes on the face of a board or a beam, but for most cabinet-scale work, it's just too massive. If you work with large, thick stock, this may be the jig for you.

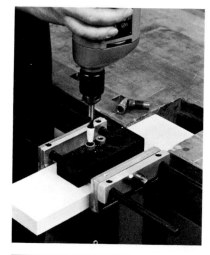

Disston Dowel Magic	Sugg. price $11.40 (¼-in.)	Dowel sizes ¼, ⁵⁄₁₆, ⅜

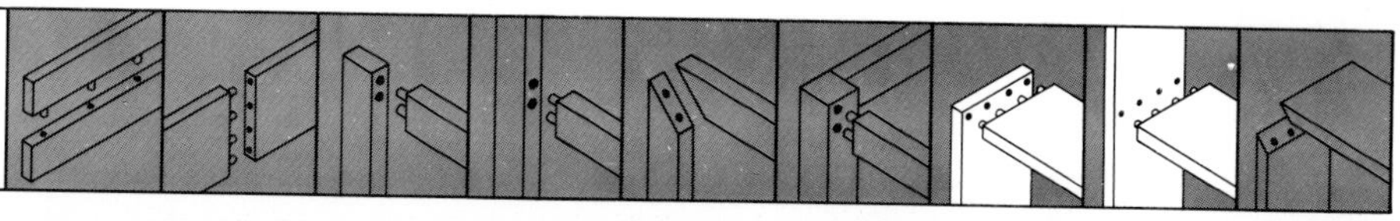

Wolfcraft Dowel-Master	Sugg. price $19.95	Dowel sizes ¼, ⁵⁄₁₆, ⅜

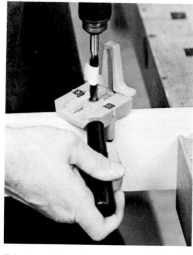

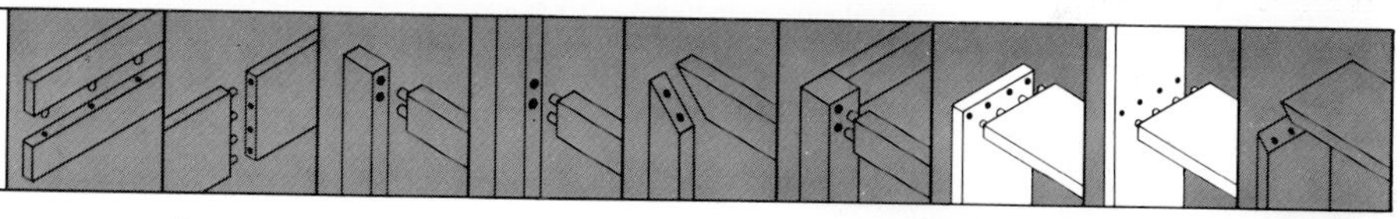

Disston Dowel Magic—This plastic contraption, imported from West Germany, drills only one size hole. You must buy a separate jig to change dowel sizes. At $11.40 for the ¼-in. model, it was the least expensive jig tested. The same jig is sold under the Coastal label.

Two plastic posts protrude from the square face of the jig, flanking a steel drill-guide bushing. A pair of machine screws with nuts clamp a sliding plastic fence to the base.

The Dowel Magic makes only 90° edge-to-face corner or "T" joints, a job it does quickly and well. It can handle stock of unlimited width, up to 1¼ in. thick. You place the jig posts astride the board's edge, which automatically centers the hole, and drill. The indexing marks don't work for edge-drilling, so you have to eyeball the location, which I found fairly easy to do. Then you slide the jig along the edge to drill more holes. Next you put dowels in the holes and clamp the mating board flat on top of the first. When you invert the jig, its slotted fence fits over those dowels to locate the holes on the face of the second board.

I tried both the ¼-in. Disston and the ⅜-in. Coastal. Base sections that were solid plastic on the Coastal were ribbed or hollow on the Disston, but this was the only difference I found, and it didn't seem to affect performance.

I wasn't thrilled about the plastic construction, but it keeps the cost down, and I don't think metal would work any better. The drill was a sloppy fit in the guide bushing. The square nuts that held the fence fell off and got lost.

Wolfcraft Dowel-Master—Similar to the Dowel Magic in design and operation, this German-made jig is very well

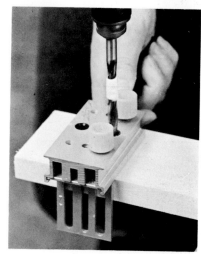

built. Unlike the Dowel Magic, one size jig can drill all three hole sizes (¼-in., ⁵⁄₁₆-in. and ⅜-in.). It's also more durable—aluminum extrusions, with steel drill guides. It uses dowels in the edge of one board to locate holes in the face of the second board, and it's limited to corner joints or "T" joints.

My only complaint: When I flipped the jig to drill the second board, I had to reset the depth gauge on my drill. Other than that, the jig performed well and was convenient to use.

(continued on next page)

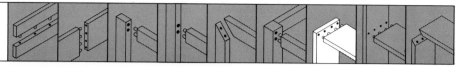

Disston Doweling Jig Clamps	Sugg. price $27.30	Dowel sizes $\frac{1}{4}$, $\frac{5}{16}$, $\frac{3}{8}$

Disston Doweling Jig Clamps

Disston Doweling Jig Clamps—This German-made, die-cast aluminum jig consists of two clamps: one with steel drill guides ($\frac{1}{4}$-in., $\frac{5}{16}$-in. and $\frac{3}{8}$-in.), and one without. The clamps are used to hold one board flat on the benchtop and the other board on edge at 90°. This jig can make only a 90° corner joint, in stock up to $\frac{15}{16}$ in. thick.

To use the jig, you set up the boards with one clamp at each end, drill a hole in each board, loosen the clamp with the drill guides, move it, retighten it and drill two more holes, and repeat for each pair of holes. When you get to the board's other end, you have to switch the clamps to drill the last set of holes.

I liked not having to set up extra

clamps, but the jig clamps' $2\frac{3}{4}$-in. throat capacity couldn't grab my 4-in. thick benchtop. It was easy to line up the jig's indexing marks with my pencil lines on the face and edge of the boards, so I got the holes exactly where I wanted. The clamps held the boards firmly for drilling, but the drill was sloppy in the guide bushing. I also found it tedious to unclamp, move and reclamp.

When I drilled the $\frac{1}{4}$-in. holes, I discovered that they were way off-center: $\frac{1}{8}$ in. from one edge and $\frac{1}{2}$ in. from the other edge of my $\frac{7}{8}$-in. thick board. There is no way to remedy this. The $\frac{5}{16}$-in. and $\frac{3}{8}$-in. holes were slightly better—$\frac{3}{16}$ in. from one edge. This doesn't affect the alignment, but the dowels are too close to the outside corner.

Disston's jig (also sold under the Coastal brand for $19.95) comes in a box marked "best," while their Dowel Magic is marked "better," but I found the latter more useful and a better buy. Although the Doweling Jig Clamps made a joint with good alignment, they were inconvenient to use and will probably end up gathering dust in my shop.

HIT Products Precision Doweling Jig	Sugg. price $25.95	Dowel sizes $\frac{3}{16}$, $\frac{1}{4}$, $\frac{5}{16}$, $\frac{3}{8}$

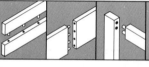

HIT Products Precision Doweling Jig

HIT Products Precision Doweling Jig—This aluminum and steel jig is radically different from any other jig on the market. The two boards to be doweled are clamped edge-up, one on each side of the $\frac{1}{2}$-in. thick aluminum vane on

the bottom of the jig. An aluminum arm, which holds a steel drill-guide bushing ($\frac{3}{16}$-in., $\frac{1}{4}$-in., $\frac{5}{16}$-in. and $\frac{3}{8}$-in. bushings are supplied), swings from side to side over the edges. You adjust a bolt on each side of the jig to stop the arm

where you want the hole. Once the arm is set, you lock it with a wing nut, drill one hole, loosen the wing nut, swing the arm over the other board, and repeat the procedure. All the holes are the same distance from the edge of the board, though not necessarily on-center. The jig reaches to the center of a $1\frac{1}{2}$-in. thick board; thicker stock can be doweled, but with holes off-center.

It took a long time to set up this jig, and using it wasn't easy. I needed a vise, a clamp, a wooden "T" spacer block (supplied with the jig), a $\frac{7}{16}$-in. wrench to change bushings, scrap pieces, and four hands—the "T" block kept falling out whenever I tried to clamp the two boards in the vise. I finally got all my holes drilled, but despite careful rechecking, the alignment was off by $\frac{1}{16}$ in. I blame the wing nut, which is supposed to lock the arm tight. It doesn't, so the arm wobbles around when you're drilling. I was intrigued by this jig's design, and impressed by the quality of construction, but in use it was a big disappointment.

		Dowel sizes								
Stanley No. 59	Sugg. price $44.45	3/16, 1/4, 5/16, 3/8, 7/16, 1/2								
General No. 840	Sugg. price $24.95	3/16, 1/4, 5/16, 3/8, 7/16, 1/2								

Stanley No. 59—This well-made, die-cast metal jig has a built-in screw that clamps on stock up to 2⅞ in., and a sliding guide-bushing holder that can be set anywhere on the board. The jig comes with six loose guide bushings (3/16-in. to 1/2-in.), which fit one at a time in the holder, and a useless, one-size-fits-all depth gauge (my favorite depth gauge is a piece of tape wrapped around the drill bit). This jig doesn't center automatically. To center a hole, you line up a mark for your bushing size on the graduated scale (which is accurate), then lock it with a thumbscrew.

The American-made No. 59 was easy to set up and performed well—one of the better ones. I liked it best for drilling a series of holes for a mortise. But the loose bushings and lack of a self-centering feature dampened my enthusiasm.

General No. 840—Also sold by Sears under the Craftsman brand ($21.49), this die-cast aluminum jig seems to be an attempt to improve upon the Stanley No. 59. It has a revolving turret with six drill-guide holes (3/16-in. to 1/2-in.), instead of Stanley's loose bushings. The turret clicks in place to index the desired hole. Like the Stanley, this jig fastens on the edge or end of a board with an integral clamp. The carriage slides on two steel rods to locate holes on- or off-center. You can drill the edge, end or face of stock up to 4⅜ in. thick.

The General is not self-centering. A measurement scale on one of the steel rods lets you locate the center of the hole once you've measured the board thickness. The scale is accurate, and I had no trouble using it.

This jig was easy to work with. No extra clamps are needed to set up, and there are no loose drill guides to lose. It's well made, but the turret has about 1/32 in. of play. Surprisingly, this didn't seem to cause any major alignment problems. The depth gauge that comes with the jig is worthless—it's clumsy and it doesn't fit small drills properly.

		Dowel sizes								
Record No. 148	Sugg. price $59.90	1/4, 5/16, 3/8, 8mm, 10mm								

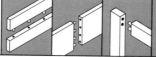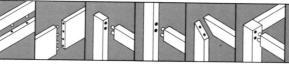

Record No. 148—This British-made jig is a complicated-looking device: Two 6-in. polished steel rods hold a stationary reference head at one end and a sliding head at the other. Between the heads, two drill-guide bushing carriers slide back and forth. You clamp a board between the heads and move the carriers to locate the holes. Five bushing sizes are supplied: 1/4-in., 5/16-in. (6mm), 3/8-in., 8mm and 10mm. The basic jig will dowel boards up to 6⅜ in. wide, but optional rods are available, in two lengths, that will extend the capacity to 12¼ in. and 18¼ in., respectively.

There are lots of adjustments, but knurled screws, some of which are slotted, so you can tighten them with your fingers or with a coin or a screwdriver, make it easy. Except for the steel rods and screws, the jig is made of painted, die-cast metal.

The illustrated manual has good, clear instructions, in four languages. I had no trouble using the jig, but I found set-up to be time-consuming, and there were loose bushings—my only complaints.

Equipped with the 18-in. rods, the Record is the most versatile of the jigs tested, but it can't handle round stock. It performed well, though it could stand some improvement. The play in the bushing-carrier assemblies, for example, could be eliminated if these were machined instead of cast and painted.

Some of the other jigs are faster and easier to use, but if you want one that does it all, this is the one to buy. □

Wood Threads

A handmade tap and screwbox

by Richard Starr

"In this remarkable and very simple and efficient tool of unknown antiquity, the great preliminary difficulty of making an original metal screw by hand with a file is escaped and nothing more precise is needed than a spiral saw kerf on a wooden cylinder, a steel point plugged therein, and a piece of sheet iron edged upon a hole."

Ancient Carpenters' Tools:
Henry C. Mercer, 1929

Two tools are needed to make screws and nuts of wood. The screwbox, or die, cuts an outside thread on a dowel that becomes the screw, while the tap cuts a thread inside the hole to be used as a nut. Because the screwbox consists of a vee-shaped gouge cutter positioned ahead of a threaded hole, the tap must be made first. It is then used to thread the inside of the screwbox.

The most common wood taps are similar to the tools for tapping metal and are made on a machinist's lathe or perhaps cut by hand with a file, laboriously. A woodworker without a lathe, or wishing a thread coarser than four turns to the inch (the limit of most lathe lead screws), is left only with commercial taps for wood. But they must be purchased paired with a screwbox, and the sets are expensive, especially in large sizes.

The wooden tap described by Mercer in the quotation above offers a solution. It is a hand tool made with hand tools, of common materials. The design is awkward in diameters under an inch, where an all-metal tap would be better. It is particularly suited to cutting the large screws needed for vises, clamps and presses. Fractional pitches and left-hand threads are no problem, and Mercer cites diameters up to eight inches. The screwbox or die design is good for any size even less than one inch.

The wooden tap consists of a helically grooved cylinder with an adjustable single-tooth cutter, and a guide block that fits behind the nut to be threaded. The sheet metal guide

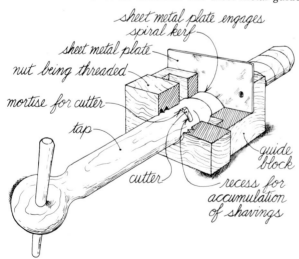

plate engages the helical kerf and draws the rotating tap through the hole. The scraper cutter pushes its shavings ahead of itself, thus requiring several passes before it reaches full depth. Its adjustability, which allows nuts to be threaded slightly oversize or undersize, is essential for a close fit and to compensate for changes in humidity.

To make the cylinder for the tap, choose a square of wood about four times as long as the deepest hole you expect to thread, plus two or three inches for the handle. The material must be a close-grained hardwood that will wear well and resist chipping along the edge of the saw kerf. I have used cherry, yellow birch, and rock maple, but hornbeam might be better. Choose a piece that is straight-grained and well seasoned to minimize changes in dimensions.

The shaft must be turned to the desired minor diameter of the nut. Use a vernier caliper rather than a pincer-type to measure accurately. Make the finish cuts with a large skew chisel, or a large gouge and a shearing cut, to leave the wood smooth and regular without using sandpaper. Sanding would leave grit in the wood, dulling tools used in later operations. A finish of hardening oil such as Watco, then wax, will help the wood wear longer.

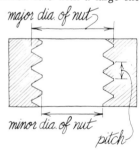

The helix cut into the cylinder determines the rate of advance of the tap, which is equal to the pitch of the screw. The cut must be shallow—around 3/16 in.—so it won't jam the guide plate or weaken the tap, but it should engage the plate snugly lest the tap widen the thread as it is backed out. The cut may be made on the band saw by tilting the table to the helix angle, holding the tap against a fence and rotating it into the blade. Or it may be cut by hand.

To make the kerf with a band saw, first determine the helix angle at the minor diameter of the nut and make a paper

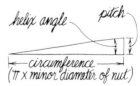

template. Choose a scrap board and cut a short kerf, as shown in the drawing. Use the template to lay out and slice off the bottom of the board at the helix angle. The apex of the angle should be at the left for right-hand threads, at the right for left-hand threads.

Richard Starr teaches hand woodworking to grade-school children and is author of Woodworking with Kids *(The Taunton Press). Starting with a clue provided by an old-time craftsman and references in old books, he rediscovered this technology.*

From *Fine Woodworking* magazine (Spring 1977) 6:22-28

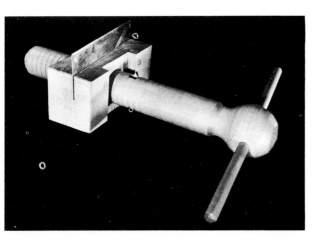

Two-inch tap (left) and die or screwbox (right) can be bootstrapped. Tap is made first, starting with a handmade helical kerf, then used

to make thread inside the screwbox, which is shown here cutting a thread in yellow birch.

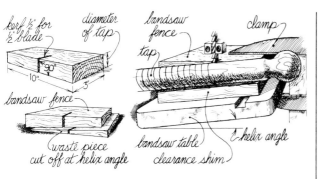

Now lay the cut surface of the board on the table and tilt until the blade lines up with the kerf. Mount the fence atop a shim for clearance, and clamp the assembly in place. Be sure the fence is square with the width of the blade.

For best results use a new, sharp blade, adjust the guide blocks close to the blade and tap, and set the blade tension high. Place the blank tap firmly against the fence and rotate it slowly into the blade. It will advance itself, creating the helical kerf. Make a test cut and measure it to check the pitch. I always make the blank overlong and use the end for the test, cutting it off afterward. If successive turns of the helix are too far apart, the table angle is a little too great, and vice versa. Adjust accordingly.

This is one of those band-saw operations where the wood is unsupported directly below the cut. The blade may grab and draw the wood quickly down toward the table, which would mar the tap or break the blade. Avoid this by holding the tap firmly in both hands and rotating it slowly, allowing the blade to cut at its own speed.

To cut the kerf by hand, prepare a ribbon of paper the width of which is a pencil line's thickness less than the pitch of the thread. Wrap this ribbon tightly around the tap, leaving the width of a pencil line between successive turns, and tape the ends down. Check the helix with dividers before marking it out. Score the pencil line with a chisel and make the 3/16-in. deep cut with a small backsaw or dovetail saw. Depth can be gauged with tape on the saw.

The cutter is ground from the business end of an old file, as shown in the drawings. Cool the metal frequently to preserve its temper. To separate the cutter from the waste, place it

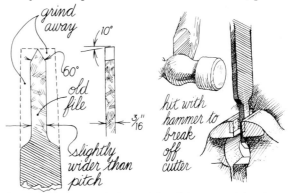

point down in a metal vise and break it away with a heavy hammer. Dub off all the edges except those that will be cutting, and sharpen on India and Arkansas stones.

The cutter sits in a through mortise and is held by a small wedge. Center the mortise hole about a half-inch beyond the end of the kerf, with one edge following a diameter of the tap. This edge will accommodate the working face of the cutter. Lay out the square by marking a line tangent to the drilled hole at right angles to the helix, and chisel it out. Be sure the blade fits snugly.

Cut the wedge an 8° taper from scrap that is just thinner than the width of the cutter, and insert it in the mortise to gauge the amount of wood that must be removed from the back face. When the wedge fits tightly, insert the cutter and mark the wedge where it emerges from the tap. Trim at both

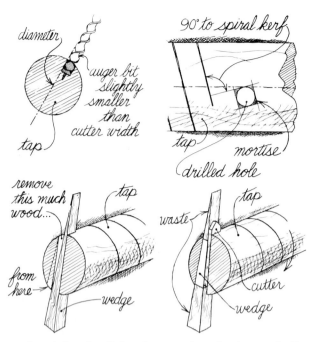

diameter

auger bit slightly smaller than cutter width

tap

90° to spiral kerf

tap _mortise_ _drilled hole_

remove this much wood...

tap

from here

wedge

waste

tap

cutter

wedge

Choose a sturdy hardwood to test the tap because strength is essential in most applications. Many woods won't take good external threads, but nearly any wood can be tapped as a nut—even pine. Drill a pilot hole in the stock the same size as the hole in the guide block. Clamp the guide block behind this stock, insert the tap and turn it a few times to ensure that

everything is aligned. Adjust the block by tapping it gently with a mallet and draw some witness marks so the guide block can be removed and replaced if necessary.

Up to now the cutter has a sharp vee point and at full depth will cut an ideal vee thread. In practice, the crest and the root of threads should be truncated to create a little flat that avoids sharp, fragile edges and provides clearance for smooth running. The truncation is obtained by dubbing off the point of the cutter, and by not setting it to full depth.

Set the cutter to project about a third of its final depth or about one quarter of the pitch. (At full depth, the cutter will be projecting about two-thirds of the pitch.) Drive the wedge in tight so the strain of cutting can't force it back in its mortise. Make the first pass through the hole and listen for the pleasant grinding sound as the cutter etches its helical path. When it emerges at the chip recess, see that it drops all the shavings before you wind it back. To adjust the cutter for the next pass, set a screwdriver or pin against its back end and gently tap it forward with a hammer. Make sure the wedge is tight after each adjustment.

It's important to take small bites, especially in very hard woods. Otherwise the tap will be difficult to turn, the thread will be rough, and the tap may be damaged. Consider that all the chips must be pushed ahead of the cutter—a 2-in. tap of 3/8-in. pitch, in a 3-in. nut, travels a linear distance of more than three feet. The little recess gouged ahead of the cutter increases chip-carrying capacity, but the tap can easily become overloaded and jam. Some roughness in the threads is normal, especially on the end-grain portions of the helix, and will occur with an all-metal tap too. Such tearing can usually be polished away by running the nut over a screw a few times with a little linseed oil or wax. I've tried to ease the cutting with beeswax or oil, but have found that any lubricant just glues the shavings together, jamming the cutter. The cutter functions as a scraper, and scrapers are most efficient on hard, dry wood. As the cutter emerges it is liable to cause some splitting and roughness, just as an auger bit would. A piece of scrap with the pilot hole drilled in it and sandwiched between the stock and the guide block will prevent this.

ends and chamfer all the edges to reduce the chance of splintering. Finally, gouge a shallow relief valley ahead of the cutter, to make room for shavings as the tool works.

The guide block has these important features: A pilot hole a hair larger than the tap so the tap will turn freely; a metal plate set in a kerf at the helix angle; a recess in front of the plate to allow shavings to drop out; and enough surface area for clamping to the nut. The notch must be wider than the major diameter of the thread and half again as deep as the pitch, to clear the cutter. For a 2-in. tap I have used a block

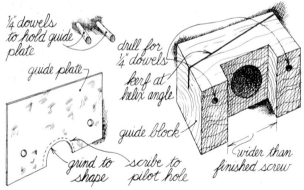

1/4" dowels to hold guide plate

guide plate

drill for 1/4" dowels

kerf at helix angle

guide block

grind to shape

scribe to pilot hole

wider than finished screw

about 3 in. by 6 in. by 2 in. thick. Center the hole and drill it; saw and chisel out the notch; then lay out the kerf at the helix angle. Drop perpendiculars on the ends of the block so the kerf will intersect about one-third of the hole, and cut it with a fine backsaw.

Any sturdy sheet of metal will do for the guide plate. I've used old saw blades and an old scraper blade. Drill two 1/4-in. holes in the block, insert the plate and mark it for drilling or punching. Two 1/4-in. pieces of dowel will secure it in place. Now use a pair of dividers to scratch an arc on the metal, gauged from the circumference of the hole to a little less than the depth of the helical kerf on the tap itself. Remove the guide plate and grind away the excess metal. Ease the corners of the arc so it won't catch in the wood, and remove any burrs. With the plate back in the block, the kerf in the tap should engage and turn freely. Drill a hole in the bulge of the tap for a tee handle, and the tool is ready to work.

The screwbox cuts threads on the outside of a wooden cylinder. It consists of a vee-gouge positioned in front of a threaded hole, and the first real job of the wooden tap is to thread this hole. When the box is rotated onto a dowel, the cutter makes a notch that immediately catches the threads, drawing the cutter around in a helical path.

The tool is usually made in two parts, although in smaller sizes it can be cut from a single block. The top half contains the threaded hole and the cutter; the bottom contains the

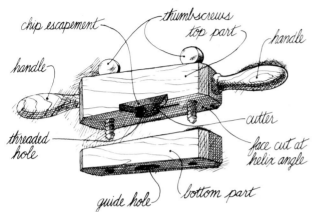

chip escapement — thumbscrews top part — handle
handle
cutter
threaded hole
face cut at helix angle
guide hole — bottom part

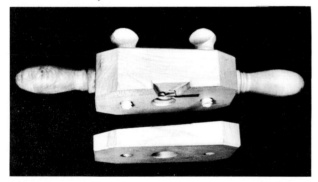

guide hole. The two halves meet at the helix angle of the screw (to be determined) and the cutter fits tightly into a mortise. This simplifies positioning the cutter and eliminates metal hold-downs for it. Metal bolts with wing nuts or wooden thumbscrews hold the two halves together. Once the thread is started the screwbox will cut with its bottom half removed, if a clamp is introduced to hold the cutter. This allows threading up flush to a shoulder.

The proportions of the screwbox aren't critical as long as the top contains at least four turns of thread, and provision is made for the handles and thumbscrews to clear the finished screw. The handles may be made separately and mortised in, or turned in one piece with the top half of the box.

Choose a dense hardwood that has been well seasoned. I have used cherry, maple and yellow birch. Square both pieces on all four sides, align them carefully and clamp them to scrap atop the bench. Locate and drill holes for the bolts through the two halves into the scrap and fasten the halves together. (If you are using wooden thumbscrews, drill and tap a pilot hole in the bottom half of the box.)

Now turn the box over and drill a hole the size of the major diameter of the screw (which for clearance is a tad less than the major diameter of the nut) through the guide plate, setting the depth gauge so the hole intrudes slightly into the screwbox itself. Reset the bit to the minor diameter of the screw and drill through.

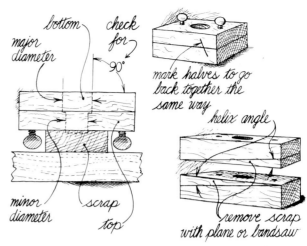

bottom
major diameter
check for 90°
mark halves to go back together the same way
helix angle
minor diameter
scrap
top
remove scrap with plane or bandsaw

Mark the two halves so they will go back together the same way (there are four possibilities at this point), unclamp the assembly and tap the hole in the top half of the tool. Calculate the helix angle at the pitch diameter (the average of the major and minor diameters). Make a paper template and lay it out. You can plane away the waste or use the band saw, but in either case the surfaces must finish smooth and flat. The two halves should go back together with all the holes aligned and the top and bottom surfaces still parallel. I prefer to finish the surfaces by running them over a long jointer plane held upside down in the vise and set very fine.

You may prefer, especially in small sizes, to make the screwbox from a single block of wood. Drill the holes and cut it apart at the helix angle. If you plan to turn integral handles, cut the box apart and saw away the excess wood before mounting it in the lathe. The turning axis should be rather close to the top surface, well clear of the angled cut.

The screwbox cutter makes a 60° thread, but because of its position with respect to the minor diameter of the screw it is ground at an outside angle of only 57-1/2°. You can visualize this foreshortening by drawing a vee and squinting at it while tilting the paper. When your eye is at the plane of the page, the vee will appear to flatten out. The front of the cutter is

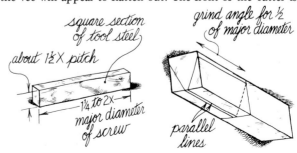

square section of tool steel
about 1½ × pitch
1¼ to 2× major diameter of screw
grind angle for ½ of major diameter
parallel lines

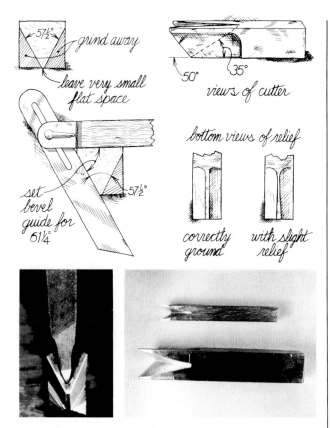

leave very small flat space

grind away

57½°

views of cutter

50° 35°

set bevel guide for 61¼°

57½°

bottom views of relief

correctly ground

with slight relief

Grind the rake and hacksaw or file the inside notch. The length of the notch isn't critical; the idea is to make a sharp cutting edge without leaving the walls so fragile that they break. The notch is cleaned out with a narrow chisel made from the end of a triangular file. First grind two surfaces of the file to an angle sharper than the interior angle of the cutter, then rake the tip back about 70°. The sharp point that results is the chisel. Tap the file handle with a light hammer to pare metal from the bottom of the notch. Finally, grind the top of the cutter down to the filed facets, and harden and temper the steel (see ''Heat Treating,'' pp. 6-8).

Sharpen the inside bevels of the cutter with a narrow India slipstone until you can feel a burr on the outside. Stone off the burr, but do not allow any outside bevel to form. Finish with an Arkansas slip.

The position of the cutter on the inside face of the top half of the screwbox is critical. It must be at the helix angle of the screw; its apex must rest on, and in fact establishes, the minor diameter of the screw; its bottom edge must be parallel to the side of the box and on a line that is almost, but not quite, tangent to the minor diameter. (Set it too high and it lifts out of the work, too low and it digs in.)

Having said all this, the cutter can best be positioned by eye. Draw lines tangent to the major diameter of the threaded

raked forward at an angle of 50° to the top of the shank. This allows the crest of the thread to be cut in advance of the root and prevents the wood from tearing.

Select a square section of tool steel and lay out the angle as shown, leaving a small flat at the apex. Grind to shape, dipping frequently to avoid burning the steel. Leave the surfaces a bit fat and clean off with a file, then file a slight relief behind the cutting edge. This allows the tool to cut smoothly.

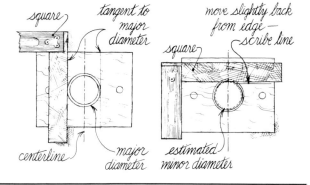

square

tangent to major diameter

move slightly back from edge — scribe line

square

centerline

major diameter

estimated minor diameter

A small tap of metal

by Trevor Robinson

hole for shavings

cavity in end

With access to a screw-cutting lathe, it's rather easy to make a small metal tap for threading wood. The tap is made from a piece of steel rod six to eight inches long and the major diameter of the nut to be threaded. For occasional use cold-rolled steel will take a sharp enough edge; a much-used tool would be made of tool steel or high-carbon steel. Common sizes are 3/4 in., 1 in. and 1-1/4 in. For all of these diameters six threads per inch is a satisfactory pitch, and a sharp 60° thread is cut for a distance of 1-1/2 in. or 2 in. from one end of the rod. From the same end about 1/2 in. of thread is then removed, just down to the minor diameter. The end is bored to a depth of 3/4 in. at a diameter sufficient to leave a wall thickness of about 1/16 in. The rod is then reversed in the lathe and turned down to the minor diameter from the far end to the start of the thread.

When this lathe work is done, a hole is drilled at the top end to take a tight-fitting tee handle, then the actual cutting edge is made by filing or grinding off the bottom end of the thread to make a face that is radial to the rod. Just in front of this face a 5/32-in. hole is drilled through into the cavity. The hole can be filed to make a triangular gouge at the end of the thread, with a sharp, inside bevel. This will direct the shavings into the cavity as the tool is twisted into the nut.

If very hard wood is to be tapped, it should be done in two steps with a starting and a finishing tap. Both have the same minor diameter, but the major diameter of the starting tap is about equal to the pitch diameter of the finished thread, or the average of the major and minor diameters. The starting tap is made with a flat-root thread, cut with a 60° bit whose end has been ground straight across for half the length of its vee. In using the two taps it is obviously essential to start the finishing tap exactly in the cut made by the starting tap.

Trevor Robinson, author of The Amateur Wind Instrument Maker, *is a biochemist at the University of Massachusetts.*

hole on the angled face of the screwbox. The major diameter is the circle that was scored by the drill as it completed the pilot hole in the guide block. Measure midway between the lines, and square a center line across the hole.

The minor diameter of the nut was established when the hole was tapped, and the minor diameter of the screw is a tad smaller for clearance. Lay a rule parallel to the edge of the screwbox at the minor diameter of the tapped hole and move the rule a little farther into the hole, to the estimated minor diameter of the screw. Scribe the line with a sharp knife. Set the cutter on the line so that the section of its edge between

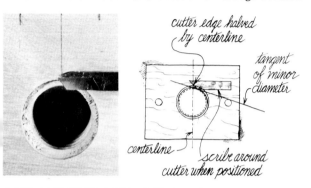

the apex and the major diameter is cut in half by the center line, and scribe closely around the shank.

Lay out and cut the chip escape channel as in the photo, making sure it clears the notch on top of the cutter, to a depth that equals the thickness of the cutter. Score the scribe marks for the cutter mortise and chop it to the same depth. Now the cutter must be sunk into the screwbox until the groove it will cut catches the threads in the screwbox. The little Stanley #271 hand router will do the job, but make sure its blade is

sharp and square to the sole before you begin. Work the mortise and chip channel together, frequently testing the cutter to make sure the fit remains snug.

Use a narrow strip of cardboard as a depth gauge. Along its edge lay out four marks exactly a pitch distance apart. Align three of the marks with the crests of the thread inside the box, and rout until the flat on the cutter exactly centers on the fourth mark. When the depth is correct, the bottom of the cutter may appear to be higher than the last ridge of thread. This is a result of the peculiar helical geometry of screws.

Finally, use the upside-down jointer to plane the surface of the box until the cutter is again flush. Since the bottom of the

Expansion bits

The expansion bit is the wooden screwmaker's cup of tea. It's an inexpensive tool that is continuously adjustable from an inch to more than three inches in diameter. Normal auger bits come in 1/16-inch increments and aren't commonly available larger than an inch and a half. Expansion bits are made for use in the drill press or the hand brace.

The most popular bits for hand use are the Irwin "Microdial" and "Lockhead." The adjustment on the "Lockhead" cannot be tightened enough to hold its setting in hardwood; the more expensive "Microdial" locks more securely. Even so, it sometimes slips to a larger size. I find it necessary to grip the drill head in a vise and bear down hard on the screwdriver.

These drills have a spur that tends to bend outward as the drilling progresses. This enlarges the hole and makes it hard to turn the brace. The cure is to file the spur to about half its original length. After the spur has been shortened it must be filed on the inside surface to reduce its thickness and to re-establish a sharp cutting edge at the top. Auger bits seldom arrive sharp enough to make a clean cut in hardwood. It pays to dress the cutter edges with a fine India stone, then an Arkansas slip.

The little scale printed on the drill is much too coarse for accuracy. I always test the setting in scrap wood, and may adjust it four or five times before arriving at the exact setting.

Auger bits will leave a rough exit hole unless you clamp a piece of scrap behind the stock and drill through into it. I like to clamp a piece of paper between the woods. When paper shavings emerge, the hole is through the stock.   —R.S.

box is also surfaced at the helix angle, it may be used as a gauge. Then remove one shaving more so that when the box is closed tight the bottom plate bears upon the cutter shank and locks it in place. Use a small gouge or knife to pare away the threads in advance of the cutter right out to the major diameter, so the dowel can enter the box.

The dowel to be threaded must be sized to fit snugly but turn freely in the guide hole. Taper or chamfer the end for an easy start and dip the whole dowel in mineral or linseed oil for lubrication because this is now a cutting, rather than a scraping, operation. Set the dowel upright in the vise and start the box with some downward pressure. Once the cut is begun, no downward pressure is needed. The box should turn easily and cut a clean thread.

Most problems result from an improperly set cutter and can be corrected by enlarging the mortise and adding shims. If it won't cut at all, the cutter is probably riding too high on the thread and the mortise will have to be widened to relocate it. If it produces a screw but is difficult to turn, check the minor diameter—a deeper cut may be indicated. If the cutter is misaligned with the thread, it will be difficult to turn the tool and one flank of the thread will bind inside the box and emerge polished. If the bottom surface is polished, deepen the mortise; if the top is polished, add shims to raise the cutter. Such misalignments affect the pitch of the finished screw. A shallow mortise rushes the thread through and lengthens the pitch; when it is too deep it compresses the pitch. The accuracy of the pitch may be checked by comparing the thread with a sliced nut.

It isn't easy to describe the quality needed in a wood to help it accept the helix of a screw with grace and strength. The wood must be strong and hard, and resistant to the shearing forces that would separate the thread from the core of the screw. Yet it still must cut cleanly across the grain.

The most common problem of wood being cut into a screw is that chunks of thread break away. In extreme cases, the screwbox leaves a shaggy, undersized dowel with no threads at all. Chips usually fall from the same position on successive turns, indicating weakness along the length of the grain. I recently cut a large screw in green elm. It had sapwood for about a quarter of its circumference. Chips fell exactly at the boundary between heart and sap along its entire length.

The only consistently fine wood I know for making screws is yellow birch (or red birch, the older heartwood of the same tree). It drips long, continuous shavings from the screwbox. Hornbeam (also called ironwood, leverwood or remin) makes a beautiful, bone-hard screw. Dogwood, juneberry (shadbush or sugarplum) and some of the fruitwoods (especially apple) also work well. Exotics such as boxwood and lignum vitae should be excellent. Oak, ash, cherry and the white birches are sometimes very good and sometimes awful.

Woods that should not be considered for screws include walnut, butternut and beech. Many commercial dowels are beech. Look for the telltale ray flecks and avoid them.

The same characteristics that make green wood cut so well on the lathe make it easy to cut in the screwbox. This is especially important when making large screws with a single-cutter tool. But green wood may check as it dries, and it will shrink. Polyethylene glycol (PEG) treatment may be an answer. But I prefer to rough out an oversize dowel and let it dry slowly until it is about half seasoned. Checking is minimized by avoiding the heart of the tree. Then turn it to size and cut the threads. Build an oversize screwbox or tap the nut undersize, and learn from experience what will work. □

Sizing threads

The dimensions of threads in wood can be figured from the same basic relationships as threads in metal. However wood is not worked in increments of .001 in. and such calculations can yield only ballpark figures. For smooth running there must be slop.

In metal threads the tolerances are precise: Truncation is one-eighth of sharp thread height, and clearance is one-sixth of basic thread height. In wood, the amount of clearance also depends on the dryness. As the wood gains and loses moisture circles will become ovals and the pitch of the nut will actually change. The threads in the photo are an inch in diameter. One is a tight fit, the other is a loose, but still good, fit.

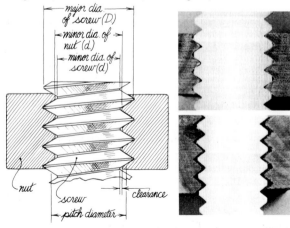

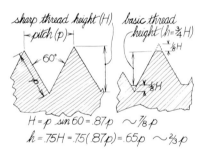

$$H = p \sin 60 = .87p \sim \tfrac{7}{8}p$$
$$h = .75H = .75(.87p) = .65p \sim \tfrac{2}{3}p$$

The maker of threading tools is likely to start with a bit with which he plans to drill pilot holes to be tapped for nuts. He chooses the pitch of the screw and calculates from there. Or he could start with some dowels which he plans to thread for screws, and calculate backward.

For example, starting from a 2-in. drill bit and pitch of 3/8 in.: The drill establishes the minor diameter of the nut. The shank of the tap is turned just a hair smaller so that it will work freely, and the cutter is set, step by step, until it protrudes about two-thirds of the pitch, or 1/4-in., from its mortise. The tool should then tap a nut with flats at crest and root.

The maker scribes this setting on the cutter and slices the test nut in half. He measures its actual major diameter to confirm that it is in the region of the minor diameter plus twice the basic thread height, or 2-1/2 in.

The major diameter of the screw, and thus of the dowel to be threaded, will be smaller than the measured major diameter of the nut by at least one-third of the basic thread height—in this example, more than 1/16 in. and less than 1/8 in.

The Scraper

A most versatile tool

by Tage Frid

The scraper is one of the most important and versatile tools for wood sculptors and cabinetmakers. It is available as a simple rectangular piece of steel, called the scraper blade, and as a blade mounted in a handle that looks like a large spokeshave, called the cabinet scraper.

Sharpening and maintaining the scraper are simple, but do take practice to learn. Many people get frustrated and give up, but once you can maintain the proper edges you will wonder how you ever did without it. Whenever I lecture, people want me to demonstrate the care and use of the scraper because few are able to learn this on their own.

The same scraper blade can be used for crude and fine work, to scrape glue or to produce a high-gloss finish with lacquer or shellac. It is better than steel wool between coats of finish because it doesn't leave tiny shreds of metal embedded in the pores of the wood. And when an old scraper gets too narrow to use it can become a tool for making half-blind or hidden dovetails.

The cabinet scraper has many uses too. It can remove old finishes without the use of solvents. It is excellent for removing paper after veneering and, like the scraper blade, it removes excess glue. If sharpened correctly it will put a fine finish on burl woods or delicate veneers.

The working edge of a scraping tool is the burr which does the actual cutting. Magnified, the burr resembles a small hook running the length of the edge. The scraper blade is sharpened by first filing the edges square. Then a medium stone removes the file marks. I prefer a wet/dry carborundum stone without oil. Then I use a honing stone, and here I prefer a Belgian clay water-stone, used with water. I hate to use oil because it mixes with particles from the stone and gets on my hands and the bench. Before I know it, the work too gets oily. The edge a water-stone produces is just as good as with an oilstone and it cuts the metal much faster. And if the stone wears hollow you can redress it yourself with sandpaper, by hand or machine.

After the edges are honed square the scraper is ready to have its cutting edge or burr put on. This is done by stroking the edge with a burnisher held at an angle of 85° to the face of the blade. A burnisher is a piece of steel that is harder than a scraper blade. The back of a chisel works just as well—I think even better—and I don't have to buy another unnecessary tool. The whole sharpening procedure is explained in the photographs on the following pages. The biggest mistake people usually make is to get too excited and burnish too hard. The resulting big hook,

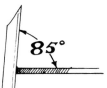

which digs too far into the wood, is fine for rough work like glue scraping. But for fine finishing you need a light touch when burnishing the cutting edge. It is just like when you had your first date and touched the other person's hand for the first time—but this time you don't have to blush.

When the blade gets dull, you can burnish the old burr down and pull it back again five or six times before you must file and stone.

For rough work I simple file the edges and don't stone it. I keep the burr left by the filing, burnish it out flat, and pull it back again. This edge will cut as well as if it were stoned, but it will have microscopic nicks that won't matter much for rough work.

The cabinet scraper is sharpened almost the same way, except its blade has a bevel and the burr is slightly larger, so it is burnished at a slightly steeper angle. As you file it, knock the corners off the blade so they don't dig into the wood.

A scraper will cut sanding and finishing time in half, and the end result will be considerably better than if only sandpaper were used. Since the rate of tree growth depends on the season, some parts of a board are harder than others. Sandpaper will remove the softer wood more quickly and the result will be a very uneven surface—which may not become apparent until the finish is applied. I never use an orbital sander because it has a flexible rubber or felt pad that will make the surface even more uneven. The best finish surface is obtained by first using a smoothing plane or cabinet scraper, then a flat scraper blade which will keep the surface flat and remove the wood quickly and efficiently. Then sandpaper.

If the first steps have been done correctly, very little sanding will be required. I use only 80-grit and 120-grit paper before applying the finish. I feel that often too much time is wasted by going any further. I always use a piece of cork for a sanding block. It is rigid, but not too hard, and it is very inexpensive. And I save the sanding dust to mix with either shellac or lacquer, depending on the finish I am using. (For an oil finish I use shellac.) This makes an excellent paste for filling small imperfections. If stain is to be applied I mix sanding dust with half Titebond glue and half water. The sanding dust will fade and shade with the wood, and is better and cheaper than any plastic preparation.

A swan neck (also called a goose neck) scraper blade is sharpened and handled the same way as the straight scraper. It is used in curved places—mostly for carvings, moldings, sculpture or sculptured furniture.

You can buy scrapers for about $2. But I always use a Sandvik #475; it costs about $4 (all 1977 prices) and is worth every penny. Its polished edges and high-quality steel produce a much cleaner burr without imperfections. You can look at various scrapers on the market and see the difference in the quality of the steel. Most people buy only one or two blades in a lifetime, so it's a good investment to buy the best.

After reading this and trying to sharpen a scraper several times, you might be the most frustrated person in the world. But don't give up. All of a sudden it will work out right, if you don't get too excited. Remember the light touch. □

Tage Frid, retired as professor emeritus of woodworking and furniture design at Rhode Island School of Design, is the author of the three-volume series Tage Frid Teaches Woodworking: Joinery; Shaping, Veneering, Finishing; *and* Furnituremaking *(The Taunton Press).*

Sharpening the scraper blade

The first step in sharpening a scraper blade is to file the edges square. Clamp the blade in the vise; curl the fingers around the file for control. →

Hold the file square to the edge and draw it along in long, even strokes.

Remove file marks with a medium stone.

Then hone with a fine stone held askew to avoid wearing a groove in its face. The edge of the blade must remain flat and square—don't rock the stone.

Finally, wipe the stone along both faces of the scraper to remove any remaining burr.

Put a drop of honing oil on all four edges of the blade to prevent the chatter of steel on steel and place the scraper on the bench with its edge extending over the side.

Use the back of a chisel as a burnisher. Hold it at an angle of about 85° to the face of the scraper and draw it back and forth until a small, even burr forms.

Two or three passes should do it, with light pressure (about four ounces).

Check the burr with a fingertip and repeat on all four long edges of the blade.

When the scraper gets dull you don't have to go through the whole process of filing and stoning. Lay the blade flat on the bench, add a drop of oil and slowly lay down the burr with the back of the chisel until you can't feel it on the top surface.

Lift one edge of the chisel to make sure you burnish the whole length of each edge and guide your finger along the bench to keep the chisel from slicing into your other hand. Then burnish to raise the burr as before.

When an old, much-sharpened scraper blade gets too narrow to use, it can become a tool for continuing the saw cut in half-blind and hidden dovetails. Set it in the kerf and tap it with the hammer. It saves a lot of chiseling.

Using scrapers, sharpening cabinet scrapers

Now the scraper is ready to test on the top of the bench. Curl your fingers around its ends and bow it slightly with thumb pressure. Start with the blade vertical and tilt it until it just bites the wood, about a 70° angle, and push. If it is sharp it will make fine shavings, not dust. ➝

The scraper can also be pulled toward you— it will cut better and more evenly if it is held askew to the grain direction, but moved parallel to the grain. Don't scrape away at one spot; reverse direction and work the whole surface so it stays smooth and even.

It won't cut properly and the blade will get dull quickly if you hold it at too shallow an angle. The correct angle is at right. If the corners dig in, press harder at the center of the blade to bow it more.

To sharpen the cabinet scraper, clamp the blade to the bench with the bevel upward and overhanging the edge. Hold the file in both hands and draw it along the bevel, maintaining an angle of 25° to 30° so the bevel is twice the thickness of the blade.

File until there is a burr on the back, then stone the edge and back on carborundum and hone with a fine stone until the burr is gone. The cabinet scraper is sharpened on both long edges—use a stick with a saw kerf as a holder so you don't cut yourself.

Then burnish the same way as the scraper blade but at a steeper angle, resulting in a slightly bigger burr. To set the cabinet scraper in its handle, remove the wing screw on the back of the handle and the two knurled screws on the front.

Place a piece of paper under the front of the sole to gauge the depth (double the paper for a deeper cut) and drop in the blade so it rests on the bench, with bevel facing upward and burr frontward. Hold the blade in place and tighten the knurled screws.

Set the wing screw until it just touches the blade and test the cut. For a deeper cut tighten the wing screw against the blade, making it bow. Always push the cabinet scraper with the blade leaning away from you. It, too, should make fine shavings.

To remove a finish, set a large burr on the cabinet scraper and tighten the wing screw so it bites between the finish and the wood. Scrape across the grain.

A scraper blade is the perfect tool for leveling a lacquer finish between coats. Just go lightly over the whole surface to remove bumps and dust. Start with the ends because they are the most difficult places.

After the pores are sealed, use the scraper to remove as much lacquer as possible without cutting through the surface. The change in color tells you you have gone too far. Work across and with the grain; be sure you don't miss any place, or the finish will streak.

After final scraping, for a glossy surface mix a pumice-and-oil paste and rub it on with a felt block. For a really high shine use rottenstone and oil. Then rub on sanding dust to absorb the oil. For a matte finish apply dry pumice with a shoe brush.

Files in the Woodshop
They're often a good alternative to abrasives

by Henry T. Kramer

Single-cut

Double-cut

Rasp

Fig. 1: Parts of a file

Files seem to be poor country cousins in a typical woodworker's shop, often neglected by even skilled craftsmen. But it's wrong to ignore a tool that can be so useful and that frequently is the best tool for shaping, smoothing or sharpening.

Files can true up all kinds of tools, especially new planes and spokeshaves. They sharpen saws, scrapers, cold chisels, axes and screwdrivers. Files can also smooth knicks and dents in everything from drill bits to drive shafts. They're efficient and economical alternatives to abrasives for shaping both wood and metal—they last a long time, and there's a size, shape and cutting grade for almost any carving or smoothing job you might encounter.

You may not consider a file a precision tool, but I've brought the badly hogged sole of a 22-in. jointer plane to within ±0.00125 in. of dead flat with only three files. And it doesn't take as much time or experience as you might think. As in any woodworking or metalworking, the slogan is "Measure twice, cut once." Stress the word "cut": you'll never learn how to use a file properly until you realize it's a cutting tool, not one that abrades the work.

More than 650 types of files are available today, but I'll discuss only 10 groups of "American Pattern" files that include about 170 files useful to woodworkers. The American Pattern designation is a traditional one stemming from post-Civil War days when Americans first began manufacturing files on a large scale, instead of importing them from Europe. These American Pattern files usually are coarser than their European or "Swiss Pattern" counterparts. I won't consider Swiss Patterns here, since they are finishing tools used by jewelers and modelmakers and too fine for most woodshop jobs, or circular-tooth files designed for soft, ductile metals such as copper, brass and aluminum.

The terms commonly used to describe files are fairly self-explanatory and probably already part of your vocabulary (figure 1). Most files have cutting teeth on both faces and both edges, but some have one or two smooth or "safe" edges so that they can be used in tight corners without accidentally damaging adjacent areas.

The "cut" of a file describes how its teeth are arranged. Single-cut files have one set of continuous, parallel teeth running in one direction. These files are designed primarily for sharpening or finishing metals. Double-cut files have intersecting sets of teeth forming sharp, diamond-shaped points designed to remove material faster. They'll cut wood quickly, though not as fast as a rasp, which has freestanding, clog-resistant teeth. Rasps and rifflers (small shaped rasps) are made primarily for woodworkers, carvers and farriers. Rasps come in several combinations of length and tooth grade, but all you really have to know is that in similar lengths and grades, the wood rasp is the coarsest, the cabinet rasp is a little finer, and the patternmakers' cabinet rasp is the finest. These cut wood rapidly, but leave a rough surface which can be smoothed with a wood file. In addition to regular rasps, there is also a tool called a shoe rasp, or four-in-hand, which is a combination of rasps and files that looks a lot more useful than it really is—its toothed surfaces are too short for an effective cutting stroke.

Any file can be used on wood, but you may find that the majority are too fine and clog up too quickly to be of much use. The coarseness of a file is controlled by two factors: the grade or size of tooth used, and the file's length. Today it's hard to find more than three grades of teeth: bastard, second-cut and smooth. Years ago, rough, coarse, dead-smooth and dead-dead-smooth grades were also available. The grade usually is stamped on the heel of the file, but this doesn't give you an exact gauge of the tooth size unless you also consider the length of the file. Within any one grade, a longer file has larger, coarser teeth than a shorter file, and fewer teeth per inch. There appears to be no industry-wide standard, but generally a file that's one grade finer and 2 in. longer has the same size teeth as its coarser, shorter counterpart. Thus, an 8-in. second-cut or a 10-in. smooth has the same size teeth as a 6-in. bastard. If you find a number on the heel of the file, it's a Swiss Pattern type; 00 is the coarsest and 6 the finest.

The two files designed for wood are the wood file (essentially a 10-in. coarse half-round) and the cabinet file, which has somewhat finer teeth than the wood file. Any double-cut bastard file, 10 in. or longer, can be effective, however, as long as you keep the teeth clean. Regardless of the type, a file's teeth face forward and won't cut anything when going backward—they'll just get dull. Don't move your file back and forth like a saw. Pick it up on the return stroke.

A file's name is based on several things: the shape of its cross section, such as flat, square, round or half-round; its use, such as for sharpening an auger bit or a chainsaw; or from traditions that no longer clearly speak for themselves—a mill file, for instance, is a single-cut flat file originally used for sharpening mill saws. The way in which files are identified in a catalog or a store may seem mysterious, but it's simply a combination of the file's length, name and tooth grade. For example, you'd ask for a 16-in. flat bastard when you really want to rip off material and have a lot of working room, or a 4-in. mill smooth when you want the smoothest surface an American Pattern file can produce.

Taper files, for sharpening handsaws, are a special case. Tapers are made with only one grade of tooth, but the size of the tooth increases according to the degree of slimness and the length of the file. The four sizes are regular, slim, extra slim, and double extra or extra extra slim. To sharpen a saw without damaging the teeth, you must use the correct size file. For a 5- to 5½-pt. ripsaw, I recommend using a 7-in. regular. For an 8-pt. crosscut saw, use a 6-in. slim, 7-in. extra slim or 8-in. double extra slim. For a 10-pt., a 5-in. or 6-in. extra slim does the job best. For an 11-pt., use a 5-in. extra slim or a 6-in. double extra slim. A 12-pt. calls for a 5-in. extra slim; a 12½- to 16-pt., a 5-in. double extra slim. The number of points on a saw equals the number of teeth per inch, plus one.

A table describing files of probable interest to woodworkers is shown at right. The metalworking files that a woodworker would likely find most useful are the 4-in., 6-in., 12-in. and 14-in. mill smooth; the 4-in. mill bastard; the 12-in. hand second-cut; the 12-in. hand bastard; the 14-in. flat second-cut; the 4-in. flat smooth; a 5-in. extra slim taper; and a 5-in. double extra slim taper.

I'm not suggesting that you immediately buy all these files, but as you learn how useful they can be, you'll probably want to, if you can find them. It's a vicious circle: merchants cannot be expected to stock files if there is no demand, and woodworkers can't be expected to demand tools they don't know about. If you do buy files, I recommend that you avoid foreign-made American Pattern files, which don't seem to amount to much. I've also found that files packed in plastic bubbles don't seem to be of the same quality as those sold in machinists' supply houses.

·   ·   ·

One of the first things you should do with a new file is put a handle on it. An uncovered tang is dangerous: you can drive it through your palm. If you want a removable handle, buy one with a threaded ferrule or built-in clamp. It's cheaper to make your own hardwood handles with ferrules of thin copper, brass or steel pipe. Once you've fitted a ferrule onto your handle blank, use a bit the size of the tang end to drill a hole slightly deeper than the tang's length. Then open the top half of the hole with a drill the size of the middle of the tang. Insert the tang in the hole, hold the file, and bang the end of the handle with a mallet or on a bench or other hard surface, driving the handle onto the tang. Another way to enlarge the hole is to take a worn-out file with the same size tang, heat the old tang to a red glow, and shove it down the hole. Keep a bucket of water nearby in case the handle catches fire.

You should use different files for wood, soft metal and steel. A file that has been used on a hard material will not cut as well on a softer one. So if you want to use a file on wood, don't use it on anything else. Except for small sharpening files, new files that will be used on steel should be broken in first, to eliminate any irregularities that might cause teeth to break off or dull. To do this, file for a total of about an hour on a soft metal such as brass or aluminum. Properly broken in, a file will last a long time, cutting about the same throughout its life. When it does go, this will happen quickly and you'll

FILES FOR WOODWORKERS

Name and cross section	Cut*	Description
Mill	S	For sharpening sawblades and scrapers, shaping and smoothing wood and metal, drawfiling, fitting, and truing. These files are tapered in width and thickness. Every woodworker should have a selection of these.
Flat	D	The standard machinists' file for shaping and quick removal of material. Tapers in width and thickness. Used for forming grooves, squaring holes and filing in sharp corners. Good for starting jobs that the mill file will finish.
Hand	D	Same as the flat file, but tapers only in thickness. Has one safe edge, making it useful for filing in corners where one surface should not be filed. Good for rough, heavy work.
Warding	D	Tapers to a fine point. Useful for getting into tight spots, such as when you are fitting plane irons and frogs.
Pillar	D	Narrower than a flat or hand file. Has two safe edges and no taper. Useful for filing slots.
Half-round	D	The flat side is useful for filing on flat and convex surfaces; the rounded back is good for filing on concave surfaces. You don't need a half-round often, but when you do, nothing else will do. The rounded backs of finer, shorter half-rounds have single-cut teeth.
Wood	D	Essentially a coarse half-round. Specifically designed to resist clogging when used on wood. Available in 10-in. length only.
Cabinet	D	Another file designed for wood. Thinner and with a shallower back and finer teeth than the wood file. Available in 8-in. and 10-in. lengths.
Taper	S	For sharpening 60° teeth on handsaws.
Three-square	D	A general-purpose file for working in angular corners of more than 60°
Square	D	A flat file with a square cross section.
Round (Rat-tail)	S & D	A tapered file used for dressing the insides of holes and small-radius curves. Round files longer than 10 in., except the 12-in. smooth, have double-cut teeth. Others have single-cut.
Chainsaw	S & D	Has special teeth designed for sharpening chainsaws. This file is not tapered.
Auger-bit	S	A double-ended file with each end tapering to a point. Has safe edges on one end, safe faces on the other end. Very handy for sharpening the cutting edge and spurs of auger bits.

* S is single-cut; D is double-cut.

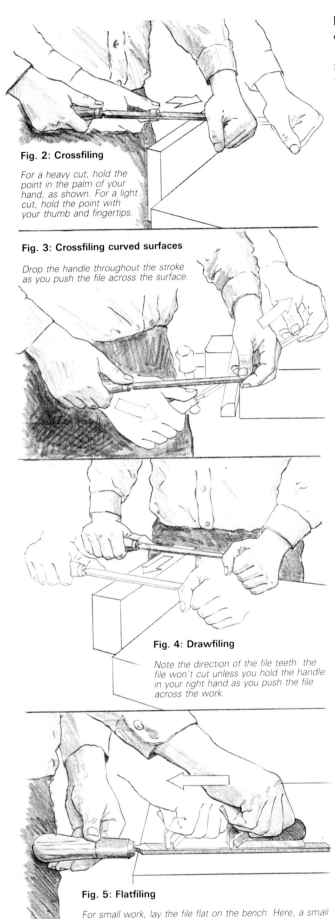

Fig. 2: Crossfiling

For a heavy cut, hold the point in the palm of your hand, as shown. For a light cut, hold the point with your thumb and fingertips.

Fig. 3: Crossfiling curved surfaces

Drop the handle throughout the stroke as you push the file across the surface.

Fig. 4: Drawfiling

Note the direction of the file teeth: the file won't cut unless you hold the handle in your right hand as you push the file across the work.

Fig. 5: Flatfiling

For small work, lay the file flat on the bench. Here, a small plane is being pulled over the cutting teeth to true its sole.

know it. Files can be resharpened, but it's impractical and dangerous in the small shop. It's best to buy a new file.

There are three common ways of filing: crossfiling, drawfiling and flatfiling. In crossfiling, which most people consider the only filing method, you usually push the file across the work, but it is sometimes done with the file held so that its long axis and the long axis of the work coincide (avoid this variation on narrow edges, or you're liable to round them). Clamp the work firmly at elbow height. Put one foot in front of the other, and stand up straight. Don't hunch over your work. For heavy filing, hold the handle of the file with your thumb on top and the point in the palm of your other hand (figure 2). To make a lighter cut, hold the handle the same way, but place the thumb of your other hand on the point and curl your fingers around the file. Think of your arms and shoulders as a parallel-motion machine swinging from the shoulders, and push the file across the work, maintaining a constant angle to the work. When filing a flat surface, first catch the vertical angle by rocking the file on the surface until it's flat. Do this each time you've stopped. On very thin material, hold the file at an angle to make a shearing cut, so the file teeth don't catch. From time to time, change the lateral angle of filing—errors in maintaining the vertical angle and any high spots will stand out clearly after only a stroke or two. If a wavy surface appears, try clamping the piece more securely, using less pressure on the file, or try a finer file.

Crossfiling with a taper file is a useful technique for notching a bar or other surface, say, to start a hacksaw cut. Notch an edge and file at a slight angle. You can crossfile a rounded or cylindrical surface if you drop the handle end of the file throughout the stroke (figure 3).

Drawfiling (figure 4), which usually is done with a single-cut mill file, is very useful to woodworkers. It's slower than crossfiling, but you'll find it easy to control the cut and produce a smooth surface. It also has the advantage of letting you file the entire surface in one continuous stroke. Drawfiling is a sharpening or finishing stroke, so don't use any more pressure than needed to feel the file cut.

Position the work so that its long axis runs away from your body, not from side-to-side. Hand position is important to ensure that the teeth are in a cutting position. If you're holding the file wrong, it won't cut—it'll just get dull. Grip the handle in your right hand, lay the file across the work at the desired angle, and grasp the point in your left. The file should be held at a right angle to the direction of the stroke. Now push. If you bear down too hard, the teeth will dig grooves and the file will walk to one side. If you are left-handed and feel uneasy with the handle in your right hand, or if the shape of the work requires it, you can hold the file handle in your left hand, but then you must use a pulling stroke. The rule is: Push stroke, handle in right hand; pull stroke, handle in left. To distribute wear evenly on the file, most workers move it slightly to the left or right between strokes.

If you want an even finer finish, wrap emery paper around the file and polish with the same drawfiling stroke. You may want to begin with 320-grit and work down to 400, then 600. Use a little light oil on the paper when sanding metal.

A good drawfiling exercise is squaring up a cabinet scraper with a 6-in. mill bastard and a 4-in. mill smooth (if you can't find the latter, use a 6-in. mill smooth or a 4-in. mill bastard, but go easy). First, use a straightedge to check that the scraper's long edge is flat or slightly convex, depending on your

Treatise on files and rasps

by Dick Burrows

BREAD RASP.

Ever try to use a rasp on bread? The practice was quite fashionable among "many of the better class of English and French people" in the late 19th century when the Nicholson File Company published *A Treatise on Files and Rasps*.

High-class bakers of the day felt that bread baked quickly and hard was sweeter and tastier than bread prepared in the conventional way, once you got past the thick, singed crust. So they ordered a curved, nickel-plated rasp (above) with an enameled handle—just the thing to get rid of the crust and create lots of bread crumbs.

The bread rasp is just one of the unusual items described in the Nicholson treatise, a catalog and description of files and rasps developed to meet the needs of every specialized trade and industry. The Early American Industries Association, which recently reprinted the book, calls the slim, 80-page volumn a classic of hand-tool literature, and the engravings reproduced from the original volumn add to the nostalgia. The work is a delight to those who favor hand tools and relish the history of tools.

Many of the files available when the book was published are no longer manufactured, but the information on using and caring for files is still pertinent. And the historical glimpses are especially informative in light of Nicholson's role as a pioneer manufacturer of machine-cut files.

The text is concise, crisp and easy to follow. The files, rasps and scrapers are well illustrated, and their uses are clearly described. There are enough details—such as discussions of the lengths of file teeth needed for penetration in various types of metals, and the relationship between tooth angle and tool control—to satisfy most students. □

A Treatise on Files and Rasps may be ordered from the EAIA, PO Box 2128, Empire State Plaza Sta., Albany, N.Y. 12220 (write for current price and members' discount). Engraving reprinted courtesy of the EAIA.

---

preference. Use the 6-in. mill to straighten the edge if needed. Then, holding the same file at a slight angle to the direction of the stroke and with the file's face flat on the side of the scraper, take off any hook left from the previous sharpening. Now drawfile the whole edge until it's square to the scraper sides. Start with the 6-in. tool and finish up with the 4-in. Crossfile lightly along the sides to remove any lip left by drawfiling, then burnish.

Flatfiling can be a useful technique for small work—work that generally is less than 3 in. long and no more than 1¼ in. wide, really too small to be handled easily with other hand-filing methods. Start by laying the file flat on a table or a bench. If the file is handled, let the handle hang over the edge, or put the file in a fairly large machinists' vise. Now draw the article to be filed over the cutting edges of the teeth. This is a handy way to flatten the sole of an ordinary thumb plane, and most rabbet planes are narrow enough to be flatfiled (figure 5). Most rectangular-section files have slightly convex faces, and some people may think that this would work against a flat surface. Actually, this convexity is intended to help achieve flatness when crossfiling, and it seems to have the same effect when flatfiling, especially if the work is reversed every four or five strokes.

Files look rugged, but like any other cutting tool, they need care. Keep them separated in racks, not thrown loose in a drawer or stuck in an old can. Given a chance, two files try to cut each other, with bad results for both.

Keep your files clean. A file card with a brush on its back is useful here. The card's stiff, short teeth work well on large-toothed files, and the short-bristle brush does the job on all files, if used frequently enough. Generally, it's best to use the brush more frequently than you think necessary. Files clog or "pill or pin up" once in a while, and this condition can both mark the work and stop the cutting. To clean a file, try a medium-grade power-driven wire wheel, holding the file so that the wires run down the gullets of the teeth. Alternatively, you can make a pinning tool from ⅛-in. brass or hard copper rod. Hammer the end of the rod to the rough shape of a double-bevel chisel and file to a smooth, slightly round edge with sharp corners. The edge should be thin enough to touch the bottom of the gullets between the rows of teeth. Put on your magnifying glasses, take a deep breath and get comfortable, and pick each "pin" out, one by one.

In addition to cleaning the files, you should also clean the metal surfaces that you file. Filing can leave metal fragments in the pores of iron, which, as in the case of a plane sole, can be transferred to the wood. Don't trust your eye: the surface may look clean, but it's not. Clean it with an oiled rag. Besides, any newly filed metal surface needs a coating of light oil right away, unless you live in Death Valley. The best lubricants and rust preventives are things people like to argue about, but anything is better than nothing. I don't think that the files themselves should be oiled, because oil can make them slip and more prone to clogging. Files will rust, however, and when they do so badly, that's it. So keep them dry. At the first hint of rust, use the wire-brush wheel. □

Henry T. Kramer, a retired reinsurance specialist, is an amateur woodworker and metalworker living in Sommerville, N.J.

Make a Hook Scraper

by Tom Vaug[h]

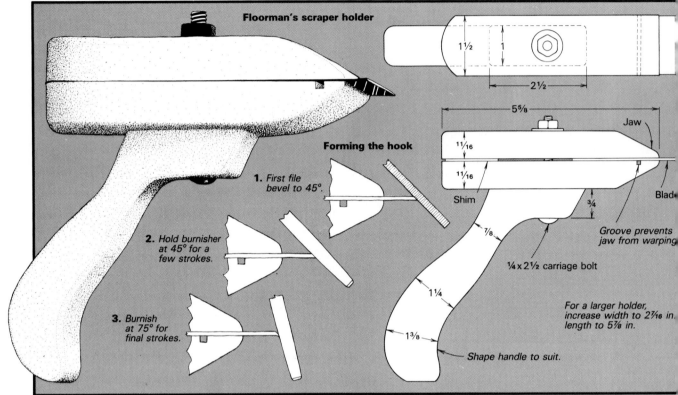

Floorman's scraper holder

1½ 1

2½

5⅝

11/16

11/16

Shim

Jaw

Blad[e]

Forming the hook

1. First file bevel to 45°.

2. Hold burnisher at 45° for a few strokes.

3. Burnish at 75° for final strokes.

Groove prevents jaw from warping

¾

⅞

¼ x 2½ carriage bolt

1¼

For a larger holder, increase width to 2⁷/₁₆ in. length to 5⅞ in.

1⅜

Shape handle to suit.

Drawing: Shearon D. Va

The phrase "laid, scraped and finished" was still part of the tradesman's lingo in 1948 when I started installing parquet flooring. Needing an efficient tool to smooth large surfaces, as well as the tight corners formed by baseboards and stairs, workmen made special hook scrapers, like the one shown here. In principle, this hook scraper works the same as a regular cabinet scraper, but its pronounced hook works better than a cabinetmakers' small burr for scraping big areas, and the wooden holder makes it less tiresome to use. A thin shim at the back of the jaws directs the pressure to hold the blade at the very tip.

You can make the holder out of any hardwood, though maple is my favorite. The drawing shows a small holder, but you could make the jaws up to 2⁷/₁₆ in. wide and ¹³/₁₆ in. thick. Shape the handle any way you wish and glue it to the bottom jaw. Blades can be made by cutting up a regular scraper blade or an old backsaw. A trick for cutting the hard steel used in these tools is to score a line on opposite sides of the blade with a carbide-tipped machinists' scriber, then clamp the steel in a vise and smack off the waste with a hammer. It should break cleanly. You can also cut steel with a tungsten-carbide blade in a hacksaw.

To form the hook, mount the blade in the holder so it protrudes about ½ in. With the holder on its side and braced by your knee atop a toolbox or an 18-in. high bench, file a 45° bevel on the top face. Work it until you have a sharp edge and

can feel a wire burr on the back side. Remove the weak par[t] the burr by passing it over a board or the edge of your toolb[ox]

Now you're ready to burnish the hook. I burnish with a [ta]pered-triangle steel (like a butchers' steel and available at m[ost] woodworking supply stores), but any smooth, rounded, ha[rd]ened steel object like a screwdriver shank will work. With [the] holder still on its side, start with the burnisher at the far end [of] the blade and draw it up toward you. Hold the burnishe[r at] 45° to the blade for three or four hard pulls, then prog[ress] to 75° for a few more passes. You should have a nice hook n[ow.]

To use the scraper, grasp it as you would a handsaw, hol[d it] at about 30° to the surface and draw it briskly toward you[. You] should pull a small shaving, not crumbs. Light scraping—[the] inside corner of a carcase, for example—can be done one-hand[ed,] but for heavier work, press downward with your other h[and] against the back of the jaws. Continual burnishing will bend [the] hook over so much that it won't cut well. You can file a [new] hook, or renew the old one for a while by inserting the poin[t of] a small oval burnisher (sold by jewelers' and gunsmiths' sup[ply] houses) under the hook and restraightening it.

Thomas Vaughn is a commercial cabinetmaker in Phoe[nix,] Ariz. He has worked at Colonial Williamsburg and at the [Na]tional Park Service in Yorktown, Va.

Two Tools

Small saw, marking gauge

by Jim Richey

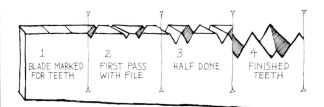

If there is a class of tools missing from modern workshops, it is those simple hand tools designed around a specific function. As a result, many of us find ourselves making a delicate little cut on a small piece of wood with a giant power saw, or designing our work around our equipment.

The planemaker's saw and a small marking gauge are members of the missing class—simple hand tools whose function has dictated their design. They are related in another way: The saw is used to make the gauge.

The planemaker's saw was originally used to cut the wedge dadoes in wooden planes. It is also quite effective for sawing through mortises or wedge slots, trimming protruding tenons or pegs without scratching the wood, and sawing curves in pierced work. In tight places it has no equal.

This planemaker's saw was made by cutting teeth into the back of an old kitchen knife. If you choose to go this route, pick a long, slim carbon-steel knife of the type readily available for a couple of dollars. Avoid the harder stainless-steel knives. Knives that taper in thickness from handle to tip are unsuitable. If you want to go through the annealing and heat-treating steps (see "Heat Treating," pp. 6-8), any scrap of tool steel about 1/16 in. thick will do.

Let your plans for the saw and the thickness of the blade dictate its length, width and taper. I needed a blade that could start its cut in a 1/4-in. hole, hence the slim design.

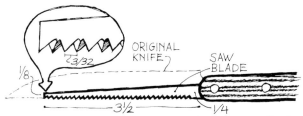

Slowly and carefully, grind the blade to shape, dipping frequently to avoid overheating. File the sides of the blade so that the front is a shade thicker than the back. Not much taper is needed, just enough to prevent binding.

Now file the business edge of the blade perfectly straight and lay out the teeth. I spaced the gullets 3/32 in. apart. To cut in the teeth, hold the triangular file level at an angle (50° to 60°) toward the handle of the saw. File every other tooth four or five strokes and turn the blade around. Holding the file at the same angle to the handle, file the remaining teeth four or five strokes. Repeat until the teeth take shape.

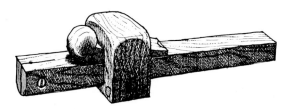

By tilting the file slightly you can give the teeth more or less rake. Old-timers claim that more rake is better for soft woods, less for hard woods. Exact angles are less important than consistency. The filing process sounds difficult but it takes only about 10 minutes.

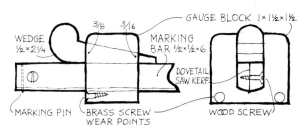

Although I have a beautiful old (but clumsy) marking gauge, I needed a small gauge designed specifically for mortise and dovetail work on thin wood. Designing the gauge around these functions resulted in the following dimensions.

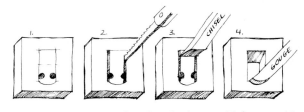

As to variations, most would prefer a wider block with more lip for general use. The wedge could be moved to the back or side. The marking pin could be installed at an angle. Design your gauge around its intended uses.

The bar was made first so that its profile could be transferred to the gauge block. The bottom rounding of the bar is quite helpful in using the gauge and should be included. I drilled two 1/4-in. holes through the block and used the planemaker's saw to cut the tapered mortise, as shown. When the mortise was trimmed so that the bar would fit smoothly, the wedge was rough-cut and trimmed to fit. I used a taper of 3/16 in. through 1 in. This is rather steep, but seems to hold well. Less taper would hold tighter.

The marking pin is a small brad held in a dovetail saw kerf with a screw. If the gauge is to be worked only one direction, the pin should have a knife-like point slightly angled so that the lip is pulled into the work. Those who mark both directions would prefer a pointed pin.

Wear points or a wear strip should be installed if the gauge is expected to have lots of use. I used two brass screws partially countersunk and filed flush. ☐

Japanese Measuring and Marking Tools

More than simple utility

墨付道具

by Toshio Odate

While I was returning home from a seminar in Atlanta recently, the word *shokunin* came to mind. This Japanese word is defined by both Japanese and Japanese-English dictionaries as "craftsman" or "artisan," but such a literal description does not fully express the deeper meaning. The Japanese apprentice is taught that *shokunin* not only means having technical skill, but also implies an attitude and social consciousness. These qualities are encompassed in the word *shokunin,* but they are seldom written down.

The relationship of a *shokunin* to his tools is very close, for it is through the tools that the work of the *shokunin* is created. When I was being trained as a *tategu-shi* (sliding-door maker), we celebrated the tools every New Year's Day. We cleaned them and our toolboxes and put them in the *tokonoma* (a special, decorated corner of the house or sometimes the shop). We put a small piece of rice paper on each box, and on top of that two rice cakes and a tangerine. This simple gesture is the traditional way of thanking the tools for their hard work and for the crucial part they play in the *shokunin*'s life.

In the past ten years, some of these tools have enjoyed popularity among Western woodworkers, but problems exist in knowing how to get the best performance from them. Though Japanese tools often look simple when compared to Western tools, they are really very complicated to use, performing best through the *shokunin*'s preparation, ability and experience. Though the knowledge is usually acquired through long apprenticeship in Japan, in America, especially, knowledge of new things is often gained through experimentation. In some countries, this freedom to experiment is unknown, but, in America, I realize that it is a natural outgrowth of interest in and respect for personal opinion, not recklessness or carelessness.

In my book *Japanese Woodworking Tools: Their Tradition, Spirit and Use,* from which this article is adapted, I had the opportunity to write about the *shokunin*'s tools. Here I will talk about some of the marking tools used by both the *tategu-shi* and the carpenter as well as other woodworkers. I will be very happy if you understand not only the tools, but a little bit about the spiritual relationship a *shokunin* has with them.

Sumitsubo—The carpenter usually begins his work by outlining on the ground with string the shape of the house to be built. Then he chooses the wooden columns and beams from the timber on the site and marks directly on them with the *sumitsubo* (ink pot) and *sashigane* (square). The same tools are used by *tategu-shi* to mark out the rails and stiles of sliding doors. The line made with the *sumitsubo* is similar to that made with a

Western chalk line (a chalk-covered string unwound from a ... stretched between two points and snapped to mark a stra... line). But instead of coarse string and chalk, the *sumitsubo* ... fine silk line and ink, which comes in both liquid form an... small solid chips.

The *sumitsubo* is an important tool, symbolic of the car... ter's spirit. When I was an apprentice, it was customary for ... master carpenter to come to the site at the beginning of ... struction and, with the *sumitsubo,* to snap one line on a ... timber. After this, his work for the day was considered d... and he was paid for the full day. An ancient custom at the ... of construction of a shrine or a temple was to leave the *st...* *tsubo, sashigane* and *chona* (adze) in the building as treasu...

Because the *sumitsubo* is such an important spiritual sym... it has maintained its ornate, formal style even though o... woodworking tools have been simplified. Today you can ... *sumitsubo* in every Japanese tool store. They are availabl... three sizes: large, about 30 cm (11⅝ in.) long; medium, ab... 24 cm (9⅜ in.) long; and small, about 18 cm (7⅛ in.) long. ... medium-size *sumitsubo* is the most commonly used.

The *sumitsubo* is used with a piece of bamboo called a *s...* *sashi.* One end functions as a pen for fine work such as mar... joints, and the other end as a brush for writing characters, n... bers and signs, as shown in figure 1. The carpenter presses ... *sumisashi* across ink-soaked cotton in the well of the *sumits...* as the ink line is being drawn out. To make a *sumisashi,* cut ... shape with a chisel or knife; use a razor blade to split the ... end into approximately 40 pieces about 1¼ in. to 1½ in. dee... separate the fibers so that they will hold ink. Then relieve ... sharp corner. This relief is called the *kaeshi,* which means ... turn." The *sumisashi* is used by pulling it toward you. W... you are making a long line and the last part of the line is get... lighter because the brush is running out of ink, you can rev... the *sumisashi* to use the ink stored on the *kaeshi,* then go ... over the line.

To prepare the *sumitsubo* for use, soak the cotton in wa... then wring it out and pull it evenly into a shape about twice ... size of the ink pot. Place half the cotton in the pot, letting ... other half hang over the side. Next, pull the end of the ... through the mouth of the *sumitsubo* from the outside, and ... it over the cotton and then through the hole between the ... and the wheel. Tie the line to the groove in the wheel the ... you would tie a fishing line to a reel, then insert the wh... Thread the handle into the wheel and start reeling in the ... Stop reeling about 2 ft. from the end of the line. Tie the ... end of the line to the *karuko,* a small piece of wood with w...

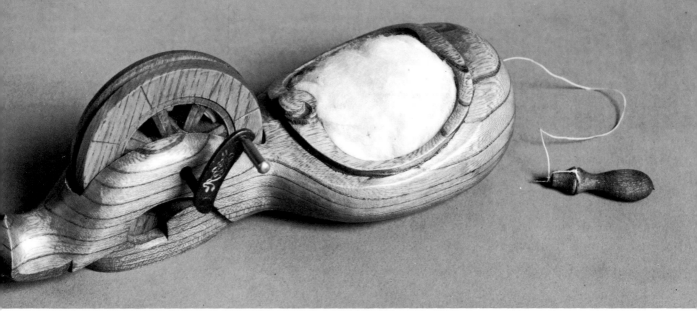

[Th]e sumitsubo, or ink pot, is symbolic of the Japanese carpen-[te]r's spirit. Used like the Western chalk line, you snap a mark by [plu]cking the silk line straight up, then releasing.

[Fig]. 1: Sumisashi (bamboo pen)

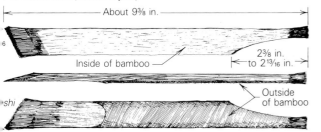

About 9⅜ in.

Inside of bamboo

2⅜ in.
to 2¹³⁄₁₆ in.

Outside
of bamboo

sashi

pull out the line, shaped so that it can be easily grasped. The *[karu]ko* (which means "porter") has a steel pin at one end with [wh]ich to hook the line after it is tied.

Put enough liquid ink into the pot to soak the half of the [cot]ton pad that is there. Spread chips of ink evenly on the cotton [in] the pot and fold over the other half of the cotton so that the [ink] is in the middle. Now pour just enough ink onto the cotton [to] soak the top layer. The chips will slowly dissolve into the [cot]ton. The next time you wish to use the *sumitsubo* and the [cot]ton is dry, you do not have to add ink—plain water will do. [No]w, to ink the line, anchor the *karuko* in a piece of wood and [pu]ll the line out about 10 ft. to 15 ft. While walking back, [pre]ss the cotton with the *sumisashi* so that the line will be well [sat]urated with ink. Then reel in the line. Do this two or three [tim]es and the *sumitsubo* will be ready for use.

[Sn]apping the line—A *sumitsubo* has many advantages. Not [on]ly can it make a long, straight line in very little time on flat [sur]faces, it can also mark straight lines on curved or twisted [sur]faces such as logs. Skilled carpenters also use it to make [bea]utiful, light, curved lines, such as for marking out the boards [for] the gable ends of Japanese roofs. They do this by snapping [the] line at an angle to the wood instead of straight up and down.

To snap a straight line, plant the *karuko* on the wood you [wi]sh to mark. Walk the *sumitsubo* back while pressing on the [cot]ton with the *sumisashi*. When enough line is out, put your [le]ft thumb between the pot and the wheel to stop the wheel [fro]m turning. Using your left index or middle finger to tighten [the] line, press down the line where you want it. Now stretch [you]r arm as far out as possible and, with your right fingers, lift [up] the line and snap it. (If you pick up the line close to its end, [yo]u won't have the necessary spring in the line.)

Sashigane—The word *kane* (or *gane*) means "steel," but in woodworking it means "square." So the woodworker saying "see the *kane*" means "check the square." A *sashigane* is used very much like a Western carpenter's framing square, but the markings, material, shape and size are quite different. The *sashigane* has a long history. I have read in *Daiku Dogu No Rekishi*, by Teijiro Muramatsu, that its predecessors came from China, where a square is known to have existed in the second century. In Japan, *shokunin* may have been using squares as early as the eighth century, but these had no measurements on them.

Today there are two types of *sashigane* used. Traditional *sashigane* use the traditional Japanese measurement system, and have different markings on the front and back. This is the square I used when I was a *shokunin*, and the one I still prefer. Modern *sashigane* have the same metric gradations front and back. Figure 2 on p. 60 shows the markings on my traditional *sashigane*. In the Japanese measurement system, there are *mo, rin* (10 *mo*), *bu* (10 *rin*), *sun* (10 *bu*), *shaku* (10 *sun*), *ken* (6 *shaku*), and *jo* (10 *shaku*). The unit *ken* (about 6 ft.) is an essential measure. The Japanese *tatami* (grass mat) measures 6 *shaku* (1 *ken*) by 3 *shaku* (½ *ken*). Japanese rooms are often proportioned according to the number of *tatami* that will be used to cover the floor.

The front face of the *sashigane* is calibrated in *sun*. The markings on both the tongue (short arm) and the body start at the outside corner of the square. These markings are only on the outside edge. On the back face, the outside edge of the body, which is based on *sun* multiplied by the square root of 2 (*sun* x 1.4142), is called *ura-me*. The uses of the *ura-me* are far-ranging. Carpenters use this edge to determine the maximum-size square timber that can be cut from a log by laying the *sashigane* across the smallest diameter of the log. This works

Fig. 2: *Sashigane* (square)

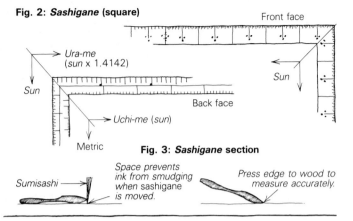

Front face

Ura-me
(sun × 1.4142)

Sun

Sun

Uchi-me (sun)

Back face

Metric

Fig. 3: *Sashigane* section

Sumisashi

Space prevents
ink from smudging
when sashigane
is moved.

Press edge to wood to
measure accurately.

Fig. 4: Judging the squareness of a *sashigane*

*Square is true if, when in second
position, it's parallel to knife mark.*

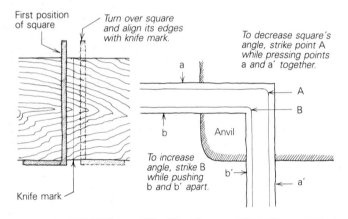

First position
of square

Turn over square
and align its edges
with knife mark.

To decrease square's
angle, strike point A
while pressing points
a and a' together.

a

A

B

b

Anvil

To increase
angle, strike B
while pushing
b and b' apart.

b'

a'

Knife mark

Fig. 5: Types of marking gauges

Suji-keshiki
(line-marking gauges)

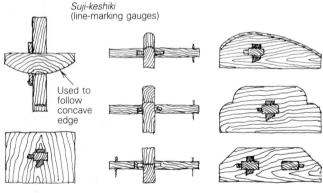

Used to
follow
concave
edge

Fig. 6: Marking-gauge blades

For softwood,
about 40°

35°

For hardwood or heavy work

15° for softwood,
larger angle for hardwood

mathematically because each side of a square inscribed in a circle is equal to the diameter of the circle divided by the square root of 2.

Until about 55 years ago, *sashigane*, like other tools, were forged by blacksmiths from iron. Today, I do not know of a blacksmiths making *sashigane* by the old method. Inste *sashigane* are made from copper, brass, German silver (an al of copper, zinc and nickel), steel or stainless steel. Steel *sashigane* rust easily, and it is difficult to see the lines, so ma *shokunin* do not like them, even though they are stronger th the others. At the time of my youth, many *shokunin* did like stainless-steel *sashigane* because the color was too bri, and its shine was cold and harsh. My master said, "It ne gives me calmness." Stainless steel does not have this effect me, and this is the type of *sashigane* I use today.

Shape and squareness—The *sashigane* is much smaller a narrower than the Western framing square, and also much m flexible. It is sensitively designed—for example, the blade is co toured so that when used with the *sumisashi*, as shown in f ure 3, the space between the edge of the square and the surf to be marked allows the square to be moved without smudg the ink. Yet by holding the edge of the square flat against surface, very accurate measurements can be taken.

The *sashigane* is the basis for all marking. If it is not squ then the entire building will not be true, so you must check t the angle is correct from time to time. I will explain how check for squareness, as shown in figure 4.

Begin by preparing a board about 1 in. thick by 12 in. w by 30 in. to 36 in. long. Dress its face as flat as possible plane one edge straight and square to the face. Then put square on the board and draw a line with a marking knife al the square's edge. Reverse the square and hold its edge to knife mark. If the edge is parallel to the mark, that is good, the *sashigane* is square. But if they are not parallel, follow th steps. If the angle is too large, strike point A gently with hammer while pressing the tongue and body together on anvil, either alone or with the help of an assistant. Don't st too hard, as you might stretch the steel badly. If the angle is small, strike point B while pushing apart at the points indica Continue this procedure and test again until the square is t

Keshiki—Marking gauges, or *keshiki*, are used mainly by *tate shi* and other woodworkers who use small materials. Many *kunin* make their own, but *keshiki* are also available in shops that carry Japanese tools. There are different sizes, sha and types for different work (figure 5). I will talk here about most common, the *suji-keshiki*, or line-marking gauge. This is used to scribe a single line parallel to the edge of the piece wood. Most *suji-keshiki* have a simple flat fence and a si beam to hold the blade. The fence, which must be square to beam, is usually held in place with a wedge, but sometimes a nut and bolt. The blade, either made from an old band blade or purchased, is a forced fit in the beam.

In general, Japanese marking gauges are similar to t Western counterparts. With the exception of the mortise ga however, all Japanese gauges use blades instead of pins, marking both across the grain and along it. A blade, which c leaves a finer mark than a pin, which scratches. Like other Ja nese tools, marking gauges are used on the pull stroke. Most adjusted in the same manner by tapping the beam with a h mer, as shown in the photos on the facing page.

Suji-keshiki are traditionally made of white or red oak, which has the hardness and tenacity the tool needs. Today, however, *suji-keshiki* are also made from rosewood and ebony. Rosewood and ebony *keshiki* should be used with a wedge of a softer, more resilient wood, such as oak or maple. Wedges made of these woods will compress when tapped to allow fine adjustment and will hold the fence tightly in position. Here are some points to consider if you are making your own *suji-keshiki*. Fences may be made in a variety of shapes and sizes. Common beam lengths are 3½ in. to 7 in. and common thicknesses are ⅜ in. to ⅝ in., but size the beam to fit your hand and work. The width of the beam may vary, and depends on the size of the blade; naturally, a wide blade in a too-narrow beam could split the beam.

The beam should slide easily in the fence, but not be loose. The wedge hole in the fence should be tapered, with the larger opening on the outside of the fence. The angle of the wedge and wedge slot have to match perfectly, otherwise the wedge may press on just one point of the beam, which could change the angle of the beam to the fence. In addition, a wedge that does not fit correctly will not hold the beam tight.

The blade of the *suji-keshiki* is beveled on one side to form the cutting edge, and that side usually faces the fence; as the blade cuts, the bevel keeps pulling the fence into the edge of the wood. Blades can be made in a number of different shapes, as shown in figure 6. I make my blades from a piece of broken bandsaw blade or any other hardened steel, but they can also be purchased. To set the blade in the beam, first insert the beam into the fence and tighten it. Then draw a line on the beam showing the location of the knife, usually about ½ in. to 1 in. from the end. This line should be exactly parallel to the fence. Now draw another line starting at the same position at the front, but skew it out one pencil-mark width at the back. (Skewed away from the fence, the blade will push away from the fence slightly in use, helping to pull the fence into the wood and allowing greater accuracy.)

Start the slot for the blade by making a small hole on the end of the line at the front of the gauge. I usually use a spade-tipped gimlet for this, or a drill. Saw down the skewed line with a coping-saw blade. If necessary, widen the top of the slot with a chisel. The thickness, but not the width, of the blade must be tight, otherwise the beam might split. (In case the blade is loose in the slot, you can add a wedge to tighten it.)

Suji-keshiki can also be made with two beams on one fence, so that you can mark two lines, as for mortising. For this, the bevels on the blades should be opposite each other, facing toward the inside of the mortise. This will leave a clear guide for the mortise chisel. *Suji-keshiki* can be adapted to do many different jobs. For example, if you have a gauge with one beam and you need to make many sets of parallel lines a certain distance apart, as when marking mortises, cut a piece of wood the width of that distance for a spacer and notch it to take the beam. Mark once with the piece in place against the fence and once without the piece. □

oshio Odate's book, Japanese Woodworking Tools: Their Tra*tion, Spirit and Use, is available from The Taunton Press,* *ox 355, Newtown, Conn. 06470. In addition to the chapter* *a marking tools, the 192-page volume covers saws, chisels,* *anes, sharpening stones and some specialized tools with no* *estern counterparts. Odate, who lives in Woodbury, Conn.,* *onducts frequent workshops on Japanese tools and teaches* *ulpture at New York's Pratt Institute. Drawings by the author.*

Most wedge-set marking gauges are adjusted in the same fashion. To check the distance from the fence, hold the marking gauge next to the rule or square with the pins or blade bevel up. Tap the beam out with the head of the hammer to move the blade out. To reduce the chances of slipping and marring the blade, tap the beam toward the fence with the side of the hammer.

Shop Math
With a little help from Pythagoras

by C. Edward Moore

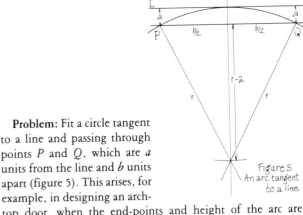

Y̲ou can use shop geometry without knowing why it works, but you will be able to solve more real-world problems if you understand the basic principles. Our point of departure is the right-angled triangle and the theorem of Pythagoras. The terms "right," "square," and "90°" all mean the same thing.

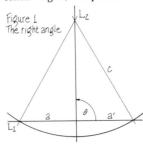

Figure 1
The right angle

The symbol θ, the Greek letter *theta*, designates any angle. In figure 1, we swing an arc of radius c whose center is on line L_2 so that it cuts through line L_1 in two places. This results in two triangles. By definition, whenever the two triangles are symmetrical $(a = a')$, the lines L_1 and L_2 form a right angle.

You use this understanding in reverse to construct a right angle, anywhere you want one (figure 2). First draw the baseline L_1 and mark the point x where you want the corner (vertex) of the right angle. Set a compass to any convenient radius (a), put the point on x, and mark points a and a' equidistantly on either side of x. Now enlarge the compass setting, again by any convenient amount (c) and scribe intersecting arcs above L_1, from centers a and a'. Connect the point thus found with x.

The theorem of Pythagoras tells us that if θ is a right angle, then $a^2 + b^2 = c^2$ and conversely if $a^2 + b^2 = c^2$, then θ is a right angle. The best-known example of this is the 3-4-5 right triangle (figure 3), where $3^2 + 4^2 = 5^2$. Carpenters have used the 3-4-5 triangle, or the 6-8-10 triangle, to square frames for centuries. With a knotted or marked rope and stakes, it is the way to lay out the corners of a building.

The circle is a set of points that all lie the same distance from a fixed point, the center. We create this relationship simply by setting a compass or trammel. On a grid of squares, with horizontal coordinate x and vertical coordinate y, we have the equation $x^2 + y^2 = r^2$, because of Pythagoras. All the values of x and y that produce the same value for r lie on the same circle (figure 4).

Problem: Fit a circle tangent to a line and passing through points P and Q, which are a units from the line and b units apart (figure 5). This arises, for example, in designing an arch-top door, when the end-points and height of the arc are known, and it is necessary to find the center.

Solution: Any tangent to a circle is by definition perpendicular to a radius. Thus the center of the circle will lie on a line drawn at right angles through the midpoint of the line PQ. Pythagoras shows that

$$r^2 = \left(\frac{b}{2}\right)^2 + (r-a)^2 = \frac{b^2}{4} + r^2 - 2ar + a^2,$$

so

$$2ar = \frac{b^2}{4} + a^2 \text{ and } r = \frac{b^2}{8a} + \frac{a}{2}.$$

This equation may be more useful in the form:

$$r = \frac{b^2 + 4a^2}{8a}$$

It can be transformed to find the third parameter of a circular arc when any two are known, that is, the width b can be found if you know the radius r and the height a, or the height a can be found if you know the radius r and the width b:

$$b = 2\sqrt{a(2r-a)} \qquad a = r - \sqrt{r^2 - (\tfrac{1}{2}b)^2}$$

These relationships apply where a is less than half of b, the same as saying that line PQ is in the top half of the circle in figure 5. When the line moves below the circle's diameter, the last equation becomes

$$a = r + \sqrt{r^2 - (\tfrac{1}{2}b)^2}$$

When working equations like these on an electronic calculator, you must either become adept at moving results into

Figure 5
An arc tangent to a line

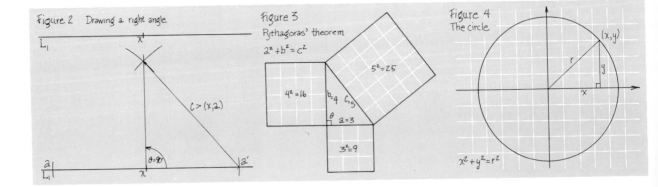

Figure 2   Drawing a right angle

Figure 3
Pythagoras' theorem
$2^2 + b^2 = c^2$

Figure 4
The circle

and out of the calculator memory, or else keep running notes with pencil and paper. In general, you start inside parentheses and work outward. For example, to solve for a, the height of an arc, when the radius r and width b are known, you would first find ½ of b, square it, and store the answer. Square r and subtract the previously stored result, then find the square root of this answer. Finally, subtract from r.

A useful property of the circle is the fact that if a triangle PQR is drawn with its long side on a diameter and its vertex touching the edge of the circle, that vertex will be a right angle. We can verify this by drawing the circle with its center at O on rectangular coordinates, and applying Pythagoras' theorem (figure 6), after showing that $(PQ)^2 - (PR)^2 = (QR)^2$. We know that wherever on a circle P is, the location of P can be described by coordinates x and y, and $x^2 + y^2 = r^2$. Since length $QR = 2r$, then $(QR)^2 = (2r)^2 = 4r^2$. We also know that $(PQ)^2 = (r-x)^2 + y^2$, and that $(PR)^2 = (r+x)^2 + y^2$. Thus $(PQ)^2 + (PR)^2 = (r-x)^2 + y^2 + (r+x)^2 + y^2$. If you do the algebra you'll find that $(PQ)^2 + (PR)^2 = 4r^2$, and we already found that to be the square of length QR. Thus the triangle PQR is right-angled ($\theta = 90°$): a diameter and any point P elsewhere on the circle always determine a right angle. Conversely, the legs of a right angle whose vertex is on the circle always cross the circle at the ends of a diameter.

Problem: Find the center of a circle or disc.

Solution: Place the right angle of a square or drafting triangle on the circle, and mark where the sides of the square cross the circle. Rotate the square about a quarter of a turn and again mark where it crosses the circle. Draw the two diameters you have thus located. They intersect at the center of the circle (figure 7).

This relationship can be used to verify whether a trough or semicircular cutout is in fact semicircular—just put the vertex of a framing square into it (figure 8). If the vertex and sides of the square all touch, the cutout is exactly half a circle. The relationship is also another way of constructing a right angle—draw a circle passing through the point where you want the right angle to be, draw in a diameter, and connect the ends of the diameter to the point.

Articles on woodworking and toolmaking often refer to proportional division by parallel lines. This is how shaper-knife profiles are derived, and a way to divide boards for dovetailing. Suppose lines L_1, L_2 and L_3 are parallel and lines M_1 and M_2 intersect them as shown (figure 9). The resulting line segments are proportional, that is,

$$\frac{a_1}{a_2} = \frac{b_1}{b_2}, \quad \frac{a_1}{b_1} = \frac{a_2}{b_2}, \quad \text{and} \quad \frac{a_1}{a_1 + b_1} = \frac{a_2}{a_2 + b_2}.$$

Problem: You have a line divided into two unequal parts. You want to divide another line of different length into the same proportions, that is, locate Q_2 below.

$P_1 \qquad P_2 \qquad P_3 \; Q_1 \qquad Q_2? \qquad Q_3$

Solution: Draw an auxiliary line through Q_1 at any convenient angle and beginning at Q_1, mark on it lengths P_1P_2 and P_2P_3. Then place a straightedge and drafting triangle so that an edge of the triangle connects P_3 with Q_3. Hold the straightedge in place and slide the triangle along it to P_2. A line drawn here will be parallel to P_3Q_3, and thus locates Q_2 (figure 10).

If you wanted to divide a line into five equal parts, you would use the same strategy: draw the auxiliary line, and

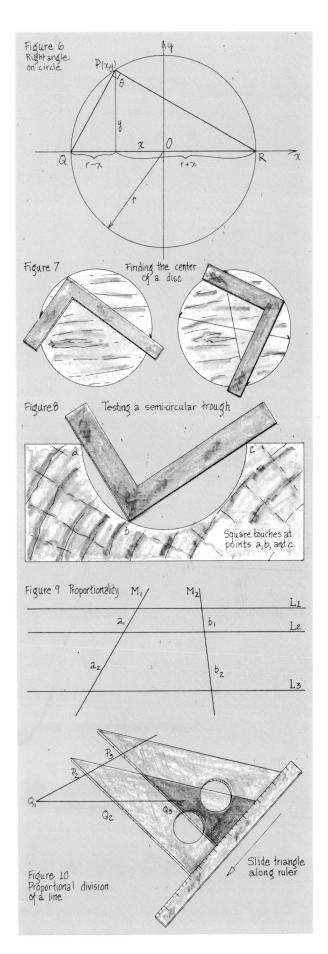

Figure 6
Right angle on circle

Figure 7   Finding the center of a disc

Figure 8   Testing a semi-circular trough

Square touches at points a, b, and c.

Figure 9   Proportionality

Figure 10
Proportional division of a line

Slide triangle along ruler.

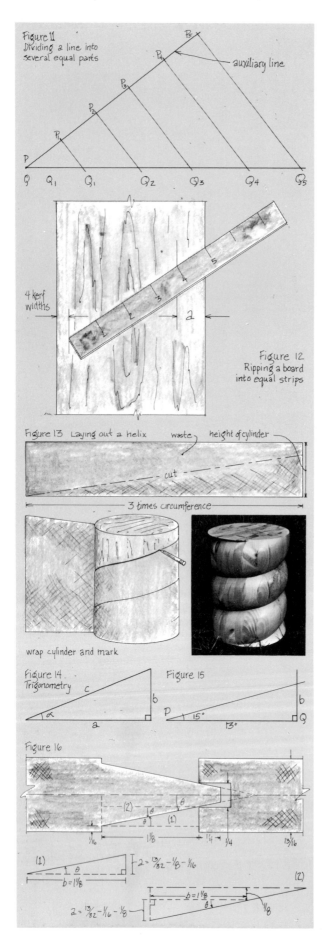

Figure 11
Dividing a line into
several equal parts

auxiliary line

Figure 12
Ripping a board
into equal strips

4 kerf widths

Figure 13 Laying out a helix

waste

height of cylinder

cut

3 times circumference

wrap cylinder and mark

Figure 14.
Trigonometry

Figure 15

Figure 16

measure five equal, but convenient, intervals along it. Then use the square-and-ruler method to drop parallels from these points on the auxiliary line to the line you want to divide (figure 11).

Practical applications: You want to rip a board into *n* equal strips, for example, five strips. First make a test cut into scrap and measure the width of the kerf. Then mark off four kerf widths from one edge of the board. Start a ruler at this point and incline it until it crosses the other edge at some multiple of five. Mark at the fourth multiple, and measure squarely from there to the edge (*a* in figure 12). The width *a* is the distance from the rip fence to the inside of the sawblade.

A related problem is marking off threads on a cylinder, as for a twist carving. My version is the laminated pine table, shown in figure 13 without its round ½-in. glass top, carved from a cylinder 17 or 18 in. high and 14 or 15 in. in diameter. I wanted the thread to go around three times, so I wrapped a string around the cylinder three times, and cut it off there. Next I cut a piece of brown paper the same length as the string, and marked off the height of the cylinder on one edge. Then I cut along the line from the corner to this point, making a long triangle, which I wrapped around the cylinder, its bottom edge aligned with the bottom edge of the wood, and marked along the long side of the triangle as I went.

Here is a brief introduction to trigonometry, the study of relations between the sides and angles of triangles. Trigonometry is sometimes seen as a fearful creature, but with an electronic calculator and a note of the basic relationships, you can tame it for shop use.

Suppose you start with some angle α (the Greek letter *alpha*) and complete the triangle as shown (figure 14) so that side *c* is opposite a right angle. The side of the triangle opposite a right angle is called the hypotenuse. Now, no matter how large or small the triangle is drawn, the ratios a/c, b/c and b/a are fixed numbers. They are completely determined by the angle α. These ratios are given names: sine, cosine and tangent. We write

$$\sin\alpha = \frac{b}{c} = \frac{\text{opposite side}}{\text{hypotenuse}}$$

$$\cos\alpha = \frac{a}{c} = \frac{\text{adjacent side}}{\text{hypotenuse}}$$

$$\tan\alpha = \frac{b}{a} = \frac{\text{opposite side}}{\text{adjacent side}} = \frac{\sin\alpha}{\cos\alpha}.$$

Pythagoras shows that $(\sin\alpha)^2 + (\cos\alpha)^2 = b^2/c^2 + a^2/c^2 = 1$, since $a^2 + b^2 = c^2$.

Problem: Suppose it is necessary to mark off an angle of 15° from the vertex *P*, where the length *PQ* is 13 in. That is, find length *b* in figure 15. We know that $\tan 15° = b/13$. From the calculator or from tables, we learn that $\tan 15° = .2679$. So, $b = 13 \times .2679 = 3.48$.

Practical application: What is the correct table-saw angle for cutting the taper on raised panels in a door?

First solution: Draw the cross section full-size or larger, and measure with a protractor.

Second solution: From the drawing, extract the relevant right-angled triangle and establish the length of two sides by subtracting known dimensions. Figure 16 shows two ways to do this, giving opposite side *b* of $\frac{7}{32}$ in. and adjacent side *a* of $1\frac{1}{8}$ in. $\tan\theta = \frac{7}{32}/1\frac{1}{8} = .09144$. You can use trig tables to identify θ or punch $\tan^{-1}(.01944)$ into the calculator and get 11°. On some calculators this operation is marked "arctan." □

Oblique Miters in Stock of Variable Thickness

by Jim Cavosie

In my job at a harpsichord shop, I had the task of mitering ¾-in. veneered plywood at oblique angles, so that both the inside and outside surfaces lined up flush. This caused me a lot of headaches because ¾-in. plywood comes from the factory plus or minus ⅟₃₂ in. The standard procedure was either to measure the thicknesses, make a drawing and measure the resulting angles with a protractor, or to rely on trial and error and experience. I found a faster and more accurate way using trigonometry and a pocket calculator. The derivation was difficult, so I'll just give the resulting equation.

To find the exact miter angles, you first need to find the length x of the line on which the two thicknesses can join flush. Measure the thickness of the two boards (a and b) and find the total angle of the miter joint (angle A plus angle B). Then find x by solving the following equation:

$$x^2 = \frac{a^2 + b^2 + 2ab\,\cos(A+B)}{\sin^2(A+B)}.$$

Once length x is known, finding the two miter angles is easy. Since $\sin A = a/x$ and $\sin B = b/x$,

$$\text{angle } A = \sin^{-1}\left(\frac{a}{x}\right)$$

$$\text{angle } B = \sin^{-1}\left(\frac{b}{x}\right).$$

If $(A+B)$ approaches 180° and a is much greater than b, it is possible for angle A to be greater than 90°. If this is the case,

$$\text{angle } A = 180° - \sin^{-1}\left(\frac{a}{x}\right).$$

When many miter joints have to be cut at any given total angle, it makes sense to calculate a table of values for angles A and B over a range of values for a and b.

Jim Cavosie lives in Carrboro, N.C.

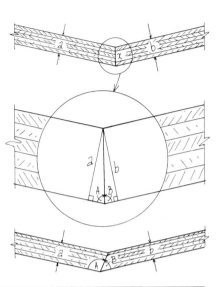

Boring Angled Holes

by Jacob N. Frederiksen

Here is a way to set up the drill press for boring angled holes, as in the seat of a Windsor chair. Most instructions call for tilting a bit brace back at some angle A, and to the side at another angle B. When using a drill press, it's easier to rotate the work through an angle of $R°$ in the horizontal plane, then, by means of an auxiliary table, to tilt the work to an angle T. The tilting table consists of two squares of plywood hinged along one edge and fixed to the drill-press table. The tilt is achieved by fitting blocks of wood under the back edge of the top piece of plywood.

The basic equations are:

$$\tan R = \frac{\tan A}{\tan B}$$

$$\tan^2 T = \tan^2 A + \tan^2 B.$$

When the angles are given in terms of R and T, they can be converted back to angles A and B using the equations:

$$\tan A = \tan T \sin R$$

$$\tan B = \tan T \cos R.$$

Here is an example. I have been building a Windsor chair using Michael Dunbar's plans, purchased through Woodcraft Supply (41 Atlantic Ave., Woburn, Mass. 01888). The rear legs of this chair tilt 13° outward (angle A) and 14° to the rear (angle B). The front legs tilt 15° outward and 9° to the front. These angles are measured from a line

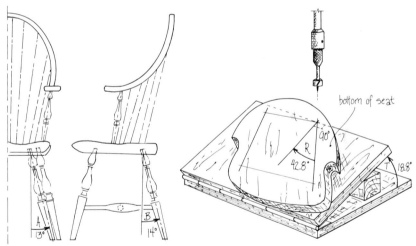

perpendicular to the bottom of the seat. For the rear legs, the work should be rotated on the table through an angle R:

$$\tan R = \frac{\tan 13°}{\tan 14°} = \frac{.230868}{.249328}$$
$$= .925962$$

so angle $R = 42.8°$.
The table should then be tilted at an angle T:

$$\tan^2 T = \tan^2 13° + \tan^2 14°$$
$$= (.230868)^2 + (.249328)^2$$
$$= .115464,$$

so $\tan T = .339799$, and angle $T = 18.8°$. For the front legs, where A is 15° and B is 9°, angle R is 59.4° and T is 17.3°.

Having done the calculations, I drew reference lines back-to-front on the bottom of the chair seat, through the points to be drilled, as shown in the drawing above. Then I added a second line through the hole centers, at angle R from the fore-to-aft reference line. I rotated the work so that this new pencil line was perpendicular to the back of the table, then tilted the table to angle T. The height of the spacer block to produce angle T can be found by trigonometry, or by trial with a protractor. The important thing is to rotate the work before it is tilted, else you will introduce error, and it is good practice to convert angles R and T back to angles A and B, to guard against mathematical mistakes. □

Jake Frederiksen, of Chevy Chase, Md., builds reproduction furniture for his family.

Drawing the Ellipse
Several ingenious methods

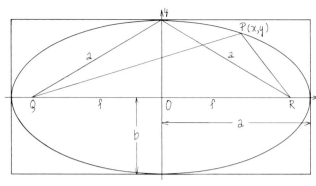

Everybody likes an ellipse. We use them for picture and mirror frames, tabletops, inlays and carved decoration. Everybody also seems to have trouble drawing an ellipse of the size and proportions he wants. First, a definition. An ellipse is a closed curve traced out by maintaining a constant sum of distances from two fixed points in a plane.

If points Q and R are $2f$ units apart and P is a point that is allowed to move so that length PQ + length $PR = 2a$ (a constant), then P will traverse an ellipse that fits into a box measuring $2a$ by $2b$, where $b = \sqrt{a^2 - f^2}$. If we place the center of this box on coordinate axes, then each point P on the ellipse with coordinates (x, y) satisfies the equation:

$$\frac{x^2}{a^2} + \frac{y^2}{b^2} = 1.$$

The major axis of the ellipse has length $2a$ and the minor axis has length $2b$. Points Q and R are called foci or focal points of the ellipse. The size and shape of the ellipse are wholly determined by our choice of a and b (half the length of the major and minor axes). These dimensions define the rectangle into which the ellipse will fit, and only one ellipse will fit any particular rectangle. If a is much greater than b, the ellipse will be long and thin. As a approaches b, the ellipse becomes more nearly circular, until $a = b$, whereupon the foci P and Q coincide at the center of a circle of radius a.

The usual shop problem is to draw an ellipse inside a rectangular box whose dimensions are given. There are a number of ways to do it.

The best-known solution (method A below), but not necessarily the easiest or best, is to draw the major and minor axes inside the rectangle, locate the two foci, drive two nails or push-pins there, and loop a string, monofilament line or braided fishline of length $2a$ around the pins. A pencil is pushed against the string and pulled around, keeping the string taut.

You can make the string come out to length $2a$ by driving a third pin at b on the vertical axis. Tie the string tightly around the three pins, then remove the third one. It doesn't matter whether you make loops at both ends of the string, or tie it into a loop around all three pins.

The distance f of each focal point from the center of the ellipse can be calculated from the formula $f = \sqrt{a^2 - b^2}$ or found geometrically. Set a compass to length a, put its point at b on the vertical axis, and scribe arcs to intersect the horizontal axis. These intersections are points Q and R, the foci of the ellipse.

With method A it is difficult to make the looped string exactly the right length. A way to do it is shown in method B. Push-pins go at the foci, as before, but the third pin goes outside

the ellipse and below the first two. Tie a loop in one end of a long string and drop it over the third pin. Run the string over the focal pins and around them twice, bringing its end over to the center of the ellipse. Then put your finger on the strings between the two pins. Pick up the last pass of string with the pencil, put just enough tension on it to keep from breaking the pencil point, and move the pencil up to the top center of the rectangle (b). Keep the string taut, and sweep the pencil to the right to draw a quarter of the ellipse. Repeat the exercise three more times, moving the third pin above the center line after completing the top portion of the ellipse.

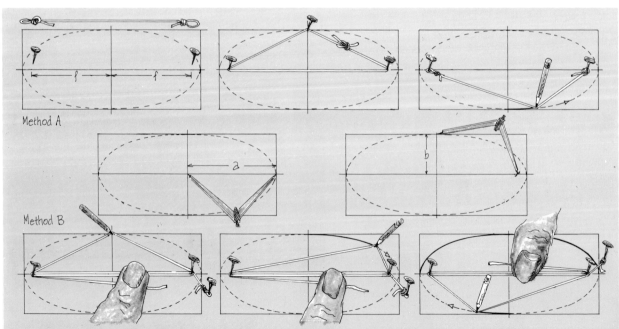

Method A

Method B

The trouble with the looped string methods is that it is quite difficult to maintain string tension and still keep the pencil at exactly the right tilt. The simplest and most accurate way to draw an ellipse is the so-called paper-strip method, which avoids focal points and string altogether.

Begin with coordinate axes and mark off length *a* to the left and right, and point *b* above and below, to define the rectangle in which the ellipse will fit, as shown in the drawing at right. On the edge of a separate strip of paper, tick a point and label it *O*. From point *O*, tick off length *a* and label it *A*. In the same direction from *O*, tick length *b* and mark it *B*.

Now, whenever this edge is placed so that *A* falls on the vertical axis and *B* falls on the horizontal axis, *O* has found a point on the ellipse. Slide the strip along the axes, mark as many points as you find reasonable or necessary, and connect them to obtain the ellipse.

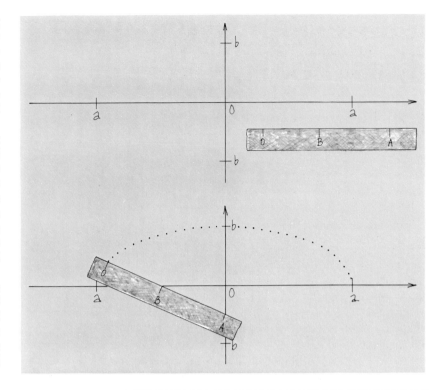

A simple device can be made for drawing ellipses by substituting for the strip of paper a trammel beam carrying two points and a pencil. You draw the axes as before, and set the trammel so that point *O* is the pencil, with lengths *a* and *b* held by the trammel points, as shown in the drawing below. If you can keep the points on the axes, the pencil will draw the ellipse. The Dominy family of woodworkers and watchmakers, who worked on Long Island from about 1760 to 1830, used an ingenious home-made trammel that ran in tracks, making it possible to draw ellipses blindfolded (photo). The track is simply two strips of wood, crossed at right angles and grooved to take the trammel points, which are not sharp but turned like a short dowel. The points slide along the beam and are fixed by wedges; thumbscrews would do as well. The Dominys probably tacked the track to the work and used an iron point to scribe the ellipse. A linkage like this might be arranged to guide a router directly into the stock, but we don't know anybody who has tried it.

One final note: to make two ellipses with parallel sides, as for a picture or mirror frame, two complete ellipses must be drawn because they will have different foci. The governing parameter for each is the box inside which it will fit, and the width of the resulting frame is the difference between the dimensions of the two boxes. □

This article was compiled from information sent by several people: Ed Moore (definitions), Rufus Winsor and Fred Johnson (string methods), C.W. Beringhaus (paper method) and Steele Hinton (trammel method). Moore, a woodworker and associate professor of math at the U.S. Naval Academy, has fielded shop math problems for Fine Woodworking's *Q/A column.*

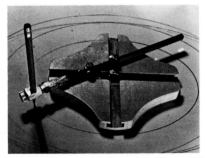

Ellipse trammel by Trevor Robinson of Amherst, Mass., has steel sliding blocks. The distance from pencil to farther pivot is half the major axis, and from pencil to nearer pivot is half the minor axis. Right, the Dominy trammel: birch beam is 39 in. long, sliding blocks are maple with satinwood wedges. Crossed tracks shown are a modern replacement. Photo from With Hammer in Hand *by Charles F. Hummel, courtesy the Henry Francis du Pont Winterthur Museum.*

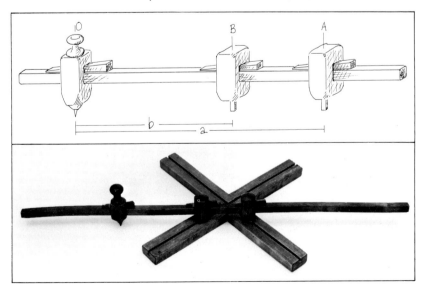

Two Tools

Push-stick; duckbill scriber

In ripping lumber on the table saw, the operator protects his fingers by using a saw guard and a push-stick. A push-stick feeds the stock forward and provides lateral force to guide the board firmly against the fence as well as hold-down force to keep the lumber on the saw table. The traditional push-stick is simply a stick with a notch in one end. This dangerous device has serious disadvantages. Boards (especially at the forward end) cannot be held firmly enough against the fence for accurate ripping. There is little control over the upward thrust of the lumber that results from the friction of the board against the rear edge of the saw blade. These shortcomings tempt the operator to use his free hand to help guide the board, to discard the push-stick entirely, or to decide that the saw guard is in the way and remove it. Here the guard has been removed to take photographs.

Careful analysis of the ripping requirements—feed, guide and hold-

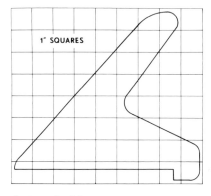

Basic push-stick pattern

down—produces a safe, single-handed push-stick. This improved design applies force at a point well forward on the board to provide enough leverage for firm hold-down. The rear overhang ensures forward feed. The grip of the long bottom surface is enhanced by a covering of thin rubber, rubberized fabric, rug underlayment or abrasive paper, fastened with an adhesive such as silicone rubber or contact cement.

Although the improved push-stick will handle most routine ripping, no single push-stick design will cover all sawing situations, and therefore details of shape and size should be modified to suit the job at hand. Narrow models should be made for ripping narrow strips; wide ones provide greater lateral stability. A double-footed pusher offers maximum control; its two feet may straddle the saw blade and carry narrow cuts safely beyond. This style also is a perfect accessory for the jointer.

It is best to make push-sticks of hardwood plywood, because it resists splitting. I don't recommend softwoods and low-density hardwoods, except for wider models. One-piece push-sticks can be bandsawn to shape from plywood sheets by simply tracing or sketching the pattern on the stock.

—R. Bruce Hoadley

The duckbill scriber is easy to make and doesn't require a lot of tools or skill. It is used for scribing frames, moldings or anything that has to fit to an uneven surface such as plaster walls or anything else out of plumb. And I guarantee you, every house has some wall out of plumb. The tool is also handy when leveling the legs of a chair or table.

The only things needed are a piece of hardwood (preferably maple) 1-1/4 in. x 1-1/2 in. x 4-1/2 in., a piece of brass or steel 1/16 in. x 3/8 in. x 1-1/4 in. with two countersunk holes, two 3/8-in. No. 2 flathead screws, and one bolt at least 1/8 in. x 1-1/2 in. with a wing nut to fit.

First shape the block, drill the holes for the bolt and pencil, and cut the groove in the bottom for the metal plate. Then cut off the two outside pieces at 1/4-in. thick and remove the half-round chunk from them.

To assemble it, bolt the three pieces together, then screw the metal plate to the two outside pieces. Be sure to drill pilot holes for the screws and put soap or wax on them before you insert them. File the plate until it is flush.

To scribe a cabinet to a wall, stand it in place or a little bit out. Place the brass plate side of the duckbill against the wall along the line the cabinet is to fit, and open it so the pencil touches the work. Tighten the wing nut. Now you merely run the duckbill along the wall, and the pencil reproduces all its hills and valleys. To level a chair, stand it on a flat surface and block up the legs until the seat is the way you want it and it doesn't wobble. Then lay the duckbill on the table and circle each leg, and you have your cutting lines.

—*Tage Frid*

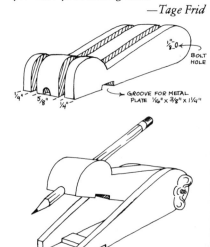

Improved push-sticks are safer.

From *Fine Woodworking* magazine (Spring 1977) 6:53

wo Dovetail Layout Tools

by Jim Richey

you don't cut dovetails regularly, laying them out is a time-consuming and
metimes error-fraught chore. Here are
tools I use in my shop to speed up the
. The first helps with spacing and the
ond is a pre-set bevel gauge that is
ier to use than the larger and more
kward adjustable bevel gauge that it re-
ces. You can make both in a couple of
nutes out of shop scraps.

The pin-spacing gauge consists of two
rts: a 6-in. slotted rub block and a
oden blade that fits into a ¼-in. slot in
block. The blade length is variable.
ke it long for dovetailing a wide car-
e side, short if you're doing a bunch of
wer sides. I made up several blades,
ne with even pin spacing, others with
ied spacing.

To make the spacing tool, mark out
proportional spacing of pins and tails
the blade. Use any spacing you like. I
rmally use multiples of ¼ in. or ½ in.
cause they are easy to lay out. Just
ke sure that the pattern is wider than
boards to be joined and leave enough
gth at one end so it can be gripped in
block. Position the tool as shown in
drawing and mark out the pin spac-
g. It will automatically maintain the
oportions you lay out on the blade, re-
rdless of board width. Take care not to
the blade pivot in the block, otherwise
spacing will be inaccurate.

With the pin spacing set, you are ready
mark the pin bevels with the other
uge. This gauge consists of a blade
etal, plastic or wood) let into and
rewed to a hardwood block. If you
rk-out with a knife, as I do, a metal or
astic blade will survive an errant cut.
e taper angle can vary from the 1-to-7
n-to-rise (80°) of the fine pins in tradi-
nal furniture to the coarser 1-to-4 ratio
5°) of most commercial dovetail rout-
bits. The other end of the blade
ould be square to the block, for carry-
g down the pin lines on the faces of
e board.   □

*n Richey edits and draws Methods of
ork for Fine Woodworking. He lives in
ity, Texas.*

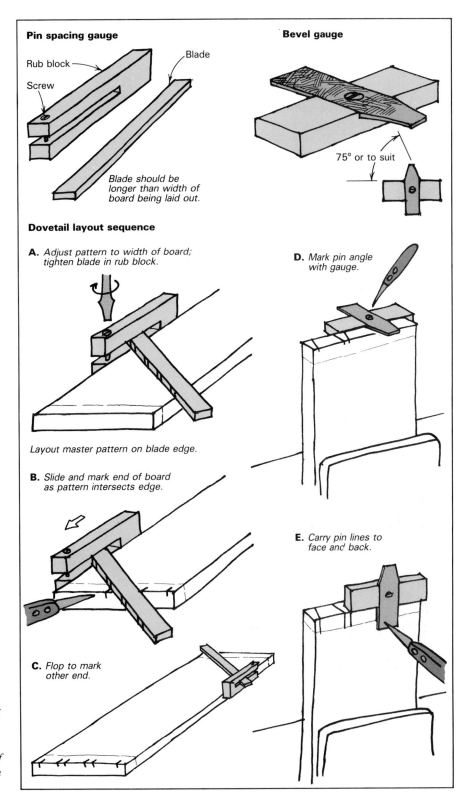

Pin spacing gauge

Rub block
Screw
Blade

*Blade should be
longer than width of
board being laid out.*

Bevel gauge

75° or to suit

Dovetail layout sequence

A. *Adjust pattern to width of board;
tighten blade in rub block.*

Layout master pattern on blade edge.

B. *Slide and mark end of board
as pattern intersects edge.*

C. *Flop to mark
other end.*

D. *Mark pin angle
with gauge.*

E. *Carry pin lines to
face and back.*

Sawing by Hand

Bowsaw is best; keep it sharp

by Tage Frid

A handsaw can replace a machine-powered saw for every cutting operation. The correct use and maintenance of handsaws should be practiced until they are second nature. To saw properly, coordination of the joints in the hand, elbow and shoulder must be achieved. The biggest mistake most people make when using a handsaw is to hang onto it as if their lives depended on it, bearing down much too hard. This makes it hard to start the saw, and once the cut is started, it is difficult to follow the line. A handsaw should lie loosely in your hands. No pressure should be applied, particularly when starting the cut. Once experience is gained, a slight amount of pressure can be applied after the cut is started. Use your thumb as a guide when starting the saw.

There are many different handsaws on the market, and each one is designed for a special purpose. Handsaws are sold by length and by the number of points—a six-point saw has six teeth per inch.

The bowsaw, scroll bowsaw, offset dovetail saw and rip panel saw are the saws I have found most useful in my many years as a cabinetmaker. I don't like and would never buy a backsaw; they are clumsy and heavy. Maybe they are all right in miter boxes, but a bowsaw will do the job faster.

For general sawing, I would recommend buying a 26-in., six-point and an 18-in., eight-point bowsaw. (Lengths might vary, because most bowsaws are made in Europe and so are measured metrically.) I would also buy a 26-in. scroll bowsaw, preferably with interchangeable blades, and a 10-in., or longer, 15-point offset dovetail saw. A 24-in. rip panel saw (the standard American carpenter's saw), six to seven points, is useful for cutting big pieces such as plywood, where the bridge of the bowsaw would be in the way.

Japanese saws are good for special work. I have some but hardly ever use them, except in cramped space where I can't get in with a regular saw. The Japanese ripsaw cuts on the pull stroke. This makes the line fuzzy and hard to see when cutting joints. On the crosscut, the teeth are long and might bend when hitting a knot. Also, the saw is hard to resharpen.

For scroll work, I would of course use a band saw if I could. Or I might use a saber saw. But a scroll bowsaw will cut as fast or faster than a saber saw, and no electricity is needed. The blade on the scroll bowsaw is considerably longer than that of any other scroll saw or coping saw.

Starting the cut: Frid holds saw loosely, left thumb guiding blade, with eye, blade and cutting line all aligned vertically. Blade is angled so frame will clear wood as cut proceeds.

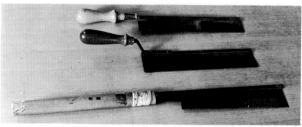

Dovetail saws: straight (top), offset and Japanese.

From *Fine Woodworking* magazine (Fall 1977) 8:56-59

Sharpening Vise

You can make a sharpening jig out of two pieces of 3/4-in. plywood. The dimensions can be changed to suit your individual needs. Glue two pieces of maple or another hardwood on the ends of the plywood, as shown at right. These will be the jaws of the jig. When the glue has set, put the two halves together and attach butt hinges at the bottom. Screw or glue on the two side pieces, which keep the jig from falling through the vise. Then cut the jaws parallel, and saw the outside bevel. If you use a table saw, slide a piece of wood in between the two pieces of plywood, below left, to prevent the jaws from binding on the saw blade at the end of the cut. Or handplane the jaws parallel and plane off the bevel, below right. Planing a little off the bottom of the two jaw pieces ensures a tight grip at the top.

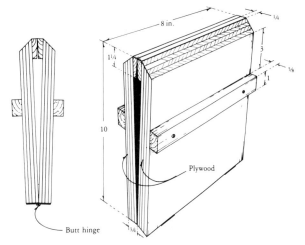

Butt hinge

Plywood

Whatever saw you use has to be kept sharp and set right. There are many vises you can buy that hold the blade during sharpening. But I make my own—it is simple to do and considerably less expensive.

For some strange reason, most new handsaws are filed for crosscutting. The first time I sharpen a crosscut saw I change it to a ripsaw (by changing the teeth from a point to a chisel edge). This makes ripping faster and easier, of course, and I find the saw works better even for crosscutting.

Before sharpening, check to see if all the teeth are the same height. If not, level them off with a mill file. Then file each tooth to a sharp point, and the saw is ready to be set. After setting, file two strokes on each tooth the length of the saw.

All handsaws have an alternating tooth setting; that is, the upper part of each tooth is bent out to one side or the other, to create a kerf that is wider than the saw blade. If the saw is not set enough it will bind. If set too much, the cut will be wide and rough, and the saw will cut more slowly. If the teeth are set more to one side, the saw will favor that side. To correct this, both sides must be reset. A properly set saw that is started correctly, with little pressure, will easily follow the cutting line. There are many good saw sets on the market. I prefer the Sandvik because it is light, easy to adjust and simple to use. It allows you to see what you are doing. Each tooth should be set approximately 1/64 in.

If the teeth are too small for a saw set, use a small screwdriver instead. Press it down between every second tooth and twist it the same amount each time.

Now the teeth are ready to be filed, with a new triangular file. Use only one edge for each saw filing; by using the same

number of strokes and the same length of the file on each stroke, all the teeth will be sharpened uniformly. The file gradually gets dull, but so gradually that all the teeth will remain the same length. Turning the file to a new edge in the middle of a sharpening is a mistake, because the new side will cut deeper than the worn side. I never use an old, worn-out file. Use a new file—you get three sharpenings from each one. This way the teeth stay the same length and you won't have to level them off for many years.

When filing, press down straight on the file, just enough so the file works and doesn't skip over the metal. File both the

To level the teeth, a mill file is run the length of the blade.

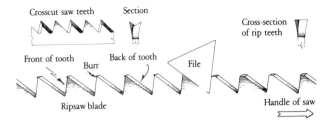

As teeth take shape, tiny burr points in direction of cut.

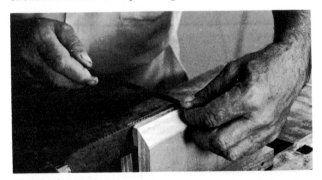

Pliers-like saw set alternately bends teeth away from plane of blade, about 1/64 in. to each side. Set must be even.

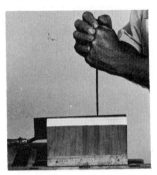

Screwdriver twisted in every second gullet will set small saws.

With fingers as stops, whole length of file is used on each stroke.

Tensioning string is wrapped four times lengthwise, woven to finish.

front and back of the teeth at the same time, working from the front toward the handle of the saw. Thus the final stroke on each tooth will be on the back, and the burr that appears when the tooth just comes to a point will be aimed in the cutting direction. Be sure to keep the file strokes at 90° to the blade. Never file or stone the face of the blade, because this would change the set of the teeth. Don't file the teeth of a ripsaw alternately, as is usually recommended in textbooks.

The saw can be refiled four or five times before it needs resetting. Of course this depends on how dull you let the saw get before you refile it. I always file my saws as soon as the tips of the teeth get shiny white. This means the saw has started to get dull. If it isn't too dull, two file strokes on each tooth should be enough to sharpen the saw.

If the wood tears up in the back when crosscutting or ripping, one or more of the teeth are too long. In this case I file across the top to even the teeth, and then refile all the teeth before setting. If the teeth still tear, as is likely to happen in softwood and especially in plywood, scribe a line where the cut will be and make a vee-cut with a chisel on the underside of the piece. This will prevent tearing.

The bowsaw is my all-purpose saw. It takes longer to learn to use than other handsaws, but once you get the hang of it, you will use it for most cutting. All my advanced students use a bowsaw, and I don't brainwash my students. Its advantage is that because the blade is narrower, there is less friction in the kerf. The blade does not whip because it is kept in tension. Because the steel is thinner than in a panel saw, the bowsaw advances more quickly, and it is easier to cut a line.

When you buy a bowsaw that uses string as a tensioning system, you usually get the saw in pieces. Even if it comes assembled, you must know how to string it in case the string breaks. Clamp the saw in the bench so that there is tension in the blade when the string is applied. Wrap the string four times lengthwise, then finish the stringing by weaving the end in and out of the strings about 10 times. Then place the piece of wood that controls blade tension between the strings. Release the tension when the saw is not in use.

When I rip with a bowsaw I clamp the board down on the bench. I can cut faster this way because I am sawing up and down and can put force into the down stroke. I use both hands so I don't tire as easily. Also, by positioning the board with the portion to be ripped extended over the bench, I have to clamp the board only once. If I stand it up in the vise, I have to keep clamping and unclamping to move it into position. If I were cutting a long board, say 8 ft., I would need a ladder if I stood the board up in the vise. The board would vibrate so that it would be just about impossible to cut.

When I rip a board with a bowsaw, I hold it so the blade is perpendicular to the board. All the force is from the right hand, with the left hand acting as a guide. I saw away from myself so that I can see the line, and so that I can move along with the cut with my arms in a comfortable position. On a 3/4-in. thick piece of basswood clamped horizontally, 10 strokes with a 26-in. bowsaw cut 9 in. With the wood vertically in the vise, the same number of strokes cut about 5 in.

For crosscutting, I use the rip-sharpened bowsaw. I lay the board flat on the bench, with the piece I am cutting off to my right, and hold the wood down with my left hand. Then when the cut is almost through I plant my left elbow on the board to hold it, and reach between the blade and the bridge of the saw to catch the off-cut.

Making a Bowsaw

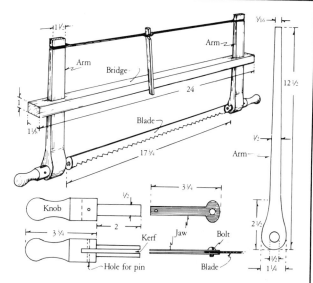

If you want to make a bowsaw, the first thing to do is to buy the blade, so you can design a saw with the right relationship between the arms, bridge and blade. A bowsaw should be as light as possible. I would use teak or mahogany for the arms, clear pine for the bridge, and maple for the knobs.

To make the arms, drill 1/2-in. holes in the arms first, then mark the wood and cut the taper using a band saw, scroll saw or scroll bowsaw. The arms should be identical. Sand the pieces and break the edges, especially where you will hold the saw. Leave the arms square where they pass through the bridge. The bridge is rectangular in section and has a through mortise near each end for the arms.

Make a 1/8-in. saw cut in the knobs for the two pieces of steel that will hold the blade. Then turn the knobs.

The steel jaw pieces are the most difficult parts of the saw to make. Two pieces go in each knob and sandwich the blade between them. One, 19 gauge, has a hole so the screw can slip in easily; the other, 17 gauge, should have a threaded hole to fit a 3/16-in. roundhead bolt, 1/4 in. long. Remember to put the knobs through the arms before fastening the steel to the knobs with a pin.

For a 17-3/4-in. blade I would make the arms 12-1/2 in. long; for a 25-3/4-in. blade I would make the arms 14-1/3 in. long. Personally I would not go to all the trouble to make a bowsaw. The wood parts are easy, but the metal parts take time, and I can buy a good bowsaw ready-made for about $20 (1977).

When I have to resaw by hand, I start the same way as sawing a tenon; if started correctly it will naturally follow the line. I mark a line on both ends and along one edge of the board and saw down on one corner, cutting the whole end and part of the top. Then I turn the board around in the vise and saw from the other corner. The saw drops into the first kerf, which guides it along. (Using a slightly thinner blade for the first cut gives a little more accuracy for this guiding process.) For cutting up plywood, I place the panel flat on sawhorses and climb right up on top of it.

For very small work I use an offset dovetail saw. With the offset, I can see the line more easily and I can use the saw for cutting flush anything that protrudes above a flat surface. I also change it from crosscut to rip the first time it needs filing. I don't like the reversible offset. It is very bulky, and because I change it to a ripsaw I can only use it one way anyway.

[Editor's note: Bowsaws are sold by Frog Tool Co., P.O. Box 8325, Chicago, Ill. 60680; Garrett Wade, 161 Ave. of the Americas, New York, N.Y. 10013; Silvo Hardware, 107 Walnut St., Philadelphia, Pa. 19106; Three Crowns, 3850 Monroe Ave., Pittsford, N.Y. 14534; and Woodcraft Supply Corp., 41 Atlantic Ave., Box 4000, Woburn, Mass. 01888. Olson Saw Co., Route 6, Bethel, Conn. 06801, makes blades for most types of frame saws.]

When ripping (left), left hand guides cut and right hand powers whole length of blade downward. Scroll bowsaw (center) also cuts on down stroke, away from sawyer. As saw nears end of crosscut (right), sawyer reaches between blade and bridge to catch wood.

Shopmade Bowsaw
Tailor its size to suit the job

by Simon Watts

Although an ancient tool—they've been used at least since Roman times—bowsaws still have some distinct advantages over either powered bandsaws or saber saws. They need no electric power, are light and portable, and take up little space when dismantled. Also, they can be fitted with different-width blades—narrow ones for sawing tight curves, wider ones for more general work. Bowsaws are especially useful when you have to saw a curve with a changing bevel. I find my saw an excellent tool for cutting the curved transoms and sculling notches in the lapstrake boats I build.

You can tailor the bowsaw described here to your spec needs. For example, you might want a deeper throat, more less blade length, a handle at each end or no handle at all. Y could also make different-size stretchers to accommodate sevo lengths of blade. I've found the saw shown here to be a con nient size, well-balanced and not too heavy. The blade is 20¼ from pin to pin, one of several standard sizes available. Bla can be bought, or you can make them from broken bands blades, just as long as they're sharp and still have some set. cut the blade, just touch it to the corner of a grinder and snap

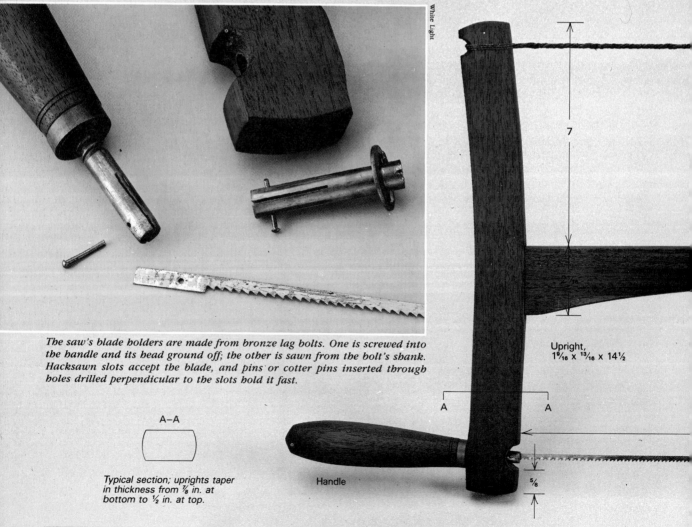

White Light

The saw's blade holders are made from bronze lag bolts. One is screwed into the handle and its head ground off; the other is sawn from the bolt's shank. Hacksawn slots accept the blade, and pins or cotter pins inserted through holes drilled perpendicular to the slots hold it fast.

A–A

Typical section; uprights taper in thickness from ⅞ in. at bottom to ½ in. at top.

Handle

Upright,
1⁹⁄₁₆ x ¹³⁄₁₆ x 14½

7

5⁄8

Photo: White

off. Drill ⁵⁄₃₂-in. holes at each end, but as a kindness to your twist bits, soften the spring steel first—heat the ends red-hot with a torch, then let them cool slowly.

Use any strong, straight-grained hardwood for the frame. Mahogany is my first choice because it looks good with copper and bronze, and I like the way the color gets richer as the wood matures. First make patterns in cardboard for the curved uprights and stretcher, then cut out rectangular blanks for these parts. Mark out and cut the mortises before doing any shaping. To form the notches for the blade holders and tensioning cord, clamp the uprights together edge-to-edge and drill a ⅛-in. dia. hole with a sharp Powerbore or machine spur bit centered on the crack. Inevitably, half the hole will be in each upright, neatly forming the notch. Drill ⅜-in. holes for the blade holders, shape the uprights, and cut the tenons on the stretcher, which should fit without forcing. For looks and lightness, I tapered the uprights in thickness from ⅞ in. at the bottom to about ½ in. at the top.

I turned the handle on a lathe, but you could equally well carve it by hand—an octagonal section might give a better grip than the more usual round. Without a metal collar, called a ferrule, the handle would eventually split, so I made a ferrule by cutting a ½-in. long section off a piece of ¾-in. thin-walled copper pipe. I tapped the ferrule into the end grain of the handle's rough blank, then used a heavy vise to press it into the end grain, flush with the surface. I then turned the blank to the shape shown. If you have a chuck center for the tailstock, drill the handle for the blade holder while it's still in the lathe; if not, you would do best to drill it before turning.

For the hardware, you'll need two ⅜-in. by 4-in. bronze lag screws and a ⅜-in. bronze washer. I use bronze only for the looks and because it doesn't rust. You can get bronze hardware from Jamestown Distributors, 22 Narragansett Ave., Jamestown, R.I. 02825. You could perfectly well use cheaper and more easily obtainable steel lags, however. For this saw, I pinned the blade in the holder with brass escutcheon pins I happened to have around, but they bent when I tensioned the frame. Stainless-steel cotter pins would do better. Make the blade holders as shown in the photo on the facing page. Mount the blade and tension it by looping nylon cord—¹⁄₁₆-in. to ⅛-in. dia.—loosely three or four times around the notches in the upper end of the uprights and then twisting it with a tapered piece of hardwood. You'll find that thinner blades need more tension than thicker ones.

Bowsaws can be used with the teeth pointing either way—you can cut on the push stroke or the pull. There's no need to reverse the blade—just turn the saw around and grasp it by the upright. I usually use bowsaws two-handed, especially when cutting tight curves with a thin blade. Speed and assurance come only with practice, but it's well worth persevering. □

Simon Watts is an FWW contributing editor who spends his summers in Nova Scotia and his winters in California teaching boatbuilding.

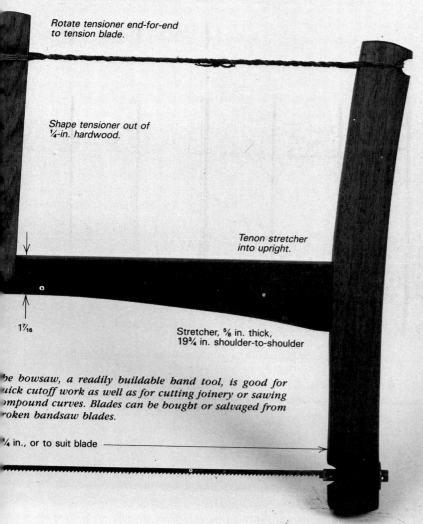

Rotate tensioner end-for-end to tension blade.

Shape tensioner out of ¼-in. hardwood.

Tenon stretcher into upright.

1⁷⁄₁₆

Stretcher, ⅝ in. thick, 19¾ in. shoulder-to-shoulder

The bowsaw, a readily buildable hand tool, is good for quick cutoff work as well as for cutting joinery or sawing compound curves. Blades can be bought or salvaged from broken bandsaw blades.

¼ in., or to suit blade

To bore notches for the blade holders and tensioning cord, clamp the uprights together and center the bit line between the parts.

The Backsaw

How to buy, use and sharpen this basic tool

by Ian J. Kirby

Backsaw is the generic name for any handsaw with a metal stiffening strip along its top edge, opposite the teeth. A backsaw works like any handsaw that cuts on the push stroke, but a finer cut is possible because the saw's reinforcing strip allows a thinner blade. This saw shouldn't be overlooked by the machine woodworker—it's a versatile tool for cutting tenons, dovetails and other joints, and for clean crosscuts.

Of the better-quality saws now manufactured, there are two main types—the tenon saw and the dovetail saw. The tenon saw is the larger of the two, and it is commonly sold in three lengths: 10-in., 12-in. and 14-in. Selecting the length is really a matter of personal preference. The 12-in. length is probably the most useful; the 14-in. is heavier and therefore more difficult to use. Tenon-saw blades are about 4 in. wide and usually have 13 or 15 points per inch. The dovetail saw looks like a miniature version of the tenon saw. It is commonly 8 in. long and about 3½ in. wide, with 20 points to the inch. Dovetail saws with blades 2 in. wide are sold. These usually have a turned rather than a pistol-grip handle.

The dovetail saw's finer teeth leave a smoother surface than does a tenon saw, inviting its use for cutting tenons. Don't yield to the temptation, because dovetail saws are quite delicate and should be reserved for sawing thin wood. A good rule of thumb is that the dovetail saw will keep an accurate cut 1 in. deep in 1-in. thick maple, maximum.

The best-quality backsaws available in North America are brass-backed and English-made, though steel-backed saws of good quality are sold. If you order a saw through the mail, inspect it carefully before you accept it. First, hold the saw end-on at arm's length with the handle away from you and sight down the blade. The sides of the brass back should be parallel to the sides of the blade. Misalignment doesn't affect the way the saw cuts, but sighting along the back is the easiest way to keep the saw upright, and learning to compensate for one that is askew is a skill you can do without.

Next, turn the saw teeth up and sight along them for straightness. A slight curve at one end or the other can be gently bent out of the blade, but an S-curve should be rejected. Rotate the saw 90° and view it again to check the blade for wind or twist. A slight twist can be corrected by bending it the other way. An inaccurately mounted handle may make the blade appear twisted, a difficult condition to adjust.

Finally, sight the back for straightness. This isn't easy, because the metal is folded and distorted during manufacture, but you can at least gain an impression.

Using the backsaw—The backsaw can cut along the grain, as when sawing tenon cheeks or dovetails, or across the grain,

Ian J. Kirby, an educator, designer and cabinetmaker, directs Kirby Studios, a school of woodworking and furniture design, in Cumming, Ga.

Skill with the backsaw comes easily if you learn how to hold the tool and how to stand comfortably. Sawing is primarily an arm movement and it's encouraged by the stance illustrated above. Kirby saws right-handed, so he places his right foot farther back and bends slightly at the knees. You should modify this stance to your own comfort. He grips the saw much like a pistol; the pointed index finger is important, as it spreads and strengthens the grip, and helps you keep the saw vertical.

as in cutting boards to finished length or sawing tenon shoulders. For each type of cutting, there are refinements of technique, but the basic operation of the saw is the same.

Grip the saw with three fingers wrapped around its handle, the index finger pointed alongside the handle toward the saw tip. Extending your index finger is important: it spreads and strengthens your grip, and it helps you keep the saw vertical. Wrap your thumb around the back of the handle so that it just touches your middle or ring finger.

From your grip to your shoulder, the saw, wrist, forearm and upper arm should be in a straight line when viewed from above. From a side view, the forearm should be in a line that, if extended would intersect the saw at about the center of its length. Work to be sawn should be positioned on the bench at a comfortable height (which obviously varies with the individual) that gets you closest to this alignment. The rest of the body doesn't do anything when you're sawing—the action is entirely an arm movement—but you must position yourself so that you can easily move your arm like a piston. If you are off to the left or right of the line of sawing, your wrist will turn and the saw will jam.

Stand comfortably away from the workpiece and lower your body to a crouch by placing your right foot (if you are sawing right-handed) farther back and bending your knees

From *Fine Woodworking* magazine (March 1983) 39:96-98

lightly. Standing with your feet too close together bunches up the whole flow of movement and is an almost universal fault among beginners. You'll never get your foot back far enough by inching it back, so put your rear foot ridiculously far back, then inch it forward.

Before you actually begin to saw, you will have to learn to position the saw correctly on the work. This is best done by sighting down the saw back and developing a feel for where the saw is, relative to the work. You want to hold the blade vertical, at right angles to the surface you are cutting, and at the same time learn to sense the angle at which the line of teeth strike the wood. To sense verticality, you could have a friend stand in front of you and simply tell you when you are tilting the saw—a warm gesture but pretty much a waste of time for your friend. A better method is to prop a mirror in front of you on the bench and make the observation solo. You could also set a small square next to the saw for reference, but I think that this method is less accurate than the mirror.

Learning to control the angle at which the teeth strike the board is just as important, otherwise you may pitch the front of the saw—which is at the opposite side of the workpiece and difficult to see—so it cuts deeper than you intend, past your marks when making tenons or dovetails. The sense of angle comes with practice. Start by holding the saw with all the teeth flat on the bench. Memorize this feel and you'll be able to tell precisely where the saw's cutting edge is, and you won't be surprised by an overcut.

Before you begin, boards to be crosscut, tenons, and dovetail pins and tails should be marked out with a knife, gauge or pencil. You must, of course, decide whether you will split the line or cut to one side of it. In most instances, it doesn't really matter which you choose as long as you are consistent. When crosscutting a board or sawing a tenon shoulder, however, it is advisable to cut to the waste side of the line and then trim to it with a chisel or a plane.

Boards must be held firmly and at a height that will encourage a comfortable stance. For crosscutting, a bench hook or sawing board (for a bench hook, see photo, center right) is helpful; it gives you a way to grip the board, while protecting the bench from a wayward blade. For tenons or dovetails, mount the work in the vise.

Whether you are sawing along the grain or crosscutting, the cut is started in the same manner. Place the saw's forward-most teeth on your mark at the far edge of the board, with the saw pitched up 10° or so at the handle end. Using your thumb and/or index finger to position and guide the blade, make your initial cut about ⅛ in. deep, then gradually pivot the saw down and carry the kerf over to the near side of the board. If you are crosscutting a board to length, complete the cut with the saw held flat in the kerf. Don't force the saw by bearing down on it. A steady hand and a light touch will give the best results.

To saw tenon cheeks, start the cut as before, but once you've carried the kerf over, pivot the saw down farther at the handle end and saw down the tenon cheek line facing you to the shoulder line. Don't lift the saw out of the kerf when you pivot it. Reverse the workpiece and saw down the other cheek line. Then hold the saw flat in the kerf and saw almost to the shoulder line. Complete a tenon by crosscutting the shoulders.

For dovetails, after starting the cut, keep the saw flat in the kerf, and saw to the knife line at the base of the pins or tails. Finish the joint by sawing the waste with a coping saw and

The fine teeth and thin blade stiffened by a brass or steel back make the backsaw an ideal joint-cutting tool. Backsaws are of two types: the larger are called tenon saws, the smaller are dovetail saws. Shown above are a 12-in. English-made brass-backed tenon saw, an 8-in. dovetail saw, and a 7-in. dovetail saw with the straight turned handle preferred by some craftsmen.

Kirby grips a board in a bench hook to demonstrate a crosscut. Start the cut by placing the saw's forward-most teeth on the mark at the board's far edge. Then tilt the saw up about 10° from the handle end and begin the cut with a slow, firm thrust. Use your index finger (not the bench hook's block) to guide the blade. Make the initial cut about ⅛ in. deep, then carry the kerf across the board to guide the saw and complete the cut.

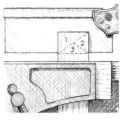

To saw tenon cheeks, mount the workpiece in the vise at about a 60° angle as shown above and start the cut at the edge of the piece opposite you. Carry the kerf over, and without lifting the saw out of the cut, pivot it toward you and saw down the cheek line until you reach the shoulder. Reverse the workpiece in the vise and saw down to the other shoulder line.

paring to the line with a chisel. Some woodworkers clamp the work in the vise at an angle so they can hold the saw vertical, but I think it's better to clamp the work upright and learn to control the angle of the saw.

A couple of recurring problems plague novices learning backsaw use. One is holding the saw at too great an angle to the wood when starting the cut and forcing it on the first stroke or two. Keep the angle about 10° and hold the saw with no more than its own weight on the wood, less than its own weight if starting problems persist. Another problem is learning just the right arm movement so that all but the three or four teeth at each end of the blade are used. Using only the middle four inches of the saw is inefficient, but burying the ends of the saw in the cut frequently jams the blade. Try sawing in slow motion to get a sense of where you should be taking the saw for optimum results.

As with any tool, practice is essential. A common fallacy is that you should make finished joints to practice with tools. The end results, of course, bear all the scars of bad workmanship. So practice first, and soon enough you will have the skills to use the backsaw to its fullest advantage. □

To saw dovetails, clamp the workpiece upright in the vise, and hold the saw to match the tail and pin angle. Guide the cut with your thumb and, keeping the saw flat in the kerf, saw down to the line marking the base of pins and tails.

Sharpening the backsaw

Many woodworkers send their saws out to be sharpened. Yet sharpening a saw is as easy as grinding and sharpening a plane iron or a chisel, and we don't send either of them out.

Half the battle is won by having the correct tools: a saw vise, a setting tool and the right files. Vises are available from several mail-order tool outlets, or you can make your own out of wood (see pp. 71 and 85 for two simple versions). You can buy a saw set or make the simple anvil described in figure 2, a particularly good one for setting dovetail saws, whose teeth are usually too fine for commercially made sets. (For more on files, see pp. 52-55; for more on using files for sharpening saws, see pp. 71-72 and 85-86.)

Tenon saws and dovetail saws have more teeth than regular handsaws, but they are sharpened in much the same way. Sharpening itself consists of four separate steps: topping, shaping, setting and sharpening.

Topping is essentially getting the teeth in a straight line so that none projects above its mates and all cut evenly. Use a straightedge to see if the teeth are of uneven height. If so, clamp the saw in the vise and file the teeth into line with an 8-in. or a 10-in. mill file held flat.

Shaping will restore the proper profile to any teeth flattened by topping. You are aiming both for uniform gullet depth and for the approximate profile of the other teeth on the saw or for the

profile shown in figure 1. To shape the teeth, use a slim or extra-slim, 4-in.-taper triangular file held horizontally and at right angles to the blade's length. Remove metal from both the front and back of the teeth.

To keep the saw from binding, the kerf must be about 1½ times as wide as the blade itself. This is done by setting the saw—bending the outer half of each alternate tooth outward. Using the setting anvil shown in figure 2, place the

Fig. 1: Tooth profile and sharpness angles

60°

15°
rake angle

Mount saw with gullets just beyond vise jaws.

Fig. 2: Saw setting

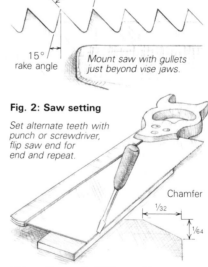

Set alternate teeth with punch or screwdriver, flip saw end for end and repeat.

Chamfer

1/32

1/64

Make setting anvil of ¼-in. steel bar stock. 2x10. Grind or file 1/64-in. chamfer.

saw teeth on it so that their upper halves project just beyond the edge of the chamfer. Then, with a screwdriver (grind the blade down if necessary), set every other tooth, flip the saw end for end and set the rest of the teeth.

Sharpening is the final step. Before you begin, rub a piece of chalk over the teeth so you can keep track of which ones have been filed. Put the saw in the vise and, starting at the saw tip, work toward the handle. You can sharpen your backsaw as a ripsaw, with the front and back of each tooth filed at 90° to the saw's length, or as a crosscut saw, with the fronts and backs alternately beveled. If you bevel the teeth, make the angle slight—less than 15°—or you'll remove too much metal and weaken the tooth. Whether you bevel or not, position the file in the gullets so you are filing the front of one tooth and the back of the adjacent tooth at the same time. Four to six light file strokes per tooth should do it.

Test your sharpening job on a scrap of wood. The saw should start easily and cut quickly and smoothly. If it grabs or catches, one or more teeth may be overset and should be dressed into line with a benchstone rubbed lightly along the side of the blade. If you get in the habit of sharpening your saws before they become too blunt, you shouldn't have to do anything but set and file the teeth. Topping and shaping won't be necessary. —*I.J.K.*

Top to bottom: a kataba, ryoba *and* dozuki, *each approximately 22 in. long.*

Japanese Saws
Thin, flexible blades cut on the pull stroke

by Robert Ghelerter

The *kataba, ryoba* and *dozuki* are the three primary hand-saws for the Japanese woodworker. The *kataba* and *ryoba* roughly correspond to the cabinet saw or carpenter's saw, and the *dozuki* is equivalent to the backsaw or dovetail saw. They differ from their Western counterparts in that all the teeth face back toward the user—they cut on the pull stroke rather than on the push. This allows the blades to be very thin and light. My *ryoba* weighs less than 6 oz. All in all, I find them less tiring to use and more accurate than Western saws.

In Japanese the words *"kataba," "ryoba"* and *"dozuki"* are often followed by the word *"nokogiri,"* which means "saw." *Kataba-nokogiri* is a saw with teeth on one side; *ryoba-nokogiri*, a saw with teeth on both sides (one edge for ripping and the other for crosscutting); and *dozuki-nokogiri*, a saw with guard adjoined.

The first saws came to Japan from China via Korea between the 14th and 15th centuries. The Japanese were never on friendly terms with the Chinese, and everything from China came via Korea. There is some evidence of saws before this time, but they weren't widely used. The first saws introduced were large, for felling and resawing trees. The other saws evolved from them.

The *ryoba* is relatively new, created about 100 years ago. Before this combination saw, woodworkers needed two *kataba*, a rip and a crosscut. Both *ryoba* and *kataba* are for rough cutting and can be used with one or two hands. The saws are versatile and can bend to get into difficult places. When cutting flush to a surface, I prefer the *kataba* because its back can be rested on the wood without scratching the sur-

face. The blades of both *ryoba* and *kataba* are thinner in the center than at the edges to reduce friction in the kerf.

The *dozuki* is used for accurate work, and when cutting angles a guide block can be used. To trim a board to length, draw lines on four sides of the board with a square and a sharp pencil; a thin pencil line will be easier to see, especially on light wood, than a marking-gauge line. Begin the cut at the far corner of one side, gradually leveling the saw until the kerf is about ¼ in. deep. Then turn the board and do the next side. When all four sides have been started, the cut can easily be completed, the kerfs guiding the saw.

The *ryoba* and *kataba* can be used this way too, and the same method cuts shoulders on tenons. For crosscut work I find these saws superior to electric saws in that they leave no tear-out. They are especially handy for cutting 4x8 sheets of ¼-in. paneling. They can be every bit as accurate as a machine and often faster. Although *dozuki* are usually filed for cross-cutting, their teeth can also be shaped for ripping.

There are a few different styles of *kataba, ryoba* and *dozuki* to choose from. The *ryoba* and *kataba* usually come with the teeth in a straight line, but sometimes carpenters prefer a saw with a convex cutting edge (*anabiki*) to begin cuts in the middle of a board or panel. On *dozuki*, the teeth are always in a straight line but the amount of arch in the stiff back varies,

EDITOR'S NOTE: In 1980 a 210-mm *ryoba* saw cost $46.50 at Woodline/The Japan Woodworker, 1004 Central Ave., Alameda, CA 94501; and $11.75 at Tashiro Hardware, 109 Prefontaine Pl., Seattle, WA 98104. Many mail-order catalogs also offer them: Garrett-Wade, $17.50; Woodcraft Supply, $17.40; and Leichtung, $10.95.

Dozuki *with guide block cuts the beveled shoulder for a beveled mortise-and-tenon joint.*

Board is cut to length by sawing in from each of the four sides in turn.

Ryoba *crosscut edge trims tabletop.*

changing the angle of the handle to the saw body. There is also a small version of *ryoba* known as *azibiki*. Its blade is usually no longer than 100mm (4 in.), is thick and will not flex much. The cutting edges are convex. I have seen these saws used only by carvers for roughing out, though I understand they are also used in joinery.

When choosing a saw, first consider usage. Carpentry and cabinetmaking saws differ in size, flexibility, hardness and thickness. Standard blade sizes are as follows:

	Cabinetmaking	Carpentry
Kataba and *ryoba* length	210mm to 240mm (8¼ in. to 9½ in.)	270mm to 420mm (10⅝ in. to 16½ in.)
Dozuki length	210mm to 240mm 8¼ in. to 9½ in.)	240mm to 315mm (9½ in. to 12⅜ in.)
Dozuki depth of cut	40mm to 55mm (1⅝ in. to 2 in.)	60mm to 95mm (2⅜ in. to 3¾ in.)

Carpenter's saws are bigger, thicker, harder and have fewer teeth per inch than cabinetmaker's saws. *Dozuki* usually have from 25 to 30 teeth per inch. *Kataba* and *ryoba* crosscut blades range from 15 to 20 teeth per inch, and ripsaws have from 6 to 8 teeth per inch. *Kataba* and *ryoba* teeth are slightly smaller near the handle, for starting the cut.

There are three grades of Japanese tools based on the quality of the steel: "Yellow" is the lowest, "white" the middle, and "blue" the highest quality. It is difficult in this country to distinguish these grades except by price. Saws of the yellow rank (their blades have a yellowish tinge) are cheap ($2 to $13) and not used by serious craftsmen. Most middle and high-grade tools are made from white steel and can cost from $20 to several hundred dollars. A few extremely expensive tools are made from blue or sword steel. The handmade ones are easily differentiated from machine-made saws; the surface is rough and they can cost several thousand dollars (all 1980 prices).

For general cabinetry, a good saw to start with would be a 220mm *ryoba*. For fine joinery you should also have a *dozuki*—240mm is standard. Beginners should stay away from the thinnest (paper-thin) *dozuki*, which, although more accurate, are harder to control and can easily break. A good saw maximizes hardness and flexibility; it will bend considerably (the *ryoba* and *kataba* into a half circle) and still return to its original shape. Yet because it is thin, it will break before it deforms. Cheap saws are thicker, softer, less flexible, and less likely to break.

Good saws generally come with the handles unattached. The handles are usually wrapped with bamboo cane, for strength. Some are wrapped only at the end where the saw fits in, others the entire length. Handles come with a hole for the tang, but the holes are usually too small and should be enlarged with a keyhole saw. Cut only a little at a time, trying the saw tang for fit. Push the tang into the handle and strike the handle end with a hammer. Never strike the saw itself.

In Japan most woodworkers send their saws to a shop for sharpening by hand. Saws can be sent back to the factory to be sharpened by machine, but hand-sharpening, which leaves the teeth rough from the file, is considered superior. It is not difficult and with a little practice can be done rapidly. If this is your first time sharpening a saw, before beginning, cut a kerf in a piece of wood so that the newly sharpened saw can be compared to how it was before.

If the blade is warped or kinked, sometimes a result of friction-caused heat expanding the metal at the cutting edge, hammer it out with the same hammer that will be used to set the teeth. The saw is placed on a piece of iron, concave side of the warp down, and struck lightly to stretch the metal evenly. Never heat the blade; you can easily ruin its temper.

Sometimes the blade of the *dozuki* slips a little from the backing. It is held only by pressure and is not actually bonded. A loose blade can become badly kinked, but is easily remedied by tapping the saw's back on a piece of wood. After straightening, hold the blade in one hand, resting on a firm surface, and joint the teeth. The Japanese use a special tool, but a flat metal file serves the same purpose. Two or three strokes ensure that all the teeth are the same height. Now the saw is ready to sharpen.

Sharpening must be done with a special feather file (a thin diamond in cross section), which should be available where the saw is purchased. It is best used only once and comes un-handled, so it's a good idea to make a simple, reusable

Photos: Robert Ghelerter

A special tool, left, joints the teeth. The saw vise alongside the sharpener's knee is used with a diamond-profile feather file, as at right, to sharpen the lead side of a rip tooth.

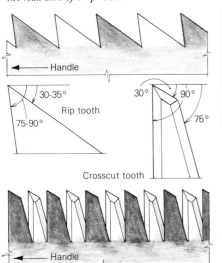

After filing, gentle tapping sets the teeth.

handle. The Japanese prefer a thin branch from a cherry tree, but a piece of dowel stock with a drilled hole to receive the tang will work as well. To hold the saw, the Japanese use a flat, wide vise whose two jaws, hinged in the middle, are driven together with a wedge at the bottom. The jaws are shaped so they grasp the saw only near the teeth. Two shaped boards held together with screws and wing nuts will suffice.

Rip teeth and crosscut teeth have different shapes and are filed differently, except that filing is always done on the push stroke and on teeth that point away from you. For the rip teeth, hold the file 90° to the saw body and file the lead side of every other tooth (the side closest to the handle), then turn the holder around and file the lead side of the remaining teeth. Push simultaneously sideways and down, to cut a little into the body of the blade. One or two strokes are adequate. Next file the trailing side, also 90° to the saw body, once again doing every other tooth, then turn the holder around to file the remaining teeth. File until a new point is formed.

Japanese crosscut teeth are quite unlike any Western saw teeth, in that each is sharpened with a bevel not only on the leading and trailing edges but also at the apex of each tooth. The leading and trailing edges of adjacent teeth are filed on the same stroke, then the top facet is filed. Start with the handle of the saw on the right. Hold the file at a 60° angle to the saw body, pointing toward the handle. One stroke, pushing down and toward the left, should cut the leading

edge of the tooth set away from you, while the other side of the file rubs lightly on the trailing edge of the tooth to the right, set toward you. Next file the top of each tooth set away from you, trying to duplicate the existing angle, which is about 60° to the saw body, but slanted away from the handle. Again, one stroke is adequate. Then turn the holder and with the handle and file pointed to the left, and applying more pressure on the stroke to the right (on the leading edge of a tooth set away from you), file the other teeth.

Because the blade is so thin and sharpening can bend the teeth, they are set after filing. A hammer with a face no wider than a single tooth is used. Hold the edge of the saw on the rounded edge of a piece of flat iron so the tooth to be struck almost touches the iron. Bring the hammer down lightly, or allow it to fall of its own weight. The small crosscut teeth require considerable skill. Look down both sides of the saw to make sure the teeth are in line. *Dozuki* teeth need little set, although the amount can vary with personal preference. If in use the saw is difficult to guide, the teeth may need a little more set. After setting, deburr the saw by running a piece of metal along both sides of the teeth. Occasionally, rub a little oil into the blade to keep it from rusting. □

Robert Ghelerter spent a year and a half studying wood-working in Japan, then returned to the United States. He now builds furniture in Berkeley, Calif.

Scroll Sawing
Filigree revitalized with a saber saw

by Ron Pessolano

About six years ago, I was involved in a form of aesthetic expression called string art, or in my case wire art. One day, when I realized that wire was not giving me the spiritual, emotional or financial rewards I'd hoped for, I trudged down to the lumberyard and invested in a couple of square feet of plywood, to see what I could tease from it with my saber saw.

I cut the 24-in. square into an abstract, amoeba-like shape, then made a similar inside cut to leave an unusual (strange, some called it) picture frame. Then I beveled and sanded all the edges, so that the laminations would show up well and add to the design.

I had made something, without a doubt. But I couldn't come up with a single painting, print or "thing" that looked good framed by it.

The next day a friend suggested I in-

Solid-core birch plywood can be saber-sawn into delicate filigree.

stall a mirror instead of a picture. So I bought a mirror, attached it to the frame, and suddenly got the feeling that my life would be taking a turn for the better. I spent the next few weeks drawing and sawing every amoeba-like design I could think of.

Later that year, 1976, while I was exhibiting some of my work in a shopping mall, someone asked if I could make a small square frame with the outline of the Liberty Bell inside. Sure. Why not?

I was soon designing *within* the frame, instead of making the frame itself the design. As I became more skilled with the saber saw, I began to devise patterns based on stained glass designs. For a while I fitted them with fabric or grasscloth backings instead of mirrors, mainly because the reflections in a mirror tend to overpower the delicate filigree. But lately I've gone back to mirrors because they sell better. Most of the fabric-backed panels were meant to be wall hangings, but many became glass-covered tabletops, door or window inserts, room dividers and free-standing screens.

Each piece begins as a single panel of plywood: ½-in. for larger or less stable pieces, ⅜-in. for smaller ones; ¾-in. plywood is thicker than necessary and slow to work. Baltic birch, Finnish birch and alder plywoods are the only ones I've found that will hold together.

After drawing or tracing the design, I drill a hole in each area to be cut out, insert the blade, and cut along using a hand-held saber saw.

The saw—When I began this work six years ago, I already had a Sears autoscroller saber saw, model #17280. Sears was the only tool store I knew of at the time, and I bought the saw because it was on sale. I've scoured the market since, looking for a better design, but for my money that old saw has them all beat. Its wide, stable base is even better than the new Sears model.

I'd bought the saw for straight-cutting the backboards for my wire art, but when I took my first crack at the Liberty Bell design, I began to realize just what that knob above the blade is for. It rotates the blade—in a complete circle if necessary. You can push the saw with one hand while steering the blade with your other hand. Thus, the body of the saw doesn't have to point in the direction of the cut. Without this feature I'd have to either work on a round bench (to walk around the piece) or be a contortionist. You could attempt this work with a jigsaw, but you'd have to swivel the entire piece around the blade, and detach and reattach the blade to move from cut to cut.

One problem I encountered with this saw is that the screw that's supposed to

Frame, 4 ft. high, awaits mirror.

From *Fine Woodworking* magazine (May 1983) 40:86-87

For the tight curves pictured above, Pessolano makes narrow, set-tooth blades by grinding standard blades (right) and mounting them upside down in a blade holder modified to take a larger setscrew. The blades cut on the downstroke, limiting tearout to the back of the plywood. A shim made from a broken blade spreads the blade holder's clamping pressure.

hold the blade securely in the blade clamp doesn't—it's too small. The blade tilts backward under pressure. The best solution I could come up with was to drill and tap the clamp to accommodate a ¼-in. Allen screw. This holds if I insert a small flat piece of metal (the top part of an old blade) between the screw and the blade to spread the pressure.

Two months after solving the first problem, I realized I'd created another. As a result of my enlarging the hole, the blade clamp split. I noticed it was made of sintered metal (powdered and molded into shape) rather than of a stronger, solid piece. So I went to a local metal shop and asked what it would cost to have one made from solid metal. At least $200, they told me. Ouch. Instead, I ordered two dozen blade clamps from Sears, and I just change them when they crack.

Blade modifications—I've tried out just about every blade you might find in a random search of hardware stores and lumberyards. I was lucky to come across some 18-tooth and 24-tooth set-tooth blades made by the Vermont American Co., of North Carolina. These blades outlast all others I've used by at least five to one, and they're also less expensive than most. Their set teeth make a wide kerf that allows tight turns.

You can get a smoother cut from straight-tooth scrolling blades, but they are not stiff enough for my work, and they burn the wood around tight curves. They're best for straight cuts, and for wide turns in stock ½ in. and thinner.

Before I use a blade, which is about ⁵⁄₁₆ in. wide, I make some modifications, as shown in the photo, above right. First, I grind the width down to ⅛ in. to ³⁄₁₆ in. (sometimes less for really tight work) so that it doesn't bind in tight turns. Such a thin blade tends to weave and tilt, and despite six years of practice I still run into trouble once in a while. It's necessary to keep the saw directly over the blade as you turn the curves.

Second, because the blade cuts on the upstroke, sometimes the plywood splinters and obscures the line I'm trying to follow. To prevent this, I reverse the blade so that it cuts on the downstroke and leaves the burr on the underside. I use a 5-in. disc sander (a grinding wheel would work as well) to remove the set from the bottom teeth so that the blade can sit flat in the clamp. Otherwise the pressure of the clamp screw will crack the blade. There are commercially made, reverse-tooth blades, but those I've seen have straight teeth, so I recommend that you adapt your own.

Supporting the work—I used to work standing and leaning over a workbench, with the piece clamped and extended

over the edge, which I don't recommend unless you can tolerate back pain. I finally made an open-framed draftsmen's-type table that clamps to the bench and enables me to work while seated. I clamp the stock with only a slight overhang so that my work area is solidly supported.

On most pieces, I start cutting in the center, reclamping and radiating outward. This maintains maximum strength in the board and leaves enough wood at the overhanging edge to support the weight of the saw.

Sanding and finishing—I round off the edges of the cuts with a shopmade drum sander in a high-speed electric drill. This is tricky work, particularly on springy parts, and more than once the drill and the work have ended up going in opposite directions. If the surface needs any smoothing, I use a belt sander. It shouldn't be necessary to sand the blade marks in a design with a lot of tight curves and small openings. Visually, the marks are regular enough to become part of the design.

After sanding, I stain the piece, then finish with Watco Danish oil. A few days later, I attach the mirror with screw clips, fit the frame with a hanging wire, and make drawings for the next one. □

Ron Pessolano lives in Dedham, Mass.

Sharpening Saws
Principles, procedures and gadgets

by Jules A. Paquin

Crosscut saw with reconditioning apparatus.

A handsaw is a tool with a blade of tempered steel in which teeth have been cut. Different kinds of saws are made to perform different functions. The number of teeth to the inch and their shape vary according to the work the saw has to accomplish. The two basic woodworking saws are the crosscut saw, designed to cut across the grain of the wood, and the ripsaw, designed to cut with the grain. The crosscut-saw tooth cuts like a knife. The ripsaw tooth cuts like a chisel.

The teeth of a saw become blunt from regular use, particularly from sawing hardwood. New saws have been shaped, set and sharpened by precision machines at the factory, but many saws can be improved, and old saws reconditioned, by following the step-by-step instruction offered in this article. It is not always necessary to go through the complete sequence, but wherever you start, you should follow through the rest of the order.

For regular maintenance it is a good idea to file the teeth lightly as soon as they have lost their sharpness. One or two filings of this kind will not affect the set of the teeth. Generally it will take three or four filings before resetting is needed. At this stage you can check the shape of the teeth. If the previous filings were done with care and attention, and the saw has not been misused, only setting and filing will be needed. If the teeth have been damaged or made uneven by excessive filing, it will be necessary to go through the five restoring

operations: jointing, shaping, setting, filing and honing.

The only equipment you need is a saw set, an 8-in. smooth mill file and a fine-cut triangular file, slightly tapered and with 60° angles to match the angles between the teeth of most handsaws. The saw sharpening vise and various filing guides shown here you can easily make yourself.

Jointing — This operation consists of filing the points of the teeth with the mill file to make them even or in line along the saw. The jointing guide (figure 1) will keep the file flat on the tips of the teeth and square with the blade. Run the file gently along the top of the teeth, holding the guide flat on the side of the blade. This cuts a flat on the tip of the teeth, which varies in width according to how far out of line each tooth was. Jointing must touch all the teeth but cut none down more than is necessary to bring them in line. If the teeth are very uneven and a considerable amount of jointing is necessary, you should alternate jointing with the next operation, shaping, otherwise the shape of the teeth may be lost.

Shaping — This operation restores the teeth to their regular form. Place the saw in the sharpening vise (figure 2), the teeth close to the top so the thin metal will not vibrate when filed, and clamp the saw vise in the bench vise. Inserting the tip of a triangular file firmly on a tilting guide (figure 3), file straight across the saw, at right angles to the blade. Note that there are two tilting guides, one for ripsaws and one for crosscuts. Shape first the teeth that have been leveled most. The jointed flats or brights on the tips of the teeth will be taken off in two stages: The triangular file will wear half the flat on one tooth and half the flat on the next tooth. Take care that the top of the tilting guide remain horizontal while filing and that the stroke of the file be perpendicular to the blade. Don't file the gullet too deeply. To make the teeth equal and regular, often you will need to press more against the front of one tooth than against the back of the next tooth, or vice-versa. After shaping, all the gullets should be of equal depth, the front and back of the teeth at the proper angle and all the teeth the same size. Check by looking at the saw from the side. All the teeth will have been shaped from the same side of the saw and there will be no bevel toward the front or back of the teeth. Before setting, rub both sides of the saw with an oilstone to remove the burr left by the file, and brush away any oilstone residue left in the gullets.

Setting — The goal of setting is to make the kerf that the saw will cut wide enough so the blade will not bind. This is accomplished by bending outward the upper part of each tooth. To work properly, a saw should have no more set than is necessary. Only one-third of the height of the tooth should be bent, producing a saw kerf that is a little less than one and a half times the thickness of the blade, thus the set on each

Fig. 1: Jointing guide

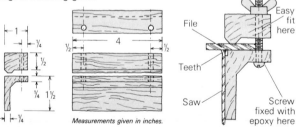

Measurements given in inches.

File
Teeth
Saw
Easy fit here
Screw fixed with epoxy here

To joint the teeth, place the saw in the bench vise and a smooth mill file in the jointing guide. Hold the guide flat against the side of the blade and run the file gently over the top of the teeth. The saw vise pictured on the bench is used in subsequent steps.

From *Fine Woodworking* magazine (May 1980) 22:62-64

Fig. 2: Sharpening vise

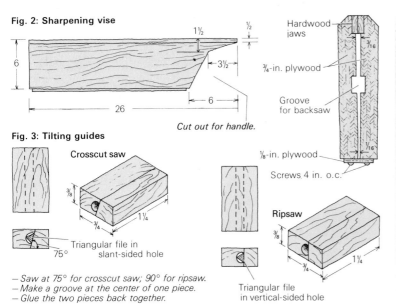

6

1½ ½

26

3½

6

Cut out for handle.

Hardwood jaws
¾-in. plywood
Groove for backsaw
3/16
1/16
⅛-in. plywood
Screws 4 in. o.c.

Fig. 3: Tilting guides

Crosscut saw

⅜
¾
1¼

Triangular file in slant-sided hole
75°

Ripsaw

⅜
¾
1¼

Triangular file in vertical-sided hole

— Saw at 75° for crosscut saw; 90° for ripsaw.
— Make a groove at the center of one piece.
— Glue the two pieces back together.

Shaping is done with the saw in the saw vise and a tilting guide on the tip of a smooth-cut triangular file. The stroke should be level and at 90° to the sawblade.

Fig. 4: Saw set

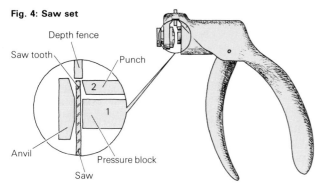

Depth fence
Saw tooth
Punch
2
1
Anvil
Pressure block
Saw

side should be one-quarter the thickness of the blade. Trying to bend the teeth too much may break them off or cause a crack at the bottom of the gullets. Work in hardwood requires less set than work in softwood.

Setting is done with a special tool called a saw set, which operates with handles like those of a pliers. The principle is to press the tooth with a beveled punch against a little anvil. There are several styles of saw sets on the market. The most practical one (figure 4) does two operations simultaneously: A block presses and holds the sawblade on the anvil, and a beveled punch pushes the tooth onto the inclined part of the anvil. The saw-set anvil is usually an adjustable wheel with numbers around it. These numbers correspond approximately to the number of teeth to an inch of the saw. Bring the number to the appropriate index mark, and the anvil is in po-

sition to set all teeth to the same proper inclination. Set first the teeth that point away from you on one side, then turn the saw around and set the other teeth. Never reverse the set of a tooth. When you are finished check to see that you have not missed a tooth. The set must be the same from end to end of the blade, otherwise the saw will not cut straight, but snakey.

Filing — Filing sharpens the saw and is the most important operation in reconditioning. Depending on the point size of your saw, select a slim triangular file: for 11 to 18 points per inch, a 5-in. file; for 7 to 10 points, a 6-in. file, and for 4 to 6 points, a 7-in. file.

Except for differences in tilting and bearing angles, filing crosscut saws is the same as filing ripsaws. Mount the saw in the saw vise, the bottom of the tooth gullets ⅛ in. above the vise jaws and the handle of the saw to your right.

For a crosscut saw, place the bearing guide (figure 5, next page) on the top of the teeth, and the crosscut tilting guide (figure 3) on the tip of the file. The bearing guide may be placed to the right or to the left of the tooth being filed, but as close as possible to it without getting in the way. It is a device with which to line up the file by eye and is moved along the saw as needed. Start at the toe of the saw and place the file in the gullet to the left of the first tooth set toward you. The file should be parallel to the bearing guide, and the tilting guide should be horizontal. Push the file straight forward, holding it firmly at both ends. Exert slight pressure on the forward movement, but lift the file on the backward movement. The

Reconditioning a saw			
Process	Aim	Necessary	Recommended
1. Jointing	To make the teeth the same height.	If the teeth have been seriously damaged by careless handling of the saw.	After several filings to make the teeth the same height.
2. Shaping	To restore the shape of the teeth.	If the jointing has left a large flat top at the tip of some teeth.	If the flat on the teeth is not nearly the same.
3. Setting	To widen the kerf by bending alternate teeth in opposite direction.	If you have done processes 1 and 2.	After four or five filings not preceded by processes 1 or 2.
4. Filing	To sharpen the teeth.	Processes 1, 2 and 3 are always followed by filing.	When teeth become dull.
5. Honing	To remove the burr that appears on the sides of the teeth.		Highly recommended for delicate saw work.

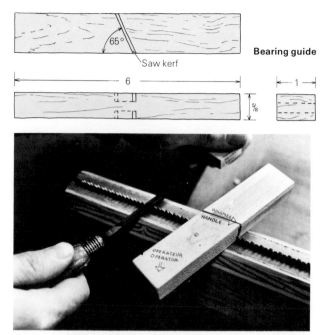

Bearing guide

Crosscut-saw filing is aided by a bearing guide on the saw and a tilting guide on the file. Maintain consistent pressure for an equal number of strokes in each gullet, with a tooth set toward you always closest to the saw handle.

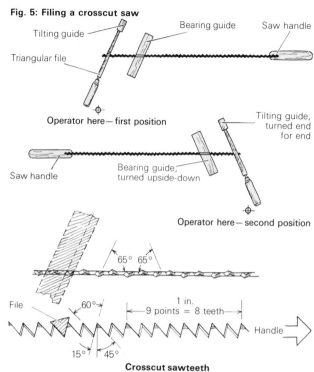

Fig. 5: Filing a crosscut saw

Tilting guide / Bearing guide / Saw handle

Triangular file

Operator here—first position

Saw handle / Bearing guide, turned upside-down / Tilting guide, turned end for end

Operator here—second position

File / 65° 65° / 1 in. 9 points = 8 teeth / Handle

60° / 15° 45°

Crosscut sawteeth

stroke should be always horizontal. This operation will wear both the front of the tooth set toward you and the back of the preceding tooth set away from you. Count the file strokes and note the pressure you exert because you will have to repeat the same number of strokes and the same pressure all the way along. After the first gullet go to the third gullet, skipping the second; then go to the fifth, skipping the fourth; and so on every second gullet up to the handle.

Turn the saw around so the handle is at your left. Turn the bearing guide upside-down and the tilting guide around, end for end. Work the other side of the saw in the same manner, starting at the toe and in the gullet to the right of the first tooth set toward you. After filing a few teeth on this side, check them. The filing should have brought the teeth to a fine point with a bevel to the front and to the back of each tooth. Do not remove any more metal than is necessary to make the bevels meet at the top of the tooth. Continue filing along the length of the saw.

A crosscut saw is filed well if you can slide a needle between the tips of the teeth without it falling.

For a ripsaw (figure 6), place the ripsaw tilting guide (figure 3) on your triangular file and file perpendicular to the face of the saw; rip teeth have no bevel. A well-trained eye and hand can easily keep the stroke perpendicular without the aid of a bearing guide. File the first gullet, the third, the

fifth, etc. Turn the saw and file the other gullets so the filing will be uniform on each side; otherwise the saw will cut on a slant. For ripsaw teeth, the alternation of the direction of the stroke and its evenness are the only differences between filing and the earlier operation of shaping.

Honing — Filing leaves a burr or wire edge at the sides of the teeth. A burr won't make any difference in rough work, but for fine work it is best to get rid of it. To do this, put your saw flat on your bench and run a fine oilstone gently against the teeth on both sides. Honing will also correct small irregularities in setting.

The angles I use are good. I have adopted them with satisfaction. But there are other workable angles and they should not be ignored. For a crosscut saw some prefer a bearing angle of 55°, and others 60°. Some prefer the handle end of the file about 10° below the horizon. For a ripsaw some prefer a tilting angle of 8° instead of 0°. You can adopt the standards that best fit your needs, but when you have made your choice, be consistent. Remember, though, you will have to alter the guides shown in the figures accordingly.

Those who haven't tried it think that maintaining a handsaw requires a lot of time, but this is not the case. Here is the time it took me to recondition completely a 24-in. crosscut saw, with 12 teeth per inch. The work, which was performed without haste, took only 47 minutes. Jointing and shaping required 17 minutes; setting, 8 minutes; and filing and honing, 22 minutes. If the same saw were to require only filing to renew the cutting edge, it would take no more than 12 to 15 minutes.

Take good care of your handsaws. When not in use, keep them in a tool rack that will protect them from damage. Wipe the blade frequently with a lightly oiled cloth. □

Jules Paquin, of Laval, Quebec, is a wood patternmaker and an amateur woodworker.

Fig. 6: Ripsaw teeth

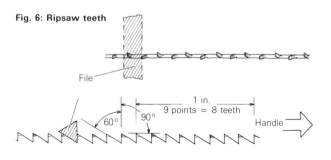

File

60° / 90° / 1 in. 9 points = 8 teeth / Handle

Tiny Tools

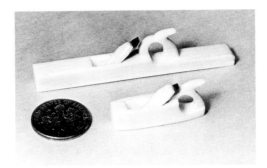

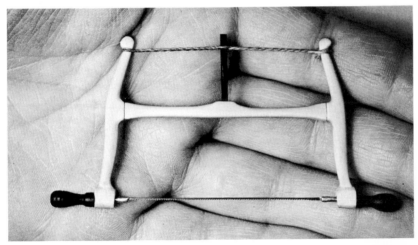

Paul B. Kebabian is an active member of the Early American Industries Association and owns a major collection of 18th, 19th and early 20th-century woodworking tools. His book, *American Woodworking Tools,* was published by the New York Graphic Society. Professionally, he is director of libraries at the University of Vermont. Obviously, Kebabian has little time to spare, but when he has some time he makes little tools.

He got started several years ago after a visit to Vermont's Shelburne Museum, where he noticed a tiny plane that was missing its cutter. Kebabian set out to make only replacement parts for the museum's tool, but he soon found himself reproducing the whole plane. He has been making lilliputian tools ever since.

Kebabian is deeply interested in the history of tools and in the men who made them, and he uses the design skills and techniques of two centuries ago to make his miniatures. None are slavish copies of existing tools—they are redesigned to suit the needs and tastes of the maker. And all of them actually work.

Kebabian finds it difficult to explain his fascination for making these gemlike objects. "It's a challenge, a little like climbing mountains," he says.

—*Richard Starr*

From the top: Shipbuilder's jointer with razee stock and smooth plane with closed tote, both made of ivory at 1/10 scale and reproduced actual size.

Plough plane with sliding arms, made of ebony with ivory wedge, depth stop and keys, about 1/4 scale.

Turning bowsaw made from boxwood and ebony, about 1/7 scale.

Coachmaker's rabbet planes of ebony, boxwood and ivory, about 1/6 scale.

Hewing
Axwork shapes log directly

by Drew Langsner

There are three basic types of axwork: chopping, where the axman works diagonally to the grain, as in felling trees and bucking logs; splitting, where the wood is cut with the grain, as for firewood; and hewing, the most sophisticated of the three, in which the woodworker combines techniques of chopping and splitting. Hewing used to be common practice, and still has a place in the modern woodworker's repertoire. Craftsmen who traditionally hewed wood include post-and-beam carpenters, turners, furniture makers, coopers, boatbuilders, carvers of woodenware, wheelwrights and makers of tool handles and agricultural implements. Wood sculptors have also used hewing techniques to advantage. Hewing is perhaps the fastest and certainly the most direct way of bringing a log to approximate size, shape and flatness.

Axes — There are two basic types of hewing axes. Symmetrically beveled axes are shaped and sharpened on both sides of the blade. These may be similar to woodpile axes, except that the blade is usually slimmer and more perfectly maintained. Many have specially shaped handles, and there is a wide variety of ax-head patterns—the result of local traditions, different needs, and available materials. Symmetrically beveled axes permit a scooping action, good for concave cuts. They are also excellent for convex cuts, rough and complex shaping, and fine carpentry.

Broad axes (named after the massive axes used to hew timbers for buildings, railroad ties and bridges) have a bevel on only one side of the head. The other side is flat from the eye straight down to the cutting edge. These axes work like super-broad chisels, and generally are used to create smooth or moderately convex planes. The flat side allows the ax to work at a close angle, skimming the surface in a straight line.

Symmetrically beveled axes and broad axes are also available as hand hatchets—handle length, not head weight, is the determining factor here. Hatchets have shorter handles, and while they are generally lighter (1½ lb. to 2 lb.), some hewing hatchets weigh upward of 5 lb. Axes weigh from 2 lb. to 12 lb.

The evolution of axes probably reached a peak in the Middle Ages, when a wide variety of special types were made for various trades. Though industrialization resulted in the large production of a limited variety, it is still possible to find some special styles of axes in junk and antique shops.

Almost any hatchet or ax can be reshaped or sharpened for use in woodworking, but common hardware-store hatchets tend to be too thick in cross section. The short bevel necessitates chopping at a wide, unwieldy angle, and the thick head has more of a wedging effect, which means the wood is more likely to slip out of control. You can more easily slice into

---

Drew Langsner is director/instructor at Country Workshop, a school for traditional woodworking in Marshall, N.C.

wood at a close angle with greater precision using a hatchet of thin cross section.

Woodworkers' hatchets and axes also tend to have a longer cutting length than common camp axes. Many craftsmen prefer a shape that flares back from the eye to allow gripping close to the cutting edge, which makes the cut easier to control. An ax or hatchet with a straight cutting edge can be used on thin stock like a chair post. However, a curved edge facilitates severing the grain and is therefore easier to use for hewing wider pieces, shaping the exterior of a large bowl, for instance, or hewing a beam.

The handle of a woodsman's chopping or splitting ax is generally made as thin as possible for a slight whiplike effect and to help absorb shock. Woodlot ax handles require a smooth finish so that the user's forehand can slide freely with each swing. In hewing, the craftsman generally uses a much shorter stroke, keeping both hands in one position—a comfortable grip therefore results from a thicker handle and a rippled or whittled surface.

Handle length and shape are matters of taste. The handle on a heavy broad hatchet may be shorter than a foot, while the handle on a Japanese broad ax may exceed 4 ft. I prefer a handle that gives good leverage, but which is not awkward—about 28 in. long. The axis from eye to handle foot should be straight except in broad axes, where a single or double bend ensures the knuckles will clear the work during each swing.

Ax handles should be split from clear, straight-grained hickory, ash, birch, maple or oak. Green handles are shaped about 10% oversize, then seasoned for at least one month before fitting. Handles made from preseasoned rough blanks can be fitted to the ax eye early on, which allows testing for feel and alignment as shaping progresses.

Broad-ax handles can be bent green immediately after fashioning or after fitting to an ax head. I boil the fitted handle for a half hour, then bend it in a jig (photo facing page, bottom right) and let it set for two to four weeks. After it has cured, I touch up the handle with a knife or rasp, sand it a little, and finish with linseed oil.

Hatchet hewing — Hatchets can be used on stable massive timbers, such as in post-and-beam construction and boatbuilding, but they are generally used for much finer work that must be held in place by hand. For this kind of work, you'll need a support to prop the stock against. A waist-high hardwood stump set in the ground or on the shop floor is ideal. You can also make a small chopping block from a slice of a log and place it directly over a leg on top of your workbench, handy in shops with limited space or where hewing is only an occasional undertaking. A shallow depression on one side of the chopping surface, made with a hatchet or chain saw, keeps the wood from slipping, especially when you're hewing at an angle. The edge of the stump or slab can also be

From *Fine Woodworking* magazine (March 1980) 21:64-67

used for support. Keep the striking surface clean—dirt and grit will dull a hatchet fast.

Hatchet weight and shape and your strength and speed will determine the effectiveness of your hewing strokes. Fine hewing is easier if you hold the hatchet at an angle, thereby slicing into the wood. For delicate work I sometimes wrap thumb and index finger around the hatchet head. In hatchet work both hands are busy, as you must also pay attention to the non-hewing hand that holds the work. All axes and hatchets are easier to control in vertical strokes, so it is constantly necessary to invent ways of holding the wood.

In most cases, begin hewing a few inches above the end set against the stump. Progress upward with succeeding strokes. You can start at the upper end and work down, but there will be more risk of the wood splitting or going out of control. Hew notches and concave shapes with conventional hatchets and axes, beveled on both sides. Place the wood on the stump, end grain down, and hew toward the center of the desired shape. Work from both sides to make a *V* or *C* shape with small, easy strokes to avoid splitting. Making a sawcut down the center of a concave shape to full depth also helps prevent splitting.

Hewing a spoon blank.

Any hatchet is effective for hewing close to the grain angle. But you can chop a steep angle only with a sharp hatchet and the work well supported (hold the work over the edge of the stump), taking small shavings with each stroke.

Hewing a beam — Most areas grow at least one timber species that is suitable for log work. Some typical hewing woods include the pines, fir, spruce, redwood, tulip poplar and oak, but you can also hew other woods such as black locust or maple. Within a species, certain trees will be more suitable than others. Knots add to the work involved, and the butt section of a tree is often much tougher than wood a few feet farther up the trunk. Most projects call for relatively straight trees. In North America, logs are generally worked green, but most European craftsmen prefer to hew seasoned logs, which are less likely to check, split or warp.

Before beginning, it's important to be aware of the prob-

lems in dealing with a material as heavy as logs, which weigh green between 40 lb. and 70 lb. per cubic foot. It's often difficult to get a log moving, but when gravity takes over, the log becomes hard to stop. Always be careful when lifting or moving logs. Learn to use leg muscles, which strain less easily than the back. Make use of levers, fulcrums, block and tackle, and rollers. Large and small peaveys and cant hooks are almost indispensable. I like to lift and haul logs with a partner on the other side of a timber carrier (photo top left, p. 91). It consists of a pair of grab hooks that hang from a swivel in the center of a 4-ft. or 5-ft. pole. Each person lifts an end of the pole; the front end of the log is in the grab hooks between them, the far end is supported by a pair of wheels in a wooden truss.

Most log hewing is done with broad axes, but though they're wonderful tools, you don't need one to try hewing. In fact, some beginners find a 7-lb. to 10-lb. broad ax intimidating, awkward and backbreaking.

The broad ax that I use has a 9-lb. head with a 13-in. cutting edge. An important feature of this ax, often not understood, is that the inside face of the head is not flat. The side curves along a horizontal line, forming an arc about 3/16 in. deep. This causes the ax to cut with a slight scooping effect. Vertically, the inner face is perfectly flat from the cutting edge to the poll. Broad-ax handles vary in length from 15 in. to 30 in. For most hewing techniques, the handle must take a radical bend immediately behind the head where the lead hand is positioned. This provides the necessary clearance between the hewer's fingers and the log.

The method of hewing I use was developed by Peter Gott, an accomplished craftsman who has refined his hewing technique and style during 18 years of log-building. Many axmen hew by eye, snapping one or two chalk lines down a log, and then hewing. This can be tricky because logs taper, bend and bulge, making it difficult to eyeball a flat plane. Gott's technique, which practically guarantees good results, uses a series of accurate pencil and chalk guidelines that are all perpendicular or parallel to one another, and can be used for hewing one, two, three or four surfaces. Flat planes facilitate notch work, mortise-and-tenon joints and other detailed refinements. You can also adapt Gott's technique to carving and sculptural projects.

Begin hewing by barking the log. Some trees (such as tulip poplar) peel in large slabs, others require more work. Slash a narrow strip with an ax, then try to peel by inserting a barking

At left, hatchets (top to bottom): A symmetrically beveled Kent hatchet, characterized by a diamond-shaped flange around the eye, a well-defined poll and symmetrically flared shoulders; a German broad hatchet; a Japanese daiko ono, *whose light head (less than 1 lb.) and extremely back-flared blade (you can hold the hatchet directly above the blade) make it maneuverable enough for making furniture and chopping bowl exteriors; and a reproduction of a 12th-century Viking hatchet, probably an all-purpose tool used for woodworking, butchering and self defense. Axes and hatchets are of two basic shapes. The broad ax (center photo, left) is flat on one side and ideal for smoothing plane surfaces. The symmetrically beveled ax (center right) cuts with a scooping action and is best for roughing out and for concave cuts.*

Handle-bending jig (for broad axes) is made from 1-in. thick board, two C-clamps, a wooden wedge and a piece of twine. Heat the handle in boiling water, clamp the head to the board and bend the handle up, by hand, to an angle slightly more than is needed (to allow for springback). Slip the wedge between plank and handle, and tighten the twine with a winding stick to pull the handle into a reverse curve. Shape the handle to align your two hands and the ax head in a straight line.

Hewing a beam

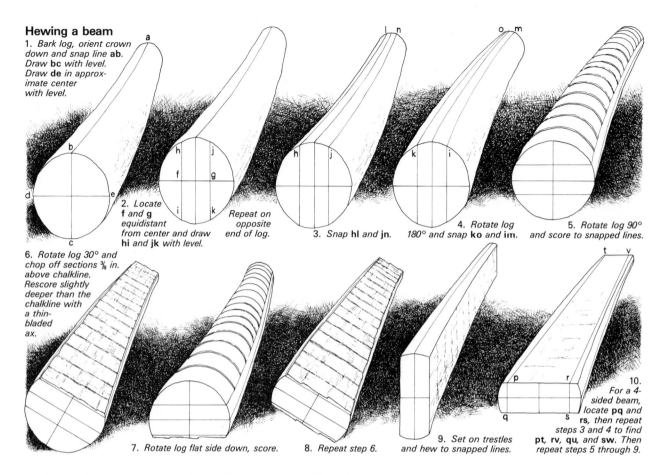

1. *Bark log, orient crown down and snap line* **ab**. *Draw* **bc** *with level. Draw* **de** *in approximate center with level.*

2. *Locate* **f** *and* **g** *equidistant from center and draw* **hi** *and* **jk** *with level.*

Repeat on opposite end of log.

3. *Snap* **hl** *and* **jn**.

4. *Rotate log 180° and snap* **ko** *and* **im**.

5. *Rotate log 90° and score to snapped lines.*

6. *Rotate log 30° and chop off sections ⅜ in. above chalkline. Rescore slightly deeper than the chalkline with a thin-bladed ax.*

7. *Rotate log flat side down, score.*

8. *Repeat step 6.*

9. *Set on trestles and hew to snapped lines.*

10. *For a 4-sided beam, locate* **pq** *and* **rs**, *then repeat steps 3 and 4 to find* **pt, rv, qu,** *and* **sw**. *Then repeat steps 5 through 9.*

spud or garden spade at the cambium. You can also ax off bark or use an extra-large barking drawknife.

Move the clean log onto a pair of cribs (3-ft. to 4-ft. cross logs with center notches to prevent rolling). Sight the log from each end to determine dominant swag or crown, and, with a short peavey or cant hook, rotate the log so that it is crown down. Put an awl through the loop of a chalkline and stick the point into the approximate center of one end of the log. Reel out the line and stick a second awl into the other center, pulling the string taut. A chalk line snapped on a rounded surface can easily result in a curve—avoid this by locating the angle for snapping the line with a vertically held carpenter's level. This is particularly important when working on nonlevel ground, as it's difficult to judge plumb by eye.

Draw a vertical line down the end of the log, using the level as a straightedge. Then draw a perpendicular line somewhere near the middle. Locate the edge(s) to be hewn by drawing vertical lines across the perpendicular line. (On a log to be hewn on two sides, these lines are equidistant on either side from the original vertical line.) Use your level.

When your lines are drawn, knife a small *V*-notch where they meet the side of the log. Repeat this procedure at the other end of the log. Snap new chalklines along the length of the log to locate the hewing lines, using the *V*-notches to hold the chalkline in place. Rotate the log 180° (crown up) and snap parallel hewing lines along the crown.

Rotate the log 90° so the side to be hewed faces up. Remove bulk waste by first scoring to the hewing line every 8 in. to 24 in. on center, using a symmetrically beveled ax, a handsaw or a chain saw. Then rotate the log 30° and remove the end chunk, placing the ax edge ⅜ in. to the waste side of the

chalkline and striking the poll with a mallet. Continue down the log, splitting wood off and leaving the same ⅜-in. margin above the chalkline so the broad ax, which will be used to finish the surface, will have something to bite into. After you have removed most of the waste, chop another series of vertical scoring marks slightly deeper than the chalk hewing lines with a sharp, thin-bladed ax. These cuts should be about 4 in. apart; their pattern will show slightly after hewing is finished. Deep scoring prevents fiber from tearing inward, especially around knots, and is also more attractive than rough saw kerfs. Then flip the log and repeat the entire process on the obverse face.

Set the log on a pair of trestles about 30 in. high—diameter of log, size of craftsman and personal preference dictate different trestle heights. Place the log on edge, and temporarily hold it steady with makeshift wedges placed underneath. Use the level and a vertical guideline on one end of the log to adjust for plumb. A variance of a few degrees makes hewing considerably more difficult.

One traditional way to hold a log steady on edge is with hewing dogs—iron staples with one end driven into the log and the other into the trestle or crib log. Some large logs can be wedged upright, or you can wrap a chain with a light load binder (a lever and cam device used to tighten the chain) around the log and trestle. You can also improvise excellent bracing using 1x1s cut to various lengths and secured to the log and the trestles with box nails. With this system it's possible to make any number of lightweight staples in dimensions as needed. They're virtually free and have the advantage of being mainly wood—there is little chance of dulling an edge tool. I generally begin with two staples on either side of

Photos: Tad Stamm; Illustration: Christopher Clapp

Two-person timber carrier and trolley, left, bring log to where it can be scored with a symmetrically beveled ax, hand saw or chain saw, center. Then log is rotated 30° and waste wood chopped with a symmetrically beveled ax to within ⅜ in. of the chalkline, right.

Broad ax, left and below, leaves a smooth surface in plane.

With both sides roughed out and rescored with a thin-bladed ax, log is steadied on trestles with 1x1 staples. Finish hewing can then begin.

the far end of the log, and one nailed on the opposite side from where I begin hewing. On a long wobbly log I'll set a fourth staple after I've hewn past the first trestle.

The hand grasps used in hewing are different from those used for chopping wood. The best hewing grasp consists of holding one's accustomed hand immediately behind the ax head (thumb extended forward and fingers tucked close to the handle), with the unaccustomed hand somewhere near the handle end. Rather than lean over the log, I prefer to bend both legs, keeping my right leg well forward (something like an advance position in fencing, but not as extreme). I like to stand close to the log, so that my vision is straight ahead along the hewing line. I take short and deliberate strokes.

Carefully hew down the right-hand vertical guideline on the log end, with the length of the log in front of you. Start with short, careful strokes. Hold the ax slightly askew (outward) so that you chop a shallow bevel, trying to split the upper line, but stop after about 2½ ft. Go back and hew straight down, concentrating on the area between the log and the inner side of your ax blade.

I hew about half to two-thirds through from the upper line, then move on. It's easy otherwise to break off wood along the bottom edge, or to go off plumb. Another advantage of not hewing straight through is that I'm continually hewing into waste wood, so the ax doesn't fly free, throwing me off balance or out of rhythm.

Hewing is a skill that combines muscular exertion with subtle accuracy. It's important to find a steady rhythm. Hewing through knots takes extra muscle—extra scoring across and around them minimizes excessive tearing. Sliding your

forward hand toward the middle of the ax handle results in more power. Try to remove thin shavings.

When I get to the far trestle I remove the staple and renail it at the first trestle, if one isn't already in place. I carefully hew down the vertical end, stopping often to glance down the line. (It's not visible from the hewing posture.)

In hewing two surfaces of the log, switch staples and work down the other side. Turn the log over, restaple and finish hewing. For hewing a three or four-sided beam, continue the same procedures. Chalklines for each side of the log can be taken from the original horizontal pencil line made when the log was round. Scoring the third and fourth sides is awkward, because it's necessary to see both hewn edges while sawing. If you're using a chain saw, I recommend stationing a friend on the opposite side who can signal just as the cutters approach the chalkline.

Once you develop a feel, it becomes possible to hew fairly large slabs and to move along at a steady pace. In cool weather I hew one side of a 15-ft. log 15 in. in diameter in about half an hour. Seasoned experts are considerably faster. However, the total time needed to hew two sides of the same log, from initial barking and layout to final hewing, adds up to several hours. The job should be virtually perfect, requiring no touchups with an adze or slick. ☐

AUTHOR'S NOTE: Woodcraft Supply Corp., 41 Atlantic Ave., Box 4000, Woburn, Mass. 01888, sells a fairly nice Kent hatchet imported from England. Modified Kent broad hatchets are made by Blue Grass and True Temper, available in hardware stores. Some fine broad hatchets are imported from Germany and Austria by Woodcraft; Garrett Wade, 161 Ave. of the Americas, New York, N.Y. 10013; and Frog Tool Co., P.O. Box 8325, Chicago, Ill. 60680.

Making Ax Handles
A good handle fits at both ends

by Delbert Greear

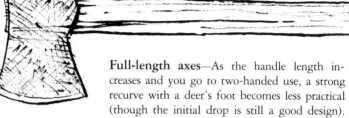

The ax has been around since civilization began and is likely to be with us for the duration. In a popular witticism, an old-timer claims to have had the same ax for forty years, only it's had twelve new handles and four new heads. This joke actually harks back to the frugal days when the ax head was regularly reforged and retempered after it had become blunt and misshapen from much use and sharpening. The old-timer's ax head could be made "new" by reforging, but a new handle, then as now, is a new handle.

While good manufactured handles are readily available at the hardware store, many woodsmen prefer a handle custom-made to suit the type of ax and the job to be done. A good ax handle will fit the ax head at one end and the ax wielder at the other.

The handle is an extension of the arm, and its main purpose is to give leverage. Too long an ax is unwieldy; one too short can result in extra work, bent posture and danger from a short stroke. Full-size axes average just under 3 ft. long. A hatchet handle may be as short as 1 ft. A camp ax, balanced for either one-handed or two-handed use, is usually about 2 ft. long, as are the small double-bit cruising ax and the light Hudson's Bay ax.

Parts of a handle—Except for broad-hatchets and broad-axes, which call for offset handles to protect the wielder's knuckles (see the preceding article, pp. 88-91), the ax handle, from top view, needs to be straight in line with the head so that the blade will strike true. An initial drop, as shown in the drawing below, puts the center of weight of the ax head a little behind the line of the handle. This helps aim the blow, reduces the tendency of the ax to twist when it strikes the wood, and somewhat reduces shock.

In side view, single-bit handles frequently have a slight S shape, and often there is a pronounced recurve and a fat knob at the end, sometimes resembling a deer's foot. The deer's-foot pattern is a good one for short handles. It provides a firm grip for the hand, and the recurve lets the wrist work at a comfortable angle, especially in one-handed work, where the elbow is held close to the body for control and the arm is never fully extended.

Full-length axes—As the handle length increases and you go to two-handed use, a strong recurve with a deer's foot becomes less practical (though the initial drop is still a good design). Most experienced woodchoppers say the deer's-foot pattern interferes with their aim and presents the blade at the wrong angle to the work when their arms are fully outstretched.

Deer's foot or no, it is good practice to extend the handle back beyond the grip for a few inches and to end it with a flare or a knob. Many axmen of the old school rely on a pull at the end of their stroke to shorten the radius of the ax head's arc, thus increasing its final velocity. A flare or a knob gives the hand a stopping place, and also dampens shock. Most people when using an ax, a hammer or any such striking tool for very long tend to choke up a little on the handle because with every blow a shock wave travels down the handle, focuses at the very butt, and transfers itself to the hand and arm. A few inches up the handle this shock is less.

Special cases—A double-bit ax needs a straight handle, usually more oval in cross section than a single-bit handle. As with the single-bit ax, the cheek needs to be deep and strong—it takes the most abuse from overshooting and other mislicks. It shouldn't be thicker than the head, however, or it is liable to fray and splinter, especially when the ax is used for splitting. Also, for a splitting ax, the main length of the handle should be as skinny as is commensurate with strength and a good grip. This gives the ax more whip and speed. A wood splitter accommodates the increased vibration by relaxing his grip as the blade meets the wood. A hewing ax needs a stiffer handle, since whip and vibration can quickly tire the hewer. And it also needs a flare or a knob. Axes and hatchets used for carving and trimming call for a comfortable handle shape for special one-handed grips, such as right behind the head, or where the ax balances best for short chopping strokes.

Handle wood—Oak, ash, maple and birch are often used, but where it is available, hickory is the woodsman's choice. All the hickories I've tried have made good handles: pignut,

Parts of an ax handle

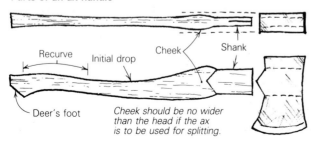

Recurve · Initial drop · Cheek · Shank · Deer's foot

Cheek should be no wider than the head if the ax is to be used for splitting.

From *Fine Woodworking* magazine (July 1983) 41:40-41

bitternut, mockernut, shellbark and shagbark. The shagbark enjoys a reputation for exceptional strength and good grain.

Unless a marked offset is needed, as for a broadax handle, straight, clear wood is best. A tree about 9 in. in diameter is likely to be nearly all sapwood, better than heartwood for a handle. And even for a long ax handle, the bolt needs to be only about 42 in. long, to allow for seasoning checks and waste. Thus a tree that might be culled in a managed timber lot may produce six or eight handle blanks. Quarter the log right away, and if it's large enough, take it to eighths. This will relieve much of the stress in the wood and prevent deep seasoning checks. Blanks that won't be used immediately should be leaned up in a sheltered place to season. Leave the bark and heartwood on to slow seasoning and prevent, to some extent, the blanks from bowing as they dry. If you orient the blank as in the drawing at right, a slight bow will actually work to your advantage.

Removing the old handle—Drilling the old handle out can be a chore if the handle is full of metal wedges. I usually burn the old handle out. This won't damage the blade if you bury the cutting edge in dirt (both edges on a double-bit ax) and keep the fire very small. You need to char the handle stub just enough so that you can punch it out. Keep the fire close around the eye, and don't remove the ax head from the dirt too soon, or residual heat may run out to the edge and spoil its temper.

Roughing out and shaping—Green hickory splits fairly easily, and it splits straight with the grain. Once it has been seasoned, however, it becomes difficult to split and is prone to run out.

Before the blank dries completely, I like to rough out a handle with a hatchet, then go to a shaving horse and a drawknife to skinny it down and refine its shape. I do most of the finish work with a knife, making the final touches after the head has been mounted. One difficulty in carving hickory is unwanted riving of the grain. Reverse directions before the riving gets out of control, work slightly across the grain, and keep the knife sharp.

A rasp works well when the wood gets hard from seasoning and the knife no longer cuts freely. The rasp leaves a rough surface that can be smoothed by scraping with broken glass or by sanding.

Sometimes when an ax is needed right away, you can make the handle and install it green, but it is almost sure to need resetting within a week or two. For a more lasting fit, allow the handle to season until it is dry and hard, and "sounds" when struck with another piece of wood.

Fitting the shank—Be sure that the shank of the handle completely fills the eye of the head in length, depth and thickness. Slip the ax head gently on the handle to check the fit, remove it, and cut away the tight spots with a knife or a rasp until the handle beds firmly in the eye of the head and protrudes a little beyond. After the handle has been wedged,

the extra length should be trimmed off flush with the head.

Sometimes the handle needs to be tapped in and the head knocked back off to find the thick spots on the shank. The best way to drive the handle into the eye is to hang the ax by its handle in one hand and strike its grip end with a maul. The handle is thus driven against the inertia of the head. Don't get the head stuck on too tight before you are ready to wedge it—it can be a real bear to remove.

Before final-fitting and wedging, woodsmen of the old school heat the end of the handle in an open flame until it is nearly smoking, but not charred. This drives out the moisture through the end grain, and shrinks and hardens the hickory. The wood later swells a little as it absorbs moisture again, tightening the fit.

Wedging—I used to saw the slot for the wedge, but an old-timer set me straight. It's easier to split the shank. Both the wedge and the split should be about two-thirds the depth of the eye. With care, the split won't run down the handle and ruin it.

A fat wedge will loosen from compression due to moisture changes, thus it tends to work out easily. The slimmer the wedge the better. In fact, if the handle fits the eye of the blade to perfection, the wedge can be dispensed with. Needless to say, this is not usually the case.

A soft but tough wood makes the best wedge—pine, spruce, cedar and gum are often used. A fibrous wood, such as honey locust, grips well. A hard wood such as oak or maple is a poor choice, as such wedges work loose. Some people apply white glue to the wedge first. This lubricates the wedge as it is driven in, and sets it firmly in place.

Laying a flat piece of steel on the end of the wedge while hammering will keep the wedge from breaking into pieces. Metal wedges are best saved for tightening up later, should the ax head start working loose. Don't hesitate to drive in a metal wedge at the first sign of movement—once an ax head begins to rock, it's surely on its way off.

Finishing—Final-sanding and finishing are best done after the handle has been fit onto the head. I like to use mutton tallow or similar heavy grease to seal the wood. Rub the grease in well and polish it dry with a cloth, for initially it makes the handle too slick to use safely. Tallow is good protection for the wood, and, incidentally, for the steel. Linseed oil will also do nicely. Many commercial handles are varnished, but varnish tends to blister the hands and soon wears off, whereas grease or oil wears in, and is gentle on the hands.

Keep any frayed wood at the cheek trimmed off, to reduce splintering. If a handle splinters badly, a roll of tape may get you through the day's work, but the handle is starting to go. The tape merely hides the extent of the damage and traps moisture, accelerating decay. A failing handle is dangerous. Before your ax handle gives out completely, go look for a hickory tree and treat yourself to some peace of mind. □

Delbert Greear lives in Sautee, Ga., where he employs himself in country woodcraft.

High-speed steel—*I've heard that a tool made from high-speed steel holds an edge much longer than a high-carbon-steel tool. Is this true?*

—*Allen B. Carstensen, Alfred Station, N.Y.*

JERRY GLASER REPLIES: Yes, high-speed steel will hold an edge longer than high-carbon tool steel. That's why it's used to make cutters for power woodworking machines. But there's a tradeoff: high-speed steel won't take as keen an edge as high-carbon tool steel.

About 30 different high-speed steels—all high-carbon steels alloyed with tungsten, molybdenum or cobalt—have been developed for cutting tools that must resist abrasion and the high edge temperatures caused by friction. The edges of high-carbon-steel tools subjected to these conditions will soften and dull very quickly. The new steels were designated "high-speed" because they didn't lose their temper in high-speed machining operations.

Lathe tools are the only hand tools that are subject to high abrasion and high temperature at the same time. Cutting an abrasive wood at high speed concentrates a lot of wear at one small spot on the tool's cutting edge and the edge can get very hot. A lathe tool made from high-speed steel will stand up to this punishment better than one made of high-carbon tool steel. This means that you will not have to regrind the edge as often.

Since plane irons, chisels and carving tools are never subjected to this kind of wear and heat, there's no need to make them from high-speed steel. High-carbon tool steel is the better choice because it takes the very keen edge that these cutting tools require.

[Jerry Glaser is a manufacturing engineer who lives in Playa del Rey, Calif.]

Battling rust—*My shop is in my basement, which is very humid in the summer. Although I run a dehumidifier, I still have rust on the machined surfaces of my tools and machines. How can I remove this rust, and how can I prevent it from recurring?*

—*C.J. Frame, Fredericksburg, Va.*

RICHARD PREISS REPLIES: You're wise to keep a dehumidifier running, though this alone won't overcome the problem. The best way I know of to prevent rust on tools and machinery is to use them every day. Short of this, your best bet is to tend to any rust as soon as possible, before it accumulates.

If rust accumulates on my tools, I remove it with Duro Naval Jelly. Apply a liberal coat of jelly and let it stand according to the instructions. Wipe the surface clean with a rag and apply a fresh coat of jelly. Rub with 00 steel wool and follow up by sanding with 32-grit wet-or-dry sandpaper until all the rust is gone. Finally, wipe the surface clean with a rag dampened with a small amount of acetone.

Preventing rust from returning is as tricky as keeping it off in the first place. Stay away from silicone-based lubricants. Silicone will get into the pores of wood and cause "fisheyes" when a finish is applied. To seal porous cast-iron surfaces and prevent moisture from penetrating, I apply a thorough coat of paraffin wax to all machined surfaces and buff it with a clean rag. This wax also reduces friction and permits work to glide more freely. Repeat this process frequently, but avoid gummy buildup with a careful and complete buffing.

Protect your other tools, especially those that aren't used often, by storing them wrapped in rust-preventive paper (available from Garrett Wade, 161 Ave. of the Americas, New York, N.Y. 10013).

[Richard Preiss runs the woodworking shop at the University of North Carolina at Charlotte.]

Cleaving Wood
Froe follows long fibers

by Drew Langsner

Many craftsmen today have little, if any, experience with the ancient practice of cleaving. Yet before factory-made saws became widespread, cleaving and hewing with an ax were the primary means of reducing wood in size or dividing it into smaller pieces. In cleaving, a tree trunk is split lengthwise into halves, then quarters and sometimes eighths or sixteenths, depending on the diameter of the log and the intended use of the wood. The resulting pie-shaped pieces are squared with a drawknife, then cleaved along tangents to the annual rings with a froe or knife into halves, quarters and so on. These tools allow the use of leverage to follow the grain, rather than a straight line, which a saw must do.

Cleaving has advantages over sawing. Because cleaved material follows the long fibers, it is much stronger than wood sawn by hand or machine. With cleaving, there is no sawdust, but more waste. Cleaved wood will take and hold bends better than sawn wood. And cleaving is faster than hand-sawing.

The crudest examples of cleaving are fence posts and rails, especially black-locust posts and oak rails, which are renowned for their strength and durability. At the other extreme are fine, yet very durable, baskets, woven from splints of white oak, ash, willow or hazel. Other traditional uses of cleft (or "rived") wood include shingles, wall lathing, tool handles, bucket staves, special dowels, "tree-nails" (pegs used in timber-frame buildings), ladder rungs, agricultural implements and small boat ribbing. The technique of cleaving also lends itself to carving projects and chairmaking.

Equipment

Cleaving requires a few basic tools. A peavey or cant hook is useful for maneuvering logs more than 1 ft. in diameter. A 6-lb. to 16-lb. wedging maul ("go-devil") or a sledge hammer, a heavy wooden cudgel, two or three iron wedges (a narrow timber wedge is handy), two wooden "gluts" (large wooden wedges) and a hatchet are useful for splitting the log longitudinally. Gluts are easily hewn from any straight-grained hardwood, usually saplings or limbs of hickory or oak. The beveled sides should be flat. Chamfer the edge around the head to prevent premature fraying. Gluts should be seasoned about one month before being put to use, lest they split and fray too easily. Gluts can be driven with a sledge or go-devil, but will last much longer when pounded by a wooden cudgel. A "brake," or hardwood crotch, holds the wood when the smaller sections are cleaved with a froe and froe club.

The design and workmanship of the froe are critical to its effective cleaving. A froe blade should be 6 in. to 10 in. long, and at least ⅜ in. thick. The cross section of a good froe has a narrow angled edge formed by slightly convex tapered sides beveled the full width of the blade. The back (striking) edge should be nicely rounded to minimize wear on the froe club. Froe eyes are forged or welded shut. The orifice must be

Hewing: With an iron wedge driven into the end of a white oak log (top left), wedges are leap-frogged along the cleft. Two 3-in. gluts and a dogwood cudgel complete the split (bottom left). Then quarters are cleaved into eighths with a pair of wedges and a 10-lb. go-devil (above). Note the splitting break at left, propped up by crossed saplings.

smooth. Froes with a tapered eye use a swollen handle, not unlike an adze or mattock haft. These seem to work loose just as easily as round eyes with parallel sides. The handle should be 1½ to 2 times as long as the blade. It may be any stout hardwood, cleaved of course, then well seasoned before fitting. A small wooden wedge should be dabbed with glue and driven into a slot sawn across the end grain.

I have found that a long narrow club is most convenient for cleaving with a froe. A short fat club tends to be in the way. Froe clubs are made from almost any dense hardwood. I've used apple, hickory, dogwood and oak. Clubs made from green saplings and limbs generally check. To avoid checks, use a quarter section from a larger tree. The club (which is unavoidably expendable) should be seasoned a few weeks so that its surface hardens before it is used.

Woods

You can cleave a fairly wide range of deciduous and coniferous woods. For work that requires strong or tough materials, select oak, hickory, ash or locust. White oak makes fine splints and is used in many bending applications. Most other eastern oaks cleave nicely, except for maul oak and swamp white oak, both of which are almost impossible to split. Hickory, of course, is famous for toughness and ability to take impact, but it is rather stringy and sometimes hard to work (especially when seasoned). Ash is lighter and very nice to split. Locust cleaves easily, but the grain usually warbles, resulting in distorted splints that are "foxy" (uneven or brittle). Beech was preferred by English chair bodgers, the itinerant woodsmen/turners who traditionally made legs and rungs for Windsor chairs.

Among the softwoods, one can choose from pine, hemlock, cedar and redwood. Very fine-grained pine makes superior bucket staves, and sometimes excellent shingles. Hemlock cleaves very easily, though the grain may twist or warp. Its main use is tobacco sticks and tomato stakes. Cedar and redwood may be cleaved into shingles, or made into long-lasting fence posts and rails.

Short bolts of many other woods, such as apple, linden, walnut, dogwood and holly can be cleaved into chunks for

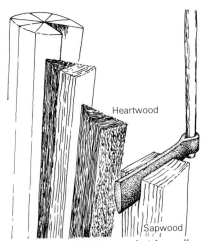

A froe is driven into the wood with a mallet, then worked along the long fibers by leverage. Long pieces of wood may be supported in a brake (far left); short chunks can rest on a stump (left). The diagram shows the cleaving sequence for basket splints. Heartwood is usually discarded; squared-off sapwood is split into halves, quarters, eighths and sometimes sixteenths. A froe makes the first cuts; finer splits are made with a knife.

carving, and bowl and spoon-making. Hazel is traditionally used for bucket hooping and basket materials. Willow rods make nice baskets, too. Until the blight, chestnut was often cleaved for fence posts and shingles.

Felling a tree

When choosing timber for cleaving, select straight-standing trees that are free of knots, scars, twists or other irregularities. White oaks for basket splints should be 5 in. to 8 in. in diameter, with minimal taper at the butt end. Trees with evenly spaced annual rings are preferred, but you can know this only if you have already taken other trees from the same site.

A large body of folklore suggests the ideal time of year, phase of the moon, and prevailing wind conditions for felling. A compilation of all this advice quickly leads to contradictions. My experience in felling trees at various times throughout the year has led to no conclusions whatsoever. I have cut white oaks for basketry that were of the same age and that grew side by side—I found one beautiful to work and the other only mediocre. In general, I recommend cutting trees for cleaving as near as possible to the time when the wood will be worked or used. Oak shingles, for instance, should be rived out and installed green; seasoned shingles may warp or split while being nailed. An exception would be where well-seasoned material is needed, such as for bucket staves, in which case the wood should be bucked and cleaved into quarter or eighth sections whenever possible.

For reasons of esthetics and conservation I prefer to fell timber as close as possible (almost flush) to the forest floor. Discard the lowermost section of stump if it's tapered or punky. Buck the log into bolts. Length depends on intended use: from 20 in. for shingles to 10 ft. for fence rails.

Cleaving the log

Using a wedge and maul, score a radial line from the central pith to the bark. If the wood is already cracked, you must follow along the cleft, because it's impossible to control cleaving once the integrity of the annual rings is broken. I begin by driving a wide, flat timber wedge into the end grain, but one can use a regular splitting wedge. In either case, the first wedge will open a cleft along the bark.

Insert a splitting wedge and drive it within an inch of its head. The cleft will lengthen as the wedge is pounded into place. Place another wedge into the cleft where it's ⅜ in. to ⅝ in. wide. Again, drive to within an inch of the head. Leapfrog the wedges one past the other until the end of the log is reached. Occasionally a wedge will stick in place. Tapping the sides of the head to the left and right will usually free it.

At this point small or easily cleaved logs simply break apart. Tougher logs require a pair of gluts. When inserting a glut try to find a place free of cross fibers. More gluts are ruined when the leading edge intersects cross fibers than by damage caused by pounding. Leapfrog gluts from one end to another, as with iron wedges.

If the log still isn't halved, roll it over and look for any incipient cracks on the reverse side. Sometimes it's necessary to clear off bark with a hatchet before any fissures are located. Drive wedges or gluts into the back side. The log should divide into halves, although it may be necessary to sever stubborn cross fibers with the hatchet. I prefer to do this kind of hatchet work two-handed. Be careful not to strike implanted iron wedges.

Follow the same procedure for cleaving quarter sections and eighths, if the bolts are still too heavy to haul to the shop. Green worked wood should be left in sections that are as large as possible, because small segments dry out much faster. Big sections, however, check more as they dry. Wood should be removed from the forest floor. Many species are subject to invasion and attack by fungi and insects. Ambrosia beetles infest and ruin oak felled in the spring and summer.

The next step is cleaving the radial sections. Most craftsmen hold the wood in place with a brake, a narrow crotch from the trunk or branch of almost any suitably shaped hardwood. The brake may be lashed to posts driven in the ground. Or lay the big end across a log and support the legs with two saplings placed opposite each other, each one running beneath the near leg and above the far leg. The saplings work against each other, and the device is surprisingly rigid and self-supporting. Insert the wood into the brake. Place the froe crosswise at the approximate half-way point, or along the division of sapwood and heartwood. Strike with the club. Once the blade is in, rotate the handle downwards. One may have to strike the protruding blade again but usually the cleft opens and the froe is simply slid downwards. With tough wood I sometimes hold the split open by placing a stick into the wide end of the cleft. If the cleft starts to run out (divide unevenly to one side) rotate the piece 180° and continue to work from the other side. For thinner pieces, subdivide each bolt in half until you reach the required thickness. Attempts to cleave into uneven pieces, such as thirds, will usually fail. One can sometimes save a wild split by reversing the wood and starting again from the other end. The splits should meet, but it may be necessary to separate the two halves with a knife or hatchet.

Basket splints

White oak splints for basketry should be made promptly after the tree is felled. If this cannot be done, submerge the bole under water, but use as soon as possible. Five to six feet is about the maximum length for fine cleaving and weaving basketry. Cleave radial sections 1 in. to 2 in. wide. Split off the heartwood. Remove the bark with a drawknife, and shape to a square or rectangular cross section. Cleave in halves and quarters tangent to the annual rings. Once the wood is reduced to a thickness of about ½ in., it becomes possible to use a knife rather than the more awkward froe. To start, work the knife across a corner of the end grain, or tap in with a light mallet. Twist (rotate) the knife to open the cleft. As soon as possible, insert both thumbs into the cleft and place the second joint of your index fingers externally just below the cleft. Begin to pull the splint apart by using successive knuckles as a fulcrum while pulling your thumbs away from each other. This process requires a "feel" that comes with practice. If the splint starts to run out on one side, pull down and harder on the other side. Sometimes the wood fibers must be pared with a knife to keep the splint running evenly.

Good white oak will cleave to less than 1/16-in. thickness. The splints may be smoothed with a spokeshave, scraper or penknife. They are sorted and tied in bundles, and may be stored until needed.

Shingles

Shingles may be split from conifers (especially cedar, redwood and some pines) or hardwoods (generally red oaks). The tree diameter can be as little as 12 in., but 24 in. or more is much better. In any case, the wood must be straight-grained and free of knots and other imperfections. First crosscut into bolts of desired length, usually 18 in. to 24 in. There are several methods of proceeding. Swiss shinglemakers often use fine-grained 12-in. pines. They halve and quarter the bolts, then split off the heartwood and thin pie-shaped segments on the sides, to form a square bolt, which is usually split into halves, quarters and eighths.

With a larger hardwood bolt, the circumference can be divided into equal segments (3½ in. is excellent), then split into halves, quarters, and then the smaller sections. Any wavy or twisted heartwood is discarded. If the resulting segment is

Top left: White oak stick supported by brake lashed to two posts is worked into basket splints. Then thin splints are held between the knees and further divided. A small knife opens the cleft (top right), then the pieces are pulled apart by inserting the thumbs into the cleft and sliding the fingers down the outside (bottom).

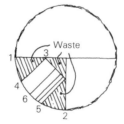
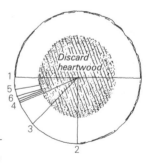

Above, Swiss system of single-splitting; right, riving shingles from a large red oak. Numbers indicate splitting sequence.

more than 5 in. wide, it is split in half. Each squarish section is split into 16 shingles.

In either case, the individual shingles are split across the annual rings. Parallel split shingles will warp unacceptably. Place the froe in the exact center of each segment, or it will run out, resulting in uneven shingles and too much waste. Most shinglemakers use a brake to hold their wood in place, but in Switzerland a leather knee pad is used to hold the material against a knee-high bench. Most shingles need dressing out—curves and bumps must be smoothed before installation. Smoothing is usually done on a shaving horse, using a sharp drawknife. The shingles should be tied into very tight bundles (use a vise to press them together) if they are not installed immediately. □

Drew Langsner is director/instructor at Country Workshops, a school for traditional woodworking in Marshall, N.C., and author of Country Woodcraft *(Rodale Press).*

The Spokeshave
How to choose and use one

by Michael Sandor Podmaniczky

The spokeshave is a marvelous tool. Compact and comfortable to use, it can, with care, perform admirable service in a diversity of jobs. I find myself using one nearly every day for cleaning up drawknifed chair spindles, shaping and fairing curved parts, chamfering anything...and on and on. The spokeshave isn't without its quirks, though, and unless you learn to live with them, it's hard to get the tool working just right.

First of all, you've got to decide which spokeshave to use for which job or, if you don't have any spokeshave at all, which to buy. A glance at the spokeshave section in my favorite wishbooks reveals an armload of choices priced from $4 to $24 (1985). You could buy them all, but the collection would leave too little room in your toolkit and too much room in your wallet. mail-order catalogs offer several sizes of metal spokeshav two generic types: flat-soled and curved-soled.

As its name implies, the working face of a flat-soled sp shave is machined flat, and apart from its extended handl looks and works like a plane with a very short, narrow so round-soled spokeshave has a straight blade, like a plane, when viewed from the front its sole appears flat. Viewed the side, however, the sole is curved to a radius of about 1½ half-round spokeshave is different altogether. It shows a con sole from the front and has a blade curved along its wid convex spokeshave is similar, but as the name implies, the is curved in the other direction.

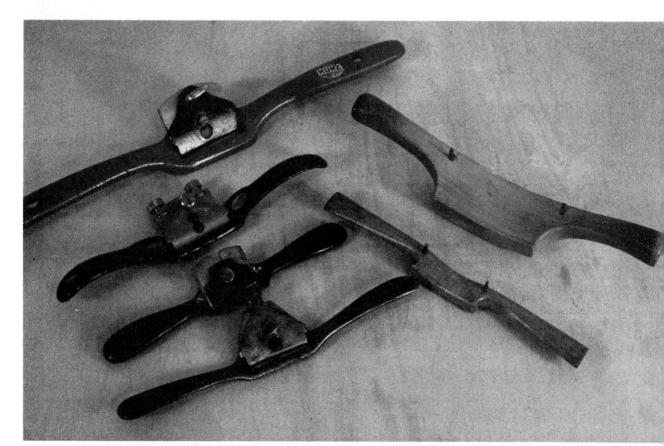

Bought from a mail-order catalog or at a fortuitous yard sale, there's a spokeshave for every purpose. Reading counterclockwise from lower right: flat-soled wooden shave; shopmade convex for shaping chair seats; cooper's spokeshave; flat-soled m with dual screw adjusters; author's favorite 9-in. Kunz (pai black); metal shave with single adjuster.

From *Fine Woodworking* magazine (May 1985) 52:50-52

hich you buy depends more on how much you want to
eeze out of your tool dollar than it does on the kind of
dworking you do. I whittle the selection down to manage-
size by first deciding what I can do without. The half-
d spokeshave, meant for shaping cylindrical parts like ban-
rails, is useless on work whose radius is larger than that of
tool's sole. On work of lesser radius, you'll do just as well
a smooth or block plane or a flat-soled spokeshave—after
tangent is tangent and there's no point cluttering up your
box with a single-purpose tool when a more versatile one
do. Combination spokeshaves are round- and flat-soled
es married by a single handle—good in theory, not so good
ractice.

cooper's spokeshave is big and beefy, and some boatbuilders
it for wearing down the inside surfaces of heavy, sawn ship
es. I've learned to work close and accurately with the band-
or drawknife, then touch up with a flat- or round-soled
keshave. Another sucker-born-a-minute tool is the adjustable-
th spokeshave. I rarely need this capability, but if I do, I
e one or two bits of shimstock or aluminum flashing behind
blade to close the mouth down, and I'm all set. Infinitely
able settings I don't need. Fine and rank will do nicely. A
nfering spokeshave—a flat shave with two adjustable fences
nted on the sole—is as specialized as an overbred show dog
I'm happy to do without both. One word about handle
s: those gull-winged spokeshaves which look like a 1960
vy in retreat are not proper. Having your hands up in the air,
y from the line defined by the blade edge makes it very diffi-
to control the tool.

it all boils down to this: Equip yourself with two simple
ght-handled spokeshaves—a flat-soled for general-purpose
othing or shaping of flat and convex or shallow and concave
aces, and a round-soled for working tight inside radii. If you
find one, I'd recommend an old wooden-bodied type of flat-
d shave—and I don't mean the adjustable rosewood models
see in the catalogs these days. I'm talking about one of those
e-a-dozen beechwood jobs (sometimes fitted with a brass
sole) that always turn up in junk shops and yard sales. These
light, well-balanced and compact; the only tool for getting
that hard-to-shape curve on a Windsor chair seat, just for-
d of the arm post. Make sure the blade has a little life left to it
that the blade tangs fit tightly enough into the wooden body
old the depth setting.

you can't find a wooden shave, the best metal ones also hap-
to be the simplest. I like the 9-in. flat- and round-soled models
le by Kunz (Garrett Wade's #19P02.01 and 3.01). Besides be-
inexpensive, these tools have another important advantage:
adjust the blade by loosening a single screw that holds the
iron in place, instead of by the cumbersome thumbscrews
d on more expensive spokeshaves, like the Record. Screw
sters just get in the way and, worse, they rattle. There's
ething evil about anything loose on a hand tool, and unless I
stop the rattle with, say, beeswax to clog the threads, I just
't use the thing. For me, using a fancy Record spokeshave is
hopping into a Delta 88 after years of driving a Rabbit. No
ks, I'd rather soup up the Rabbit.

eing an inexpensive tool, the Kunz needs some tuning. The
, the surface against which the back of the blade bears,
ld be filed flat to minimize chattering. Hollow-grind the in-
edge of the cap iron so it bears against the blade only along
eading edge, and set it about ⅛ in. back from the blade's
ing edge. True an out-of-flat or poorly curved sole with a file

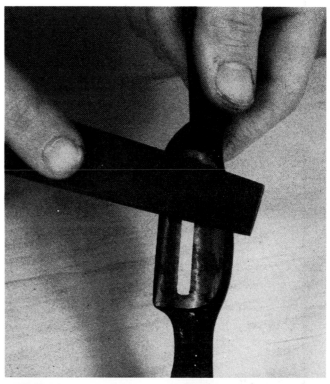

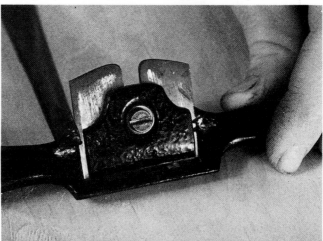

*Dressing a metal spokeshave's sole with a file improves its per-
formance. To keep it from rocking, file the sole flat across its
width. The Kunz, above, has no adjusters so author ground
pockets on either side of the frog. A screwdriver inserted into
both the pockets and the corresponding notches filed in the
blade edge aids depth-setting.*

as well, as shown in the photo above. Remember, since the
spokeshave rides on the leading and following edges of the sole,
you'll want to file these edges straight across so the shave won't
rock from side to side. To make blade setting a little easier, I
ground small pockets in the casting adjacent to the blade with a
Dremel tool. By inserting a screwdriver blade, which bears against
nicks I filed in the blade, I can finesse the cutting depth I want.

Sharpen a metal spokeshave blade as you would a plane iron.
Using an aluminum-oxide wheel, grind the bevel to about 25° or
so—you don't need to get your protractor out, just eyeball it
close. Next hone a bevel with a fine India stone, following that
with a touchup on a hard Arkansas. A wooden spokeshave usually
won't need grinding. But if it does, the metal, like a drawknife

How spokeshaves work

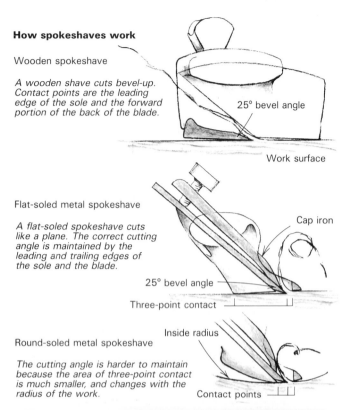

Wooden spokeshave

A wooden shave cuts bevel-up. Contact points are the leading edge of the sole and the forward portion of the back of the blade.

25° bevel angle

Work surface

Flat-soled metal spokeshave

A flat-soled spokeshave cuts like a plane. The correct cutting angle is maintained by the leading and trailing edges of the sole and the blade.

Cap iron

25° bevel angle

Three-point contact

Round-soled metal spokeshave

The cutting angle is harder to maintain because the area of three-point contact is much smaller, and changes with the radius of the work.

Inside radius

Contact points

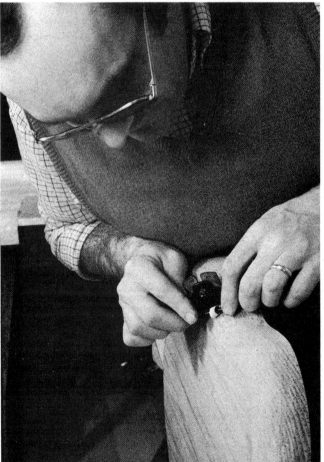

The spokeshave's short sole makes it perfect for shaping and smoothing curved wooden parts, such as the Windsor chair seat Podmaniczky is making here. Best results come when the blade is kept at the correct angle to the work; control achieved by pushing rather than pulling the tool.

blade, is often soft enough to file. Keep in mind that the b. pushes rather than slices through the work. This means that blade should not have the micro-serrations left by a fine I but the polished microbevel produced by a hard Arkansa comparable stone.

To get a spokeshave to do what you want it to, it's helpf understand what makes it tick. Although it works like a plan spokeshave is really just a jig, a holder for a chisel blade. could conceivably "plane" a surface dead-flat with a chisel, the job would require a personality most unwelcome at an mate evening over dinner. That's where the sole of a p comes in. It orients the blade to the wood surface, allowing plane to smooth a board by removing material and flatten i bridging the peaks and valleys of the wood surface. Thank the plane's frog, the cutting bevel is always positioned at just right angle.

It's not so straightforward with a spokeshave. While a p both smooths by removing material and flattens by virtue o long sole, the spokeshave is primarily a material remover. sole is far too short to bridge surface irregularities of any and is not as self-jigging, so you, the operator, have to keep blade at the right cutting angle by holding the spokeshave rectly. As you work away with the spokeshave, you must d check your progress, shave some more and check again until surface is just right. To get a consistent cut, position the too contact the work at three points—the sole's leading edge, cutting bevel, and (just barely) the trailing edge of the sole. drawing at left gives some idea of the angles involved. If rock fore or aft on the sole, the cutting angle will be wrong the spokeshave will skid over the wood instead of cuttin wooden spokeshave works a little differently: since it cuts b up, the forward portion of the back of the blade, rather than sole, serves as the reference surface. To get the right fee either type, you'll have to sharpen the blade and try it.

I sometimes pull my spokeshave for various reasons, grain direction or body position (I *hate* standing on my l while working at the bench), so I'd never say don't pull, these tools are designed to be pushed. And with just a l practice, you'll get far greater control by pushing. A nice fea on some spokeshaves are the cozy little thumb rests on ei side of the frog. Fingers need not be wrapped around the handles. If the surface being worked is quite broad and on both handles don't hang out over the edge, grab whateve comfortable around the frog and cap iron with thumb and i finger and push on the handles with the palm of your h Since *proper* handles are straight in line with the blade e (*not* gull-winged, up and away), even without a firm hand there is no tendency to roll or trip up. This grip is really hel with round-soled spokeshaves, as they can be friskier than flat ones.

If, no matter how you hold it, the spokeshave skids wit cutting, either the blade is dull or it isn't set far enough be the sole to pull a shaving. Raise the blade a little if your sp shave digs in and stops cold. Don't give up in frustration i tool misbehaves at first. Starting off with the right tool, setup procedures for use will eliminate most of the hangups that c discourage you from using it. As time goes by, you'll dev quite an affection for that versatile little fellow who lurks d in the corner of your toolbox.

M.S. Podmaniczky is a professional woodworker and l builder who lives in Thomaston, Maine.

The Drawknife
Learning to use this simple tool

by Drew Langsner

Although many woodworkers own a drawknife, I am continually surprised to learn how seldom these tools are used. Drawknives are among the most versatile handtools available to woodworkers. They are fast and easy to use for roughing out stock and for some kinds of finish work. Traditionally drawknives were needed by a wide range of skilled woodworkers. I first used one during a summer of intensive training with a Swiss cooper. Other craftsmen who once depended on drawknives include furniture makers, carpenters, turners and wheelwrights. Drawknives are perfect for dressing shingles, making tool handles, debarking poles and pointing fence posts and pickets. They're also excellent for quickly making odd-size dowels, pegs and wedges, especially from straight-grained, riven stock. There's no better tool for adding a decorative chamfer to furniture parts and even house parts.

A drawknife is a viable alternative (or addition) to machine tools for various kinds of work, especially for individual pieces or small production situations. Chairmaker John D. Alexander, Jr., for example, used to work with sawn lumber which he turned on a lathe. His book, *Make a Chair from a Tree: An Introduction to Working Green Wood* (The Taunton Press, 1978) gives good reasons for his becoming a drawknife convert. Ring-porous hardwoods can be split out quickly and shaved with a drawknife to graceful dimensions while maintaining the strong, continuous grain structure. There is also

the pleasure of working in a shop with quiet tools that run on human energy. And the waste from a drawknife is shavings, not sawdust that can cause various respiratory problems.

Old drawknives were often homemade or produced in small runs at local blacksmith shops. A good source of steel for forging a drawknife (see Ray Larsen's article, "Basic Blacksmithing," on pp. 2-5) is a worn-out file or rasp. Grind off the file teeth along the drawknife cutting edge before doing any forge work.

Early tool catalogs list a wide variety of drawknives for general and specialized uses. The basic drawknife has a straight blade, 6 in. to 10 in. long, with a handle at either end, usually at right angles and in the same plane as the blade. Most often only one side of the blade is beveled, though some old drawknives have symmetrically shaped blades, beveled like a knife or an ax. Slightly dished drawknives (with a bevel on the concave face) are used for dressing flat surfaces, such as the slats of a ladderback chair. Radically curved drawknives, called inshaves, can be beveled on either side. For hollowing (as for barrel staves) or quickly reducing the thickness of a board, a bevel on the convex surface is best. A bevel on the concave face is used for finer work.

There are also variations in the angle between the handles and the blade. Coopers and wheelwrights sometimes used a drawknife with one of the handles extending straight from

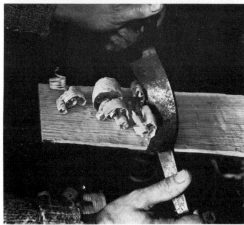

Various drawknives satisfy different needs. Above, from top to bottom, straight blade is for general-purpose work. The second can be used to slice wood with the blade at an angle or, with its straight handle out, to chamfer the inside of a bucket rim. The third has a slightly curved blade with the bevel on the concave face—best for light cuts and finishing work on flat surfaces. At top right, a similar drawknife, but with round, French-style handles, takes a fine shaving. The fourth drawknife has a radically curved blade with the bevel on the convex face. This tool makes fast work of hollowing out barrel staves, removing large shavings (photo, right). Also known as an inshave, it is the drawknife equivalent of the scrub plane.

the blade, so the tool was shaped like an *L*. It could be pulled with the blade at an angle for a slicing action without the handles bumping into the bench or workpiece. Drawknives with both handles extending straight from the blade are used for work where angled handles are in the way, for example when shaving the exterior of a bowl, secured rim down on a workbench. Like spokeshaves, straight-handled drawknives are pulled or pushed, whichever is more convenient. It's harder to control a straight-handled drawknife; standard handles provide leverage for controlling the cutting angle.

I sometimes use drawknives while standing at a workbench. However, the best workmate of the drawknife, used long before screw vises were invented, is the shaving horse, an ingenious foot-operated hold-down that grips the work fast and sure. Over the centuries various shaving horses were developed. In one style, called a dumbhead, a central arm pivots in slots mortised through the bench. Jaws on either side of the head hold the work against a ledge 8 in. to 10 in. above the bench seat. The treadle can be a cross peg or a board mortised to the tenoned bottom of the swinging arm. The English style of shaving horse, which is sometimes called a bodger's bench, cooper's shaving bench, or shaving brake, uses two lighter arms pivoted at the sides of the bench and connected by a top crossbar that holds the work, and a bottom crossbar that is the treadle. I find that I prefer the single-arm, dumbhead horse, like the one pictured at top, right.

If you've used a drawknife and been disappointed with its performance, it's probably because it was poorly shaped or dull. Many new drawknives are ground at an angle that makes them practically impossible to use. Like other edge tools, drawknives must be sharpened with care and precision. Sharpening should begin with a check of the blade bevel angle, usually 30° to 35°. Very thin drawknives, such as the Marples, work well with a 25° bevel.

The wide blade and bent handles of a drawknife require adaptations of standard sharpening procedures. Herr Kohler, the Swiss cooper I worked with, uses a small sandstone wheel whenever rough dressing is necessary. For honing, he props one handle against the work-ledge support on the shaving horse while holding the other handle in his left hand about chest height. In his right hand Kohler first lubricates with spit a small natural stone, then rubs it in circles up and down the blade. When a slight wire edge develops, he flips the knife over and whets the flat side, using the same circular motion until the wire edge disappears.

This method is slow and results in a hollow area gradually developing in the handstone. Wille Sundqvist, a Swedish woodworking instructor, teaches a method that works faster and maintains a flat whetstone. Sundqvist mounts his stone in a shallow cavity chiseled into the side of a wood block. The block is secured in a vise or with dogs and wedges on a workbench. The block's thickness keeps the drawknife handles above the bench surface when the blade is bevel down on the stone. Sundqvist begins with a coarse or medium-grit synthetic stone, depending on the condition of the edge. He holds the right end of the blade, bevel down across the far end of the stone and pulls the drawknife diagonally towards his chest and to the right, so that the left end of the blade is whetted by the end of each pass. He repeats this motion until a wire edge develops across the entire bevel. The wire edge on the flat side, Sundqvist says, should be removed using the next harder-grade stone. Usually a new wire edge forms on

Drawknife and shaving horse offer an ideal combination of direct shaping and quick, sure gripping of green stock.

Two methods of sharpening drawknives. A Swiss cooper teaches supporting the drawknife on the shaving horse, center, and rubbing a handstone first over the bevel, then over the flat face, moving it up and down the length in small circles. A Swedish woodworking instructor teaches mounting the stone in a block of wood held in a vise, above. The drawknife is drawn diagonally over the stone, toward you and toward your right, so the entire length of the blade is whetted in each stroke.

From *Fine Woodworking* magazine (November 1980) 25:92-94

Pieces that do not fit under the shaving-horse head can be held between the end of the shaving horse, in a notch or rabbet, and a roughsawn breast bib. Note that cuts do not start on the end grain; the waste at the far end of the stick will be removed after the stick is turned end for end.

the bevel side. He turns the knife and lightly whets across the bevel. The final wire edge on the flat side should be gently removed with a soft Arkansas stone. The bevel can be dressed very lightly once again with this last stone. Throughout the procedure he's sure to maintain a flat bevel at the proper angle. Whetting a microbevel is faster but necessitates frequent regrinding or coarse-dressing. Sundqvist also emphasizes keeping the flat side perfectly flat.

Drawknives are relatively easy and safe tools to use. It's almost impossible to pull the blade into your belly, though I have seen torn pants and cut legs. Skill is a matter of practice; tuning up with this freehand tool takes time. I generally work with the bevel down. The bevel acts as a slide and fulcrum for directing the angle and depth of cut. Some woodworkers use the drawknife bevel up. Drawknives with a slight bevel on the "flat" side will work in either position. The particular job and tool used should dictate the method. Practice different cuts, from shallow plane-like shavings to rougher work, shaving to ½ in. Then try curves, concave dips and other shapes. Drawknife technique is a combination of strength with the careful control necessary for doing accurate work. With practice it's possible to shape elaborate curves, using a narrow blade and pulling slowly, but with maximum muscular exertion and control—like an isometric exercise.

Drawknives work best with straight-grained woods, especially softwoods and ring-porous hardwoods. It's possible to shave dense woods like beech or dogwood, but convoluted figure requires working back and forth from each direction. This is where quick setups with a shaving horse really pay off. Wild grain may work better with an adjustable spokeshave.

A fast technique for roughing straight-grained wood to approximate size is to start a very deep shaving, then raise the handles to split off the waste wood. To drawknife very thin strips, such as basket splits and bucket hoops, place the work on a 1x2 extension stick held under the shaving-horse head. It's even possible to dress across the end grain of softwoods. Dampen the end grain a few minutes before starting. Use a keen drawknife. Work bevel up, from a low area to a high point. Pull the knife diagonally across the grain with a side-

ways slicing action, cutting only halfway across the section.

Here's a typical procedure for shaving a 1½-in. diameter chair leg from a split piece of wood roughly 2 in. square. If possible use straight and clear-grained green oak. Grip the stick on the shaving horse with the growth rings oriented vertically; radial surfaces are easier to cut than tangential ones. The first cuts will take the stick down to 1½ in. square. Start by tilting the drawknife slightly down on the right and take a shaving off the upper right corner of the stick, so the vertical side of the stick becomes 1½ in. high. Next tilt the drawknife slightly down on the left and do the same. These two cuts will leave a slight apex on the top surface. With the drawknife level, shave this off. Now rotate the stick 90°, and tilting the drawknife first left, then right, take the two shavings that will bring the other two sides of the stick down to 1½ in. Hold the drawknife level and remove the apex on the top surface. The stick is now 1½ in. square for the half of its length close to you. Turn the stick end for end and repeat the procedure to make the whole stick 1½ in. square.

The next step is to shave the square into an octagon. Tilt the drawknife 45° to the right, then 45° to the left, to shave the corners off the square. Try to make the three planes this produces equal in width. Rotate the stick 180° and chamfer the other two corners of the square. When all eight planes are the same size, you should have a regular octagon 1½ in across. Turn the stick end for end and repeat the procedures to make the whole stick octagonal.

Now to produce a perfectly round chair leg, it's simply a matter of taking thin shavings off the corners of the octagon, rotating it between strokes and checking it occasionally with a go/no-go gauge. It can be finished up with a spokeshave. Alternately shaving and repositioning the stick proves the value of the shaving horse; the hands can concentrate on the work while the feet quickly hold and release it. The dumbhead horse is particularly advantageous because the work can be slipped out the side to turn end for end, instead of drawing out its whole length from under the head, as is necessary with the English-style horse.

Slipping can be a problem with very green wood and hard-to-hold shapes. Check the shaving-horse head for height and jaw-angle adjustment. If slipping continues, place a small block with coarse sandpaper glued to both faces between the work and jaw of the shaving horse. Woodland craftsmen who continually shaved slick wood sometimes inserted a strip of serrated metal into the upper jaw. I've used a small rasp.

Sometimes it's necessary to drawknife a piece of wood that won't fit into the shaving-horse jaws. Or you may want to shape a flare or curve going into the grain at the end of the wood. A method developed before screw vises uses chest pressure to hold the piece against a rabbet or in a notch cut in the end of the shaving-horse work ledge. A breast bib (a small plank hung by a string around one's neck) distributes pressure and protects against accidents. Breast bibs are made from roughsawn wood; a planed surface will slip against the work.

For drawknifing large work use a conventional wood vise or a peg and wedge-holding system. A machinist's vise with wooden jaw-inserts is excellent for drawknifing irregular shapes or small work. The narrow jaws located above the workbench allow drawknifing at a variety of angles. □

Drew Langsner is director/instructor at Country Workshops, a school for traditional woodworking in Marshall, N.C.

Index